Attachment Theory, Child Maltreatment and Family Support

Attachment Theory, Child Maltreatment and Family Support

A Practice and Assessment Model

David Howe
Marian Brandon
Diana Hinings
Gillian Schofield

1999

LAWRENCE ERLBAUM ASSOCIATES, PUBLISHERS
Mahwah, New Jersey

First published 1999 by
MACMILLAN PRESS LTD
Houndmills, Basingstoke, Hampshire, RG21 6XS
and London

First published in North America 1999 by
Lawrence Erlbaum Associates, Inc.
10 Industrial Avenue
Mahwah, New Jersey 07430

Library of Congress Cataloging-in-Publication Data
Attachment theory, child maltreatment, and family support : a practice
and assessment model / David Howe…[et al].
p.   cm.
Includes bibliographical references and indexes.
ISBN 0–8058–3537–7 (pbk. : alk. paper)
1. Social work with children.   2. Family social work.
3. Attachment behavior.   4. Child abuse—Prevention.   5. Child
welfare.   I. Howe, David, 1946–   .
HV713.A895   1999
362.7—dc21   99–32372
                                                                      CIP

Printed in Malaysia

10   9   8   7   6   5   4   3   2   1

Contents

List of Figures and Tables

Figures

Tables

Acknowledgements

In 1996, we approached Norfolk Social Services Department to ask whether we could work with a small group of child and family social workers and their team managers. The aim was to see whether we could translate and adapt the exciting ideas that were being generated in developmental attachment theory to the world of child and family social work. Norfolk responded generously. Five social workers and four team managers volunteered to take part, curious but uncertain about what they might be letting themselves in for. We worked together for almost 2 years, meeting regularly, discussing case material, thinking through assessment implications, rehearsing possible interventions, drinking much tea and coffee, eating a fair tonnage of chocolate biscuits. We also met, interviewed and talked with many children and parents who were being seen by the social, health and psychological services. The families' help and cooperation was invaluable, and we would like to record our considerable appreciation for their time and interest. However, our greatest thanks must go to the team of social workers and team managers:

Sheila Burgoyne
Mike Chilton
Suzy Gardner
Owen Garrod
Chris Downes
Susan Lee
Jim McLauchlan
Hugh Morgan
Marilyn Smith

Throughout the 2 years, their commitment to the project did not waver and their enthusiasm was a source of great encouragement. The relevance of an attachment perspective in day-to-day work, although always apparent in theory, gradually became clear in practice. Over the 2 years, the shape of an assessment and practice model based on developmental attachment theory began to take form. The end product is the present book. Case material was also discussed individually with Dawn Gregory and Sheila Fearnley in a series of extremely stimulating sessions. Their time and expertise provided further opportunities to think through and refine our ideas. We would also like to thank Anne Borrett, Heather Cutting and Leslie Barrett who typed many of our audiotaped interviews. Our final thanks go to Julia Warner, a wizard at creating diagrams and complicated box tables, all of which helped to give graphic expression to our evolving thoughts and ideas.

DAVID HOWE, MARIAN BRANDON,
DIANA HININGS, GILLIAN SCHOFIELD
University of East Anglia, Norwich

Introduction: working with families and children

Child and family social work has always faced practitioners with situations that are intellectually and practically challenging. Work with children and their carers has to tap deep into questions about human growth and behaviour, personality development and social conduct. Asking social workers to help parents and intervene in the lives of families implies a commitment to improving the psychosocial well-being of many of society's most vulnerable people. But this responsibility requires social workers, and allied professionals, to know and understand two important things: what it is to function well as a psychosocial being, and what experiences contribute to the achievement or otherwise of this healthy and competent state.

At heart, therefore, child and family social work is a practice concerned with the developmental well-being of children. Practitioners need to understand how children develop into healthy adults, what they need from other people and what happens when these needs are not met. The fundamental knowledge base of child welfare practices needs to draw on those disciplines which study the things that help and hinder children in achieving physical safety, personal integrity and social competence. Research and theorising in the field of children's development has expanded massively over recent years, offering child welfare workers a rich, robust and highly relevant body of ideas that continues to invigorate practice. The aim of this book is to develop a practice and assessment model for working with children and their families based on such theories and the research that supports them.

The relationship histories of the children and parents with whom practitioners typically work tend to be characterised by abuse and neglect, confusion and hurt, chaos and loss, indifference and rejection. Take Melanie, a mother of four, as an example:

Melanie

Melanie was the youngest, by some 8 years, of three children. Her mother suffered mental illness and was often hospitalised for several weeks at a time. When her mother was at home, Melanie would have to take care of her, both physically and emotionally. She had not only to make sure that her mum took her medication, but also to prepare meals and do much of the housework. 'Sometimes she would slap me for no reason,' remembers Melanie. 'I never got cuddles from her. And once, when I was about 6 years old and had just got back from school, I found her trying to hang herself and I had to scream at her not to do it, not to kill herself.' From the age of 5, Melanie's father began sexually abusing her. 'I was more like a girlfriend than a daughter.' One evening, not long after she was 14, he had intercourse with her and later that night died of a heart of attack. This experience of sex with her father followed by his death left Melanie terribly confused and frightened. As a young adult, she has experienced a series of relationships with violent partners. It is suspected that these men have physically abused both Melanie and her children, but nothing has ever been admitted or proved. Her first child, born when she was 17, was adopted. However, she is determined to succeed with her other three children, but their behaviour, particularly that of her eldest son Peter, aged 7, is now becoming very difficult. 'Peter's given me a lot of grief from day one,' relates Melanie. 'He upsets other children, bites them, you know. He steals. He hasn't really got any friends.' More recently, Peter has set fire to a garden shed, has been found masturbating in the class by his teacher and killed the neighbour's puppy by repeatedly throwing it up in the air and watching it land on the ground.

Making sense of both the past and the present in cases as complex as Melanie's is no easy task, yet social workers are asked to assess what is going on. They have to act and make decisions. They have to think about Melanie as a mother as well as deal with her as a woman with needs of her own. Peter's needs also have to be considered. Can he be helped to stay with his mother, or would he better off living with a new family? His behaviour is now causing his teachers concern, but Melanie is loathe to relinquish his care, having, as she sees it, failed with her first son. Peter's 3-year-old brother, Jamie, is very quiet, but nobody has expressed anxieties about his behaviour. The baby of the family is Sue-Anne. Melanie, although she professes that she always wanted a daughter, is also nervously telling her social worker that she has never had to look after a girl before and does not feel very confident. She constantly asks for help about Sue-Anne's health and care from her doctor and health visitor. So, what is the social worker to make of Peter's behaviour? Should she be worried about Jamie's passivity? And what is she to make of Melanie's anxieties about looking after her baby daughter?

Assessment and practice in such demanding cases require much intellectual input. It is the knowledge generated by research and theory that provides the energy and stimulus for such effort. Rigourous thought is always worthwhile, and there are great rewards when theory is applied to practice. Conceptual headway can be made even in situations that threaten to sink the most doughty workers. Theoretically informed practice increases clarity, confidence and compassion. Understanding what is good for children's social and emotional development, practitioners are better placed to explain, present and defend their asessments and interventions to other agencies and courts.

Although parent–child relationships are not the only determinant of children's behaviour, we believe that a developmental perspective based on people's past and present socio-emotional experiences, particularly within close relationships, offers a powerful insight into human personality, styles of caregiving and the character of interpersonal life. We have begun to understand that the relationship between early experiences of parental care, personality growth and behaviour are, in the words of Goldberg (1997: 171), 'complexly determined' and that attachment experiences are only one element in the whole picture. However, although it is only one of the basic ingredients (others, for example, including inherited temperament, styles of parental discipline and family stress, including poverty, over-crowding, conflict), attachment theory has proved to be a major player in helping researchers to understand how the quality of early and continuing close relationships affects children's emotional development, interpersonal style and social behaviour. Developmental attachment theory has particular value for social workers. It deals with the very things that social workers are asked to tackle and can do something about – parent–child relationships, the quality of caregiving and who is best placed to provide it, and the needs of children and their development and safety within the setting of the family.

The complex interplay between the past and the present, the psychological inside and the social outside, is the dance that practitioners have to understand if they are to make sense of what is going on and intervene appropriately and effectively. It is useful to know that certain parenting styles and family relationships promote aggressive, poorly adjusted children. Foster carers and adopters need to be helped to make sense of children who seem intent on rejecting the love offered by their new family. Practitioners have to be able to analyse their observations and decide when it is safe to leave children with their parents and when it is not. Assessments are most confidently held when social workers are able to understand the links between people's experiences and behaviours. Social workers are peculiarly well placed to appreciate the psychosocial nature of children's development. They practise in those areas where the personal and the social meet, where the inner world of the self interacts with the outer world of other people (Winnicott, C. 1964; Schofield 1998). Social work has to be a relationship-based practice in the sense that relationships are the most important influence on children's development and that the quality of relationships is heavily affected by how the main participants perceive and react to the world in which they find themselves.

As we hope to show, contemporary attachment theory is complex and wide ranging, intellectually subtle yet eminently useful in practice. At a time when child welfare workers find themselves operating in a climate of increasingly prescriptive legislation, procedural guidelines and managerial visions, the ability to think is in danger of being lost. Yet informed, reflective thought is the only way for those in the thick of practice to keep their bearings and to remain present and available to both children and their parents. We believe that developmental attachment theory offers social workers and other child welfare specialists ideas rich enough to nourish and strengthen their thinking at all stages of the social work process.

In setting about our purpose of introducing attachment theory and research to social workers, we have organised the book into two main parts. In Part I, we deliberately spend much time describing the basic character of attachment theory. It is a theory with wonderfully subtle but immediately recognisable features that resonate with all aspects of our lives, both personal and professional. It deals with some of the most interesting, exciting and absorbing aspects of our everyday social selves – relationships, emotions, feelings and behaviour – particularly in times of distress and difficulty.

Part II examines how the theory can be applied to practice. We seek to do this by marrying developmental attachment theory with the basic practice process common to most helping professions. The result is a model of practice and assessment that employs a theoretical approach able to guide and orchestrate all stages of the social work process from observation to intervention. Such an approach helps us to understand how parents and children behave, relate and defend themselves. It enables us also to understand the kind of parenting that adults offer their children and how parents and social workers interact.

We believe that attachment and relationship-based developmental theories can usefully underpin and inform all the major branches of child and family social work, including child maltreatment and protection, problem behaviour, family support, assessment and risk management, foster care, adoption, residential care and therapeutic work.

All this is a forceful reminder that work with children only makes sense if it is also understood as work with parents, the family and the containing community. Attachment theory, argues Holmes (1997: 231), 'is not so much a single theory as an overall framework for thinking about relationships'. It is a theory of close relationships. Children's development is a psychosocial process, and it demands that child welfare practitioners work across the full range of the social environment – parents and teachers, the family and the community, health professionals and the police, housing departments and financial support agencies. Even in his earliest days, Bowlby (1951: 84) was aware of the need to support parents:

> Just as children are absolutely dependent on their parents for sustenance, so... are parents... dependent on a greater society for economic provision. *If a community values its children it must cherish their parents.* (emphasis added)

Child protection and family support work must therefore be based on a service that is not only multidisciplinary but also integrates the practices of all the major child and family agencies. If children's emotional understanding and social competence emerge out of interactions with their main caregivers, childcare services have to see themselves as parent sensitive, family orientated and community minded.

Part I

THE THEORY BEHIND
THE PRACTICE

Introduction

The quality and character of children's close relationships is proving to be the central concept linking the myriad of factors that have a bearing on development. Relationships provide the key experience that connects children's personal and social worlds. It is within the dynamic interplay between these two worlds that minds form and personalities grow, behaviour evolves and social competence begins. All the more remarkable then that, until 30 years ago, only clinicians appeared to be interested in relationships. 'By an extraordinary omission', admits Hinde (1995: 1), 'the psychological sciences simply bypassed what is the most important issue in most people's lives – the nature of interpersonal relationships.'

Increasingly, it is being recognised that, psychologically, the individual cannot be understood independently of his or her social and cultural context. The infant does not enter the world as an *a priori* discrete psychological being. Rather, the self and personality form as the developing mind engages with the world in which it finds itself. There is thus no hard boundary between the mental condition of individuals and the social environments in which they find themselves. It is the interaction between individuals and their experiences that creates personalities. This is the domain of the psychosocial. It is therefore becoming clear that those who are concerned about children's developmental well-being have to understand growth and behaviour as a psychosocial phenomenon.

This being the case, the quality and character of children's close relationships matter greatly, as do all the things that affect such relationships – children's innate temperamental make-up, parents' own history of relationships, the stresses generated by the social and material environment. Of course, the quality of relationships will vary from family to family. Of particular interest to social workers is the recognition that adverse relationships upset children's ability to develop sound social and emotional understanding. Children raised in such environments may find interpersonal life stressful and frustrating. These frustrations may, in turn, lead to problem behaviours. Indeed, as George (1996: 411) observes, phenomena such as abuse, maltreatment and neglect always occur in the context of *relationships*. 'What has stood the test of time', says Rutter (1991: 361), 'has been the proposition that the qualities of parent–child relationships constitute a central aspect of parenting, that the development of social relationships occupies a crucial role in personality growth, and that abnormalities in relationships are important in many types of psychopathology.'

Attachment behaviour brings infants into close proximity to their main carers. It is within these close relationships that children learn about themselves, other people and social life in general. Young children interact with their parents and other family members and, in so doing, develop an understanding of both themselves and other people. As Trevarthen (1987) puts it, young brains are designed to learn from older brains. According to Grossmann (1995: 92–3), 'Viewed properly, attachment is the very foundation for a child's ability to understand and participate in the extended social and cultural world without undue emotional conflict.'

John Bowlby's genius was to bring together an array of scientific disciplines and philosophical outlooks to puzzle over children's development from biological creatures into sophisticated social and cultural beings. Out of this inspirational blend of psychology and ethology, evolutionary theory and biology, systems thinking and cognitive science, the personal and the interpersonal, emerged the concept of attachment, which in the hands of modern-day theorists is more than just another approach to children's socio-emotional development: it is the theory that subsumes and integrates all others. It is a relationship-based theory of personality development and our psychosocial progress through life.

It is within their attachment relationships that babies first learn to organise their expression of emotion and behaviour (Grossmann 1995: 112). Later on, the understanding and display of emotions begins to take note of other people's affective states and the social context in which interpersonal life takes place. The recognition by the individual that social life involves a constant interplay between self-reflexive minds possessed of their own feelings, motives, thoughts, beliefs and intentions is a central feature of attachment theory. 'Attachment is *not* one relationship among others,' states Grossmann (1995: 115), 'it is the very foundation of healthy individual development.' Relationship experiences that are the most developmentally healthy allow individuals to see themselves as secure and autonomous but willing to accept help. Also, with its ability to throw light on healthy personality development, attachment theory has also helped us to understand how social adversity places some children at increased risk of experiencing personal distress and interpersonal conflict, and of developing problem behaviours.

In Part I, we introduce and develop the key ideas of attachment theory. We start by looking at how children learn to make sense of themselves and other people within the context of their close relationship experiences. Programmed at birth to be interested in the social world around them, it is the quality and character of that social world, particularly that supplied by caregivers, which heavily influences the kind of sense they begin to make of themselves and other people.

We feel it is important to savour the research and ideas that now make up modern attachment theory. We therefore spell out at some length the genesis of the four basic attachment patterns. Practitioners deal with people whose relationships – with their partners, their children, their parents, their peers – are not going well. Social workers meet people in distress and difficulty, and, as we hope to show, it is at such times that attachment needs and behavioural styles become most pronounced. These are times when some people become hostile and aggressive while others fall into despair and depression. It is when some children act out their mixed-up feelings while others switch to a state of listless apathy. It is when some parents bombard health and social services with one demand after another, in sharp contrast to others who avoid and disengage from the help offered by welfare practitioners. Attachment theory provides a sophisticated set of ideas for making sense of our feelings and behaviours in times of need and in the context of close relationships.

We think that engaging with this material will help practitioners to take further their professional interest and concern in the psychological state of both themselves and other people. A fascination with what makes us tick, coupled with the desire to help, is one of the major reasons why people go into social work. Developmental attachment theory provides an exciting boost to these interests.

2

Understanding attachment theory

In his early studies, Bowlby was intrigued by two findings in particular. The first arose out of his work conducted in the 1940s and 50s that looked at the long-term developmental impact on children who had either been separated from their parents for long periods of time (as war orphans or evacuees) or suffered emotional adversity in childhood (Bowlby 1944, 1951). Many of these children, Bowlby believed, went on to suffer a range of behavioural, emotional and mental health problems that he felt were in some way connected to their earlier upsets and losses.

The second finding was the series of observations made by Bowlby and Robertson in the early 1950s that young children separated from their mothers appeared to experience a recognisable sequence of highly distressed behaviours (Robertson and Bowlby 1952). The children's first reaction to the loss was to *protest* with inconsolable crying, sometimes coupled with attempts to find or follow the missing mother. This was followed by a period of *despair*, apathy and listlessness. If the separation continued over several days or weeks, the children would enter a third phase of quiet *detachment*, withdrawal and an apparent lack of interest in the lost caregiver. In this final phase, there was the appearance of recovery, but play and relationships had a perfunctory quality to them. If reunion with the caregiver did eventually take place, children showed a mixture of anger, crying, clinging and rejection.

It therefore seemed to Bowlby that babies formed a strong bond with their primary caregivers, which, if broken, caused children great upset and distress. The phase of protest seemed to be related to the *anxieties* experienced by children when they were separated from their caregiver. The second phase of despair suggested a period of *grief and mourning*. The final phase of detachment and denial was thought to indicate the operation of defence mechanisms as the young children attempted to protect themselves against the psychological distress of losing a parent. Feelings of hurt, upset and anger often appeared to be repressed.

Bowlby felt not only that these two observations needed explaining, but also that, in some way, they might be connected. Were the experiences of loss and separation, played out over the long term, somehow implicated in the appearance of problem behaviours later in childhood? In attempting to find answers to such questions, Bowlby began the extraordinary journey that took him into ethology, the cognitive sciences, information processing and developmental psychology itself. The result has been a transformation in the way in which we look at and understand children's psychosocial development.

Under the inspiration of people like John Bowlby, James Robertson and Mary Ainsworth (who worked as a researcher for Bowlby in the early 1950s), the study of parent–child relationships became more disciplined. Close, systematic observations of parent–child interactions, often in their 'natural' home setting, helped researchers to lay down the basis of a 'science of relationships' and socio-emotional development. The general rule was first to *describe* relationship behaviours in detail and then to attempt to *classify* them. The final step was to generate ideas that might connect the things observed to the suggested classification. It is *theory* that plays this connecting, underpinning, organising role. In the case of parent–child relationships, *attachment theory* began to provide the conceptual tools that helped researchers to classify and make sense of the behaviours and interactional exchanges observed.

Put simply, attachment behaviour is activated whenever young children feel distressed and insecure, and need to get into close proximity with their main caregiver. Thus, situations that lead to separation from or loss of the attachment figure not only cause anxiety, but also entail the absence of the very person who is able to help soothe the child and return them to a less distressed condition. Prolonged or repeated losses and separations of the attachment figure, whether physical or psychological, might therefore subject children to sustained periods of unresolved distress. The idea that the quality of children's relationship experiences with their main caregivers might have a bearing on their subsequent emotional development began to take shape. In particular, it seemed that if children were to thrive emotionally, they needed a close, continuous caregiving relationship. Furthermore, it was not just a case of the attachment figure being physically present. Children had to *believe* that their attachment figure was available *psychologically* as well as *physically*. Thus, attachment figures who are emotionally unavailable and unresponsive are just as likely to cause anxiety and distress as those who are physically absent. The 'making and breaking of affectional bonds' was to become Bowlby's central field of study.

Attachment theory, then, is a theory of personality development. It is a theory that demands great interest be taken in the interaction between the growing child and his or her social environment, between infants and their caregivers, between children and their families, and between individuals and other people. The character of these interactions is believed to have a profound bearing on children's social and emotional competence.

From the relatively unrefined notion that simple losses of and separations from caregivers were the cause of later psychological problems, Bowlby continued to develop and elaborate his ideas until his death in 1990. In its modern guise, attachment theory provides a powerful perspective on socio-emotional development across the lifespan. As a conceptual framework, attachment theory is providing preliminary scaffolding for the construction of a metaperspective that integrates cognitive, affective and interpersonal dynamics as well as making links between past learning and experiences, and present-day functioning (Lopez 1995: 396). It is the basis of a large, international programme of research looking at all aspects of individual development and personal relationships.

Attachment behaviour

Attachment behaviour is any behaviour designed to get children into a close, protective relationship with their attachment figures whenever they experience anxiety. For most children, their primary attachment figure is usually their mother or main carer. However, it is now accepted that children may also have a small, but limited, number of attachment relationships with other people, including fathers, grandparents and older siblings. These attachment figures are not all treated the same, the mother generally, although not necessarily, being preferred at times of stress. Throughout the book, mother, father, parent and carer are used interchangeably to denote children's main caregivers.

Three broad types of attachment behaviour have been recognised (Belsky and Cassidy 1994: 374):

1. Signalling behaviours by the child that indicate to the mother that the child is interested in social interaction. Such behaviours include smiling, vocalising and laughter. These bring the mother to the child so that they can both enjoy the interaction. Mother → child.
2. Aversive behaviours by the child, including crying, that bring the mother to the child. The mother's aim is to terminate the behaviour that she finds aversive. Mother → child.
3. Active behaviours that take the child to the mother. The child may crawl towards or try to follow the mother. Child → mother.

These three types of attachment behaviour, although expressed in a variety of ways with different people, can nevertheless be recognised throughout life. When people want emotional closeness or experience distress, they will either:

- behave in a socially appealing manner
- send out distress signals designed to invite attention and concern
- actively approach and seek out others for the things that they believe close relationships could or should provide.

The main benefits to the child of being able to get close to the mother are:

- protection from danger
- the supply of food
- social interaction that provides opportunities to learn about people, relationships and the self.

In terms of biology and evolution, the most basic of these is protection from danger. If the child fails to survive, the other two benefits are redundant. Bowlby therefore saw attachment behaviour as the product of a biological control system. Evolution has ensured that behaviours that increase survival will be genetically inherited. Thus, the child–parent relationship is normally both instinctive and reciprocal. Increased separation from the mother, in either space (too far) or time (too long), increases anxiety. Anxiety activates the attachment system, which increases attachment behaviour, the purpose of which is to get the child back into close relationship with the mother. Once close to the mother, the child's anxiety diminishes, and with it there is a drop in his or her attachment behaviour.

The behaviours and emotions associated with attachment are most clearly seen in situations of anxiety and distress, including those involving fear, danger, conflict, social challenges and threats to the caregiver's physical and emotional availability and responsiveness. These anxiety-provoking stimuli can be located in a variety of sites:

1. *within the child,* for example feeling sick, tired, hungry or hurt
2. *within the environment,* for example a frightening, threatening or confusing event
3. *within the attachment figure,* for example uncertainties about the location or behaviour of the attachment figure, including a mother who is missing, unresponsive, rejecting, lost, abusive or hostile.

When attachment behaviour is activated, the child is unable to engage in other useful developmental experiences such as exploration, play and dealing with others for reasons other than protection. Indeed, we might see that attachment systems and exploratory systems are entirely complementary, although mutually inhibiting. When attachment behaviour is high, exploratory behaviour, which encourages the child to learn about the environment, is low, and vice versa. In this apparently innocuous observation lies an important point. Children who experience continuous, regular or high levels of anxiety, for whatever reason, will have less time and energy to enjoy the benefits of exploration, enquiry and natural curiosity. The suppression of exploratory behaviour is likely to have adverse developmental consequences. Exploration promotes survival by helping children to learn about and adapt to their psychosocial environment through cognitive development.

Ainsworth suggested that the link between these two systems – attachment and exploration – might be captured by recognising that the infant uses the attachment figure as *a secure base from which to explore* (Ainsworth *et al.* 1978; Belsky and Cassidy 1994: 375).

Mother–baby interaction

In order for attachment behaviour to be biologically useful, it requires both partners in the relationship to have an interest in the condition of the other. Observations of mother–baby interactions reveal that babies appear to be very socially orientated from birth. Babies enter the world ready to interact and relate with other human beings; even very young children are socially purposeful (Bruner 1983). From the earliest weeks, babies show 'protoconversation' (Trevarthen 1979). They are expressive from birth, with the capacity for much reciprocal, emotionally synchronised behaviour with their mothers.

In turn, most mothers seem highly alert and sensitive to their baby's physical and emotional states. George (1996) calls this reciprocal response to the infant's attachment system the 'caregiving system', which is organized around the goal of protecting the child. In evolutionary terms, it could hardly be otherwise. To leave the development of an attachment relationship to the caprices of individual learning, said Bowlby (1988: 5), 'would be the height of biological folly'. Relating to others is not only what we have to be able to do in order to be recognised as socially competent beings: it is also the thing that we have to do in order to become beings who are socially and emotionally literate.

At birth, babies seem to possess a small but rapidly expanding repertoire of prosocial behaviours. Such innate behaviours seem to invite parents to respond and relate. By the end of the first month, infants can look at people, smile socially and vocalise. Each of these behaviours tends to elicit warm, social responses from others. These early, sophisticated social capacities enhance infants' appeal as responsive partners in parent–child interactions. Eye-to-eye contact helps mothers to feel in a personal relationship with their children. In other words, babies appear to do an increasing number of things that reward mothers. Parents quickly begin to see their child as an emerging social being.

Equally, mothers and other people in the child's environment seem to do many things that interest and stimulate babies. Within the early months, babies selectively respond to the human face and voice in preference to other stimuli. Tactile stimulation, often accompanied by smiling, positive facial expressions and friendly vocalisations, is attractive to babies. Significantly, babies can be soothed and relaxed by their carers when they become distressed. Mothers begin to imitate their babies' expressions and sounds. This, too, can be a source of great pleasure to infants. It also generates experiences that introduce a sense of personal control to babies. This is a most important step. *It represents the beginnings of feelings of potency and effectiveness when dealing with both the self and others.* Through their behaviours and responses, infants feel that they can begin to shape their own social environment. This marks the beginning of intentionality. Babies begin to understand themselves as active participants in family life, able to bring about responses in others in order to have their needs met. No longer helpless, no longer passive, babies increasingly become fully engaged in the social world in which they find themselves.

Koestler *et al.* (1989) see much of the mother's behaviour as part of 'intuitive parenting'. Baby talk with the use of a voice that is slow and raised in pitch ('motherese'), repetitious behaviour and exaggerated facial expressions all seem to come naturally to those who look after babies.

> Whether and how mothers feed their babies and whether they spend a lot of time holding them do not seem to be important determinants of attachment. Rather, what seems to be important is whether mothers meet their babies' needs, not only of being kept fed, dry, and warm, but also of being stimulated, of having power over their environment by being able to get adults to respond to them, of being given autonomy of action, and of being accepted. (Rosenblith 1992: 474)

Mothers and caregivers who are good at *initiating interaction* and providing stimulation, and who are appropriately *responsive* to their babies, tend to sponsor secure attachments. More generally, the particular ways in which different caregivers respond to their infant's attachment needs influence the ways in which young children behave in the parent–child relationship.

In their observations of mother–baby interactions, Ainsworth *et al.* (1971) rated mothers along four dimensions of sensitivity, perspective-taking and responsivity:

1. *Sensitivity–insensitivity.* Mothers who recognise their babies' needs and respond appropriately to their signals are regarded as sensitive. Insensitive mothers fail to 'read' their infants' signals, tending to interact according to their own thoughts and feelings, needs and wants.

2. *Acceptance–rejection.* Mothers who accept their babies recognise that looking after infants entails responsibilities, responding to another's needs, and acknowledging that parenthood involves constraints on one's lifestyle and behaviour. They also accept their babies whether the infants are in a good or a bad mood. Rejecting mothers often resent the demands that their children make on them emotionally. Their children's dependency causes them distress. However, their own rejecting behaviour, anger and lack of affection can also make parents feel guilty. They may therefore complain about their babies' irritability and their refusal to be satisfied and responsive. Rejecting parents easily feel exasperated with their babies.

3. *Cooperation–interference.* Babies enjoy having control and influencing others. Mothers who recognise, support and respect their babies' autonomy appear to 'cooperate' with their babies' needs and accomplishments. There is a preference for shared, negotiated strategies to resolve difficulties. In contrast, *interfering* mothers do not recognise or respect their children's independence. They seek to define their babies' experience, often in a manner that is abrupt, impatient and aggressive.

4. *Accessibility–ignoring.* Accessible mothers, although they might be busy on other matters, remain alert and available to their infants should the need arise. Ignoring mothers continue to be absorbed in their own pursuits. They fail to notice their children's signals, whether the signals indicate distress or a desire to be sociable and interactive. Mothers who 'ignore' engage with their children when it suits them as adults.

The positive dimensions of sensitivity, acceptance, cooperation and accessibility are associated with securely attached children. Various combinations of the negative dimensions of insensitivity, rejection, interference and ignoring are associated with the different types of insecure attachments.

Overall maternal sensitivity is defined by Ainsworth (1973) as the mother's ability and willingness to try to understand behaviours and emotions from her baby's point of view. The result sees a gradual increase in synchrony between mother and child. Within this attuned, coordinated relationship, the baby can learn to regulate his or her own feelings and behaviours. Children whose mothers find it difficult to show such sensitivity find it harder to define and regulate their needs and feelings.

During the first 2 or 3 years of childhood, four stages of the attachment process can be identified (Ainsworth 1973; Bowlby 1979; Schaffer 1996):

- *0–2 months: Undiscriminating social responsiveness; pre-attachment*
  Although babies do not selectively and preferentially respond to their main carers, they exhibit prosocial behaviour from birth. There is a preference for the human face and voice. Young babies enjoy social interaction. They track their carers visually, listen and become physically excited when other people engage with them.

- *3–6 months: Discriminating social responsiveness; attachment-in-the-making*
  Babies are now able to recognise particular people and their faces. They respond with greater vocalisation, more smiling and more crying to familiar faces than they do to strangers. As they develop throughout this phase, there is growing interest in and preference for the main carer. Hence, there is positive discrimination in favour of the attachment figure. Indeed, interaction between baby and mother is increasingly attuned, the baby being able to 'read' the mother's behaviours and moods better than those of anyone else. This ability allows the baby to interact with her in an increasingly effective and competent manner.

- *7 months to 3 years: Active initiative in proximity and contact; clear-cut attachment*
  The earlier attachment behaviours are now fully consolidated. The child shows a selective attachment to one figure. With increasing mobility, motor control and later with the use of language, the child becomes much more active in seeking out and maintaining contact with the attachment figure. The ability mentally to represent relationships increases. The child can begin to alter his or her behaviour to suit personal needs and purposes. There is the ability to choose between a range of attachment behaviours (smiling, crying and following). The child becomes increasingly purposeful and deliberate in choosing behaviours designed to bring about a response in the carer. 'Following, approaching, clinging, and various other active contact behaviors become significant. The median age for achieving this phase is about seven months' (Ainsworth 1973: 12).

- *3+ years: Goal-corrected partnership*
  Children begin to develop a more sophisticated understanding of both their own and their mother's behaviour. They can begin to see how things might appear from her point of view. They can begin to cognitively represent their carer's goals and plans, and distinguish them from their own. This allows children to control and modify their own as well their attachment figure's behaviour. These new mental perspectives allow children to enter into 'partnership' with their carers. Discussion, sharing and negotiation become the preferred way of pursuing 'goals' and relating to one another.

By the time the child is aged 2 or 3 years, there is less need to be in literal proximity to the attachment figure. The toddler needs to develop a sense of independence and thus begins to separate and operate with increasing autonomy. 'Felt security' can therefore be experienced by the use of the growing capacity to 'mentalise'. This means that emotional security is achieved by symbolically representing the parents' availability and relying less on their actual physical presence. Just knowing that the parent is, through experience, generally going to be psychologically available can be sufficient to bring about feelings of security.

Internal working models

If infants are to rise above a basic stimulus and response relationship with their environment, they need to develop ways of thinking about and representing the world around them. The advantage of being able to reflect on what might be going on is that it increases the options available. It introduces the possibility of analysing situations, planning responses and behaving in a more flexible, adaptive fashion, all of which is likely to make one a more competent operator.

Attachment theory holds that, within close relationships, young children acquire *mental representations*, or internal working models, of their own worthiness based on other people's availability and their ability and willingness to provide care and protection (Ainsworth *et al.* 1978). The ability cognitively to model key aspects of one's environment increases both understanding and effectiveness. It provides options. In terms of achieving social competence, it is useful to be able to generate a mental representation of the following three elements:

1. the self
2. other people
3. the relationship between self and others.

The young child begins to learn about the self and others as he or she experiences relationships. The most important relationship is with the main caregiver, who in most cases also becomes the child's selective attachment figure. So it is in relationships with other people that one learns to understand oneself. And by understanding one's self, one begins to understand other people. Thus, the world of relationships is both the problem to be solved and the means to its solution. However, as we shall see shortly, it is implicit in this process that the quality of these close relationships has a profound bearing on how the self, others and social interaction are viewed and understood.

In general, models contain content and information-processing rules that guide perception and memory. Based on learning from past experiences with and expectations of the caregiver, they promote more efficient behaviour when dealing with current environments. Bowlby (1980) emphasised that, in order for behaviour to be varied, adaptive and appropriate yet remain organised towards the achievement of the system's goal (for example, proximity seeking and felt security), it must be guided at the level of mental representations. That is, the child must have ideas and expectations about how the self is being viewed and understood, and the probable interest and responsivity of other people in times of distress and anxiety. These organised mental representations of the self and others (as either positive or negative) are carried forward by individuals and used to guide their behaviour in subsequent relationships.

Internal working models therefore contain *expectations* and *beliefs* about:

- one's own and other people's behaviour
- the lovability, worthiness and acceptability of the self
- the emotional availability and interest of others, and their ability to provide protection.

They also employ rules that govern how emotions, attitudes and behaviours might be deployed to regulate affect and attachment-related issues. These expectations and beliefs are built up over the first months and years of life as children experience and get to 'know' the behaviour and feelings of their attachment figure.

During early infancy, the regulation and control of affect is a property of the caregiver–child relationship. Such regulation lies outside the baby. However, as development proceeds, parent–child relationships and behaviours become represented mentally by the child in the form of an internal working model. Based on these expectations and understandings, children develop behavioural strategies to ensure that their various needs are optimally met given the characteristics of their care and their carers. 'The functions of these models', said Bowlby (1973: 203), 'is to simulate happenings in the real world, thereby enabling the individual to plan behaviour with all the advantages of insight and foresight.' It is also the case that these internal working models lay down the basic trajectory for children's subsequent development. However, changing social environments and alterations in people's responsiveness can 'disconfirm' and modify children's internal working models, leading to shifts in their pathways of development, for good or ill.

It is in these ways that the quality of external relationships gets on the child's mental inside. As attachment relationships become psychologically internalised, the quality of a child's social experiences becomes a mental property of that child. In turn, the mental inside influences the child's view of the self and others. It affects behaviour, relationship style and social competence. Each of these affects the way in which the social world is perceived and dealt with. This is, in effect, a definition of personality: 'the enduring patterns of thought, feeling, and behavior that are expressed in different circumstances' (Westen 1996: 448). This is why attachment theory is described as a theory of personality development. It explains why close relationships matter, how they are developed and how their qualities influence psychological experience, cognitive modelling and relationship styles.

Having initially modelled one's own behaviour and that of the attachment figure, internal working models then begin to organise expectations and behaviours in all other significant relationships. There is a tendency for internal working models to become self-fulfilling and self-confirming as others react to the child's expectations of how they will behave. To an extent, new relationships are created and re-created in the light of previous relationship experiences; it would be difficult to approach each new encounter totally afresh. Thus, internal working models prefer to organise experience rather than be organised by it. In this sense, mental modelling produces continuity in the way in which we behave, relate, feel and respond. Our personality begins to acquire a regular, enduring quality. We begin to expect certain things of ourselves and of others, while others feel that we are becoming more familiar and predictable to them. The defensive exclusion of information that is distressing, anxiety provoking or psychologically threatening interferes with the individual's ability to modify, refine and update their working model.

Crucial to the formation of the internal working model is the quality of the social interaction between children and their selective attachment figures. It has to remembered that children's attachment behaviour is activated when they feel distress, anxiety or heightened arousal. This propels them into a relationship with their attachment figure where they look for comfort, soothing and understanding.

However, relaxation and de-arousal is experienced only if the caregiver shows:

- sensitivity
- acceptance
- cooperation
- accessibility
- availability.

In short, parents and main caregivers should ideally be interested in, attuned to and responsive to their children. Children, as we have said, have an innate appetite for relationships and social stimulation, so the way in which parents respond to children will convey significant information to young minds about their worth, emotional state and interpersonal effectiveness.

Parents who are insensitive, rejecting, interfering or emotionally unavailable present their children with a psychological problem. Infants whose attachment system has been activated enter the relationship with high arousal, but they discover that there is no immediate or appropriate response from their attachment figure that helps them to recover emotional equilibrium. Psychologically, the children therefore need to develop a strategy that gets them into proximity and psychological engagement with their attachment figure, which, after all, is the goal of attachment behaviour. Depending on the particular mix of the parent's behaviour (insensitive, rejecting, interfering and/or unavailable), the strategy developed over time will be different for each child. Each adaptive response reflects the quality of the attachment relationship. The result is a limited number of distinct attachment patterns. Each pattern is associated with a particular type of internal working model whose characteristics have defensively formed in response to different but characteristic combinations of maternal insensitivity, rejection, inaccessibility and/or intrusiveness.

One simple way of mapping the different types of mental representation and expectation is to see, within the framework of the internal working model, whether the self is experienced in relationship to the attachment figure as either worthy of care or not, worthy of protection or not, lovable or not, likeable or not, valued or not, the subject of interest or not, socially effective or not, competent or not. In short, the self will be experienced either positively or negatively.

Similarly, children will experience their attachment figure as either emotionally available or not, responsive or not, sensitive or not, interested or not, attuned or not, rejecting or not, hostile or not, intrusive or not. In short, other people will be viewed either positively or negatively.

Reworking these assessments, it is possible to generate four combinations of the way in which the self and others are being mentally modelled within the parent–child relationship. Each model indicates the meaning and organisation of the infant's goal of seeking parental protection under stress:

1. Self (loved, effective, autonomous and competent) + other people (available, cooperative and dependable) = *secure* attachment patterns.
2. Self (unloved but self-reliant) + other people (rejecting and intrusive) = *avoidant* attachment patterns.
3. Self (low value, ineffective and dependent) + other people (neglecting, insensitive, unpredictable and unreliable) = *ambivalent* attachment patterns.
4. Self (confused and bad) + other people (frightening and unavailable) = *disorganised* attachment patterns.

After the age of about 3 years, attachment evolves into a goal-corrected partnership. Ideally, children need to balance and integrate flexibly their own attachment needs with the plans and wants of their caregivers. There is an inbuilt developmental tension between parents and their toddlers: 'The toddler endeavours to explore, learn, and individuate; the parent strives to protect and socialize' (Lieberman 1992: 562). The goal-corrected partnership is one in which parents and children 'learn when and how to compromise and rearrange their individual plans for the sake of the relationship' (Lieberman 1992: 562). If the needs of each partner are to be met, both parent and child will have to negotiate, compromise, empathise and understand.

> In addition, the child now begins to rely more on mental representations of attachment than the actual presence of the attachment figure... the goal-corrected partnership that emerges during the preschool years sets the stage for attachment across the life span. As the child grows towards adolescence and adulthood, internal working models of attachment are expected to reflect an increasing understanding of the parent's own motivations, feelings, plans, and developmental goals resulting in a relationship of mutual trust and understanding. (George 1996: 413)

According to Crittenden (1992a: 232), securely attached children can apply all of their faculties (that is, feelings, attention, perceptions and cognitions) to the challenges of life. In contrast, insecure, defended and coercive children block out or distort feelings, perceptions and cognitions. Insecure children focus attention in ways that limit their development.

Over time, characteristic ways of relating to other people become recognisable. In this way, attempts to adapt to past relationships begin to govern the way in which individuals see and manage themselves and others in current relationships. Relating competently requires empathy, seeing things from the other's point of view, self-disclosure and reflection on the nature and origins of one's own feelings. The increasing stability of the internal working model means that an individual's behavioural and relationship style becomes both more predictable and difficult to shift. However, change is possible at any time across the lifespan. New social experiences always have the capacity to alter someone's representations and expectations of the worthiness of the self and the availability of others. A child's parents might improve their caregiving behaviour. In adulthood, mental representations can be changed at the cognitive level by enjoying a new intimate relationship or benefiting from psychotherapy. In such relationships, the individual begins to develop the capacity to think about themselves and others, disconfirming old assumptions and seeing social life in a more flexible, balanced way.

Defensive strategies

It must be emphasised that the perceptions and behaviours that each model sponsors, at least for the organised infant patterns, are *adaptive responses* within the social relationships in which they find themselves. The behaviours make sense within the context of the particular close relationship. The behaviour adopted is a *defensive strategy* developed by children to help them to cope with feelings of distress and anxiety. Whatever the quality of the relationship, the attachment system is designed to bring children into proximity with their attachment figure where they will ideally be comforted and understood. This produces feelings of security. If the routes to proximity and security are blocked, rough or unpromising, children either have to develop psychological strategies that attempt to ward off the anxiety or try to seek alternative ways of psychologically securing the attachment figure.

Both secure and insecure attachment patterns therefore represent efforts by children to *organise* their behaviour to achieve some kind of proximity and, with it, a 'felt security'. According to Belsky and Nezworski (1988: 8):

> insecurely attached infants have established relationships that must be considered adapted to the circumstances of their rearing, even if they prove problematical as they move into the world beyond the family. Thus, insecure relationships are considered functional in that they serve to protect the child against anxiety, which arises in the face of a caregiver who is less than optimally available.

Children who show insecure *avoidant* and *ambivalent* attachment patterns have learned that there are 'conditions' attached to their gaining proximity to their caregiver. They therefore develop appropriate strategies that (a) increase the caregiver's emotional availability and do not cause her to withdraw, and (b) bring care and protection. These behaviours result in secondary attachment strategies. Nevertheless, feelings of anxiety and insecurity remain in relation to the parent.

Looked at in terms of defensive strategies, the four basic attachment behaviours have the following characteristics:

1. *Securely* attached children approach their carers directly and positively, knowing that their distress and upset will be recognised and responded to *unconditionally* with comfort and understanding. A sense of trust in others and a recognition of the value of cooperative behaviour soon develop.

2. Children who show *avoidant* attachment patterns experience their parents as rejecting, interfering and controlling. If these children display distress, it seems to annoy or agitate their caregiver. The result is a rebuff or an aggressive attempt to control or deny the children's attachment behaviour. In other words, displays of attachment behaviour (distress, crying, clinging, following and demanding) seems to bring the opposite of what they are designed to achieve – proximity to and felt security with the attachment figure. The best defensive strategy therefore seems to be to *minimise attachment behaviour and affect*. The child either denies or does not communicate her distress. Strong feelings are defensively excluded. Emotional self-containment is established. This allows the child to remain in reasonable proximity to the attach-

ment figure without causing him or her too much irritation, thus reducing the chances of being rejected. This downplaying of feelings and expressions of distress might be defined as a *flight* from a display of attachment needs.

3. In order for children to gain proximity and attention from carers who are insensitive, unreliable and inconsistently responsive, children who show an *ambivalent* attachment style have to *maximise* their attachment behaviour in order to break through the parent's emotional neglect, unavailability and lack of responsivity. Their attachment behaviours are therefore those of an angry approach – they show distress, they whine, cling, fret, shout and threaten. These attention-seeking strategies might be defined as ones of *fight* – demands for attention and protection. Such behaviours are most pronounced at times of upset, particularly at signs of separation, parental insensitivity, threatened abandonment and emotional unavailability. Children do not feel that they are worthy of automatic interest. Others are seen as inconsistent and not always available to soothe and provide comfort. The child's developing sense of social competence, confidence and exploratory skills is conditional on the presence, support and approval of the caregiver. 'This continuing *dependency* of self on external others retards the development of affective self-regulation capabilities and thus leaves the individual peculiarly vulnerable to stress and emotional lability' (Lopez 1995: 400, emphasis added). To the child, the other person is both emotionally desired and emotionally unreliable. This is deeply frustrating. Hence, children have feelings of ambivalence about other people and relationships. At any one time, children's relationships with their caregiver are wholly guided by strong feelings of either love or anger.

In short (Holmes 1997: 234), caregiving environments may be experienced by children as either:

- consistently responsive (leading to secure attachments)
- consistently unresponsive (leading to avoidant attachments)
- inconsistently responsive (leading to ambivalent/resistant attachments).

Thus, says George (1996: 414):

Whether guided by primary or secondary strategies, secure, avoidant and ambivalent infants have developed a set of coherent and organized rules based on experience that predict and guide their future behaviour. Bowlby... stressed that as long as the representational system is *organized*, individuals are capable of maintaining functional relationships with others. The important point to be made here is that despite their anxiety, avoidant and ambivalent infants have been able to adapt to their parents and select, evaluate and modify their behaviour in a manner that allows them to achieve proximity and contact when needed.

However, within very disturbed caregiving relationships, some children find it difficult to organise their attachment behaviour in order to feel safe and cared for. So,

4. Children who *cannot organise* their behaviour or develop a defensive strategy to achieve proximity or security find that their distress and arousal remain heightened and unregulated. These infants find it difficult to maintain a functional and developmentally positive relationship with their caregiver. This is often the case when the attachment figure is the actual cause of the initial distress. For example, parents who are either dangerous (abusive) or emotionally unreachable (psychotic, depressed or heavy drug or alcohol abusers), or fail to protect, may not respond to any of the three organised strategies (secure, ambivalent and avoidant). Whatever behavioural strategy the children use, it fails to bring proximity, care or comfort. With no clear way to regulate their aroused affect, many abused and seriously neglected children remain distressed. Their attachment behaviour becomes increasingly *incoherent* and *disorganised*, showing a confused mix of avoidance, angry approach responses, behavioural disorientation and inertia. In some cases, reunion with or proximity to the parent produces either emotional conflict, fearful behaviour, depression or profound withdrawal. Without an organised attachment strategy, children may *freeze*, either physically or psychologically.

Internal working models, patterns of attachment and resilience

To recap, different attachment experiences generate particular internal working models; different aspects of the self within each working model are viewed as either positive or negative. *The concept of the internal working model is therefore of central importance in child and family work practices that use attachment and relationship-based theories.* It helps us to understand how individuals characteristically behave when their feelings are running high, how they view and relate to others under stress. Such understandings throw a strong light on the behaviours and emotional states of parents, children and social workers themselves.

We might also note that positive views of self appear to grant the individual a degree of psychological *resilience*. When the individual's self-system is under stress, resilient people are able to maintain psychological integrity; they remain able to draw on a range of personal strengths to cope with adversity and life's ups and downs. They continue to be purposeful and focused problem-solvers. Other people continue to be seen as a resource and not necessarily part of the problem. Resiliences include self-esteem, self-efficacy, self-reflexivity, social empathy and autonomy (see Chapter 10).

3

Measuring attachment across the lifespan

Assessing attachment security and insecurity

Developmental psychologists have devised a number of methods to assess the security of attachment depending on the age of the population being studied. Mary Ainsworth's great contribution to attachment theory was to develop a procedure that attempted to measure attachment security in infants. Bowlby's theoretical genius was therefore nicely complemented by Ainsworth's empirical creativity. Her development of a practical measure of infant attachment behaviour allowed researchers to examine parent–child relationships in a rigorous, systematic and standardised way.

As attachment behaviour is activated when the individual experiences anxiety, all assessment procedures involve introducing mild levels of attachment-related emotional distress to those under study. The way in which the individual responds to and handles this distress is taken to reveal the strategy that he or she typically uses to regulate arousal and raised affect. The response also shows whether the self is seen by the individual as worthy and effective, and whether other people are seen as caring and available. Thus, the measures allow investigators to determine the individual's internal working model and attachment style. We shall briefly outline four attachment assessment procedures: Ainsworth's Strange Situation for infant attachments; projective story-telling for young school-age children; Main and Goldwyn's Adult Attachment Interview; and George and Solomon's Caregiving Interview.

The Strange Situation

Ainsworth designed an experimental procedure that 'tested' the level of security experienced by infants, typically aged between 12 and 18 months, in their relationship with their main caregiver (Ainsworth *et al.* 1978). The procedure examines the representational or internal working model that children have of their relationship with their attachment figure. The test produces low levels of infant stress, sufficient to activate their attachment behavioural system. The stresses experienced by the infant are caused by:

- the 'strange' room
- the periodic presence of a 'stranger'
- brief separations from the mother.

These stresses were chosen as relatively common, non-traumatic occurrences.

The procedure runs as follows:

1. Mother and infant together. Child has the opportunity to explore and play with toys. Mother watches.
2. A stranger then enters the room. After a short while, the stranger talks to the mother and then plays with the child.
3. Mother leaves the room. The stranger remains and plays with the child.
4. Mother returns after a short while (say 30 seconds) or as soon as the infant begins to show heightened distress (First Reunion). Mother settles the child. The stranger leaves the room.
5. Mother exits the room and leaves the infant on his or her own.
6. Stranger then enters and attempts to play with and comfort the infant.
7. Mother returns after a short while or as soon as the child begins to show heightened distress (Second Reunion). Mother settles the child. Stranger leaves.

The whole procedure takes about 20 minutes. When mothers leave the room, most children stop playing. They show separation anxiety, which normally triggers attachment behaviour. Infants protest by crying and attempt to follow the mother when she exits. This illustrates that when attachment behaviour is activated, exploratory behaviour ceases. However, more important for making a classification of the infant's attachment style is the infant's behaviour upon reunion with the caregiver. '*The infant's behavior must be evaluated in relation to the set-goal of the attachment behavioral system: parental protection*' (George 1996: 414, emphasis added). Attachment quality appears to be significantly correlated with maternal sensitivity. Initially, Ainsworth identified three types of attachment behaviour:

- insecure–avoidant (the A pattern)
- secure (the B pattern)
- insecure–ambivalent (the C pattern).

Later work by Main and Solomon (1986) recognised a fourth type:

- insecure–disorganised (the D pattern).

Close observation of mother–child patterns of interaction in the natural home setting supports the laboratory findings. van IJzendoorn *et al.* (1992), in a meta-analysis of Strange Situation classifications of non-clinical infant–mother dyads, found the following four-way coding distribution:

- Avoidant (A)   23%
- Secure (B)   55%
- Ambivalent (C)   8%
- Disorganised (D)   15%

Culture and intercountry comparisons

Cross-cultural and intercountry comparisons of attachment patterns confirm that the modal type is that of the secure attachment, typically around 55–60 per cent infant–mother dyads showing the pattern. Although the proportion of insecure types is therefore similar between cultures, minor differences in the frequencies of the avoidant and ambivalent insecure patterns are sometimes observed. For example, the proportion of ambivalent types is slightly higher in Japan and Israel than in the USA. Compared with American studies, the number of infant–mother dyads classified as avoidant appears a little higher in some Western European countries, including Germany. There are also within-country differences, but again, controlling for socio-economic and other environmental risks, the broad picture remains the same. Randolph, for example, reports that the proportions of securely and insecurely attached children are similar between black African-American families and white Caucasian samples (cited in Rosenblith 1992: 476).

Gender

Research has not revealed any significant gender differences in the distribution of attachment classifications. This is not to say that girls and boys (a) are not constitutionally different, or (b) do not get treated differently. For example, Aber and Baker (1990: 452–3) report that girls scored higher than boys on flexibility of attention and responsiveness to social stimuli. Girls exhibit less gaze aversion and a longer duration of eye contact than do boys. In many cultural contexts, girls are more encouraged to seek comfort than boys when they are distressed. Such behaviours may give the appearance that more girls are more secure than boys, but in the Strange Situation, this appears not to be the case. Aber and Baker (1990) suggest that these observational findings can be interpreted as either different socialisation histories or inherent biological differences between boys and girls that evoke different parenting styles between the sexes.

Temperament

A major debate continues about the part that temperament and biological inheritance might play in attachment, the development of personality and individual behavioural styles. This is far from resolved. There is good evidence that there is a biological basis (including sex differences) to shyness, irritability, withdrawal, sociability, competitiveness, ability to concentrate, and inhibited and uninhibited behaviour (Kagan 1989, 1994). However, there is an increasingly strong belief that, instead of seeing nature and nurture, genes and environment, biology and culture as mutually exclusive influences on development, there is a complex, subtle interplay between the two. This is not meant to suggest that the developmental trajectory followed by children is the result of a bit of nature and a dash of nurture. The emphasis is on the *interaction* between biology and environment, with influences running both ways (Plomin 1994).

For example, temperamentally difficult babies who are irritable and fussy may cause temperamentally anxious mothers to react with increasing distress and decreasing sensitivity. Temperament therefore may either bring about or amplify an insecure attachment relationship. However, temperamentally difficult babies raised by more temperamentally relaxed, sociable mothers may find themselves enjoying a more responsive, accepting style of parenting that allows them to regulate their easily aroused feelings of fret and agitation. Similarly, babies with easy temperaments may produce more adept, tolerant parenting responses by mothers and fathers who, as a result of their own temperamental make-up and attachment history, might otherwise be inclined to be impatient and flustered. In such ways might babies' temperaments bring about particular social environments. In turn, social environments can influence the expression of certain temperamental traits. Development is a 'cooperative mission' between genes and experience, and 'no behavior is a first-order, direct product of genes' (Kagan 1994: 37).

It also has to be remembered that attachment classifications are not diagnoses. An insecure attachment is not in itself pathological, although children with an insecure attachment are at increased developmental risk, but only a risk, of some maladaptive and problem behaviours. Indeed, some personality characteristics associated with insecure attachments may be functional in certain situations, producing behaviours that may be valued and seen as appropriate.

Projective story-telling

In infancy, the only way to try to understand how the children are representing the availability of the mother and the worthiness of the self (the internal working model of attachment) is to observe their behaviour in various low-stress conditions. With older children and adults, it becomes possible to examine internal working models using measures that seek to elicit more directly the way in which the individual is mentally representing the self and the other. A common technique used in early and middle childhood is get children to 'project' themselves into a story in which there are attachment-related events. The stories may be facilitated by the use of dolls, pictures or opportunities to draw.

For example, George and Solomon (1996; Solomon *et al.*, 1995) use a doll-play measure with 6-year-olds. The children are introduced to the beginnings of an attachment-sensitive story, which they are then asked to complete. In the story, a child may be playing and have hurt himself, or a monster may be seen at bedtime. Mummy and daddy dolls are available for the story's development and completion if the child chooses to use them. In the 'departure' story, the child is asked to play out what happens in the home when the parents go away for the night and he or she is left with a babysitter. In the 'reunion' story, the child is asked to enact what happens when the parents return the next day. It will be noticed that parents' leaving and returning mentally mimic the separations and reunions seen in the infant Strange Situation procedure. Differences in the content and process of the stories indicate the way in which the child typically handles anxiety and distress. In turn, these defensive methods of dealing with anxiety provide information about the child's internal working model of attachment. Again, children are classified according to the four basic attachment patterns.

Secure children develop stories in which fears and separation anxieties are deliberately raised before finally being resolved, usually by the return of responsive, loving parents.

Avoidant and ambivalent children tend not to let their attachment behavioural systems become fully activated. The stories they develop do not allow anxieties and fears to threaten safety and security. *Avoidant–defended* children tell matter-of-fact stories that appear casual and nonchalant. Nothing out of the ordinary seems to happen. The attachment system is immobilised. Distressing possibilities are defensively excluded.

Ambivalent–dependent children tell busy, happy stories about what children do in their parents' absence. Brief 'sentimental laments' are often introduced about how much the parents are loved (George 1996: 415). Attachment anxieties are dealt with by a form of defensive 'splitting' – the bad, distressing bits are temporarily ignored or denied, while the good bits are exaggerated. 'Cognitive disconnection separates positive and negative information,' says George (1996: 415), attention being diverted to positive events. It seems difficult for ambivalent children to integrate and concurrently acknowledge both anxious and positive feelings. They can only deal with one emotional perspective at a time. Things are either all wonderful and good, or all terrible and bad.

Disorganised–controlling children introduce fear and danger into their stories but seem to have no way of resolving the growing crises. Parents remain physically and emotionally unavailable or even abusive. Chaos and helplessness mount, the self and the family disintegrate, and stories are ended, often abruptly, with no resolution.

Adult Attachment Interview

The Adult Attachment Interview (AAI) is an hour-long semi-structured interview developed by Main and Goldwyn (1984–94) that explores people's general descriptions of their attachment relationships in child-hood, memories that either support or contradict the general descrip-tions, and descriptions of current relationships with parents and children (if they have any). Particular attention is paid to three primary domains:

- experiences of loss, separation and rejection
- experiences of emotional upsets, hurts and sickness
- experiences of love and acceptance, with each caregiver.

The interview was developed as an index of the way in which adults organise attachment-related thoughts, feelings and memories.

The adult is asked to talk about his or her early childhood attach-ment-related memories and to evaluate them from their current adult perspective. The coding of the interview transcripts depends less on the literal content of what is said but more on the way in which the story is told and holds together (or otherwise). The adult's childhood experiences in the three primary domains are examined – their experi-ences of love, rejection and neglect. Questions about childhood attachment experiences take the adult by emotional surprise, slightly raising levels of anxiety and stress. In their responses and reflections, individuals suddenly have to cope with affect-laden thoughts and memories about key attachment relationships, both in the past and in the present. In their attempts to regulate their emotions, adults use different strategies or rules to access, process and express attachment-related material (Main 1996).

In effect, the AAI provokes a discourse of attachment-related memories. Adults who have not yet understood and flexibly modelled feelings associated with insecure attachment experiences remain insecure. According to Main (1996: 240): 'Identification of these states [of mind with respect to attachment] is derived not from apparent life history, but rather from discourse usage involved in its presentation, and chiefly albeit informally from coherence and collaboration as identified by the linguistic philosopher Grice (1975).' Grice identified coherent, collaborative discourse as requiring adherence to four maxims:

1. quality ('be truthful, and have evidence for what you say')
2. quantity ('be succinct yet complete')
3. relation ('be relevant or perspicacious')
4. manner ('be clear and orderly').

Great attention is paid in the AAI to these four maxims. Departures from one or more of the maxims produces a degree of incoherence and non-collaboration in the adults' description of and reflections on their attachment-related experiences. Researchers are therefore interested in how individuals process distress-related information. Interviews are analysed in terms of adherence to and violations of the four maxims. Differences in coherence/incoherence and collaboration/non-collaboration in the way in which the questions are answered and memories recounted reveal the defensive and non-defensive ways in which the individual typically handles and regulates attachment-related thoughts, feelings and memories. In insecure patterns, childhood memories may be vague; detail of specific events to back a general description may be missing; there may be contradictions in the story; the detail may be rich but confused.

The presence of childhood abuse, loss or trauma does not necessarily mean that the adult is insecure. If experiences are relayed in a clear, balanced manner, if the interview is coherent and questions are answered in an appropriate and informed way, adults may be classified as secure. They may supply evidence of being able to access feelings and understand the part they play and have played in relationships. These people, termed 'earned secure' by Pearson *et al.* (1994), illustrate how good-quality relationships at any time in life can help to 'disconfirm' an insecure working model. One of the aims of attachment-related practices is to provide good social experiences that help to disconfirm old, insecure working models. Secure adults attempt to understand and control their feelings rather be controlled by them.

Current adult classifications employ four attachment patterns that correspond (although they may not be continuously related) to the four childhood patterns:

- *Secure–autonomous, free to evaluate (F)* states of mind with respect to attachment (compare infant secure B patterns). The presentation and evaluation of experiences are internally consistent. Responses are clear, relevant and succinct. Adults are able to reflect on and realistically evaluate their emotional experiences. They can think about and appraise their behaviour. Individuals may also seek social feedback.

- *Dismissing (Ds)* states of mind with respect to attachment (compare infant avoidant A pattern). Globally positive statements about parents are not supported by specific examples or are indeed contradicted elsewhere in the interview. Attachment-related and emotionally charged memories are quickly glossed over.

- *Preoccupied–entangled (E)* states of mind with respect to attachment (compare infant ambivalent C patterns). Attachment-related events are talked about in a confused, angry, ambivalent fashion. There is a preoccupation with relationships, particularly with who was loved and not loved, who coped and did not cope.

- *Unresolved–disorganised (U)* states of mind with respect to attachment (compare infant disorganised D patterns). During their answers, adults may lose the thread of what they are saying as they become lost in past, maybe difficult, traumatic memories. There are lapses in monitoring what is being asked and what is being replied.

Holmes (1997: 238) reminds us that attempts to discern an individual's attachment status assume that we are able to tap into some meaningful psychological configuration:

Attachment status seems to relate to patterns of parental handling in the first year of life, and is thus clearly an interpersonal phenomenon. The strange situation measures the *enactment* of the child's relationship to her parents. The AAI by contrast defines individuals' *description* of their relationship to their own life – a movement from mechanism to meaning, from attachment behaviour to representation of attachments. While attachment emerges from parental handling, narrative style has to do with the individual's relationship to herself. Between the strange situation and the AAI a process of internalization has taken place, which comprises an individual's awareness of herself, her significant others, the relationship between them, and her awareness of, and ability to report on, these phenomena.

In a meta-analysis of over 2,000 AAI carried out in the course of 33 studies, van IJzendoorn and Bakermans-Kranenburg (1996) found the following four-way coding distributions for non-clinical populations of mothers and fathers:

Mothers

Secure (F)	55%
Dismissing (Ds)	16%
Preoccupied–entangled (E)	9%
Unresolved (U)	19%

Fathers

Secure (F)	57%
Dismissing (Ds)	15%
Preoccupied–entangled (E)	11%
Unresolved (U)	17%

In 1987, Hazan and Shaver developed a *self-report* (rather than the AAI, which is a form of clinical interview) measure for classifying adult attachments. Other investigators have developed and refined the original three-group classification of Hazan and Shaver (secure, avoidant and anxious–ambivalent). Bartholomew and Horowitz (1991; see also Feeney *et al.* 1995) have generated a four-group taxonomy based on a 2 x 2 classification of:

- the *self* viewed as either positive or negative
- *others* viewed as either positive or negative.

This gives us:

- secure: positive view of self, positive view of others
- dismissive: positive view of self, negative view of others
- preoccupied: negative view of self, positive view of others
- fearful: negative view of self, negative view of others.

These groups do not entirely coincide with or use the same attachment-related logic as that developed by Main and Goldwyn (1984–94). However, there is a rough correspondence between the four types, the 'fearful' group showing similarities to the AAI's Unresolved–Disorganised pattern.

As with child attachment classifications, adult attachment classifications are not a diagnosis. However, individuals showing insecure patterns cope less well with stress and difficulty. Security appears to confer some protection in the face of adversity.

Caregiving behavioural system

George (1996) suggests that internal working models formed in childhood continue to guide interactions into adulthood. When adults also become parents, the models guide their interactions with their own children. 'In short', believes George (1996: 417), 'this model predicts continuity and the intergenerational transmission of relationships.' For example, Fonagy *et al.* (1991), administering the AAI on first-time pregnant mothers, were able in 75 per cent of cases to predict whether the infant would be classified as either securely or insecurely attached when assessed at 12 months. The infants of 'secure–autonomous' mothers were highly likely to be classified as securely attached. Similarly, the majority of the babies of 'insecure dismissing–preoccupied' mothers were classified as insecure. Predictive power resides, believe Fonagy *et al.* (1991: 901), not in the quality of the mother's past experience 'but in the overall organization of mental structures underlying relationships and attachment related issues'.

Internal working models form within relationships and can, of course, be modified and 'disconfirmed' at any stage in the lifespan if individuals experience new, influential attachment relationships. They are, after all, 'working' models and can be modified if people begin to react in ways (both positively and negatively) that the model fails to predict or anticipate. Intergenerational transmission of the same attachment pattern is therefore by no means automatic. However, with age, internal working models become increasingly likely to be self-confirming as people behave and react in ever more predictable ways. This means that internal working models become more resistant to change, even though change is always possible.

All behavioural systems organise distinct repertoires of human behaviour to achieve certain ends. Whatever the environment in which they find themselves, behavioural systems are goal-correcting. That is, the behaviours needed to achieve the goals (for example, proximity, felt security, protection and learning) are adjusted flexibly and adaptively within the context of the (social) environment so that, one way or another, the goal, if possible, is achieved. The result is that different physical, social and relationship environments produce different behavioural patterns, each pattern representing an adaptation to the predominant characteristics of that environment. The cognitive modelling seeks to represent:

- the environment (of other people)
- how the self is to be understood
- how the self should behave in that environment if the goal is to be achieved (proximity, felt security, learning and so on).

Such cognitive representations lead to the formation of the internal working model.

George and Solomon (1996; Solomon and George 1996) believe that the parent's caregiving system is a distinct behavioural system, comparable to the attachment and exploratory systems:

> parents' appraisals of their behavior and future plans for their children are guided by representational models of caregiving… The parent thinks about and interacts with his or her child in relation to *providing protection* and care for that child, not in terms of *seeking protection* and care for the self. (George 1996: 418, original emphasis)

This represents a mature transformation of the attachment system, shifting the individual's goal in relationships with children from wanting to be protected when distressed to providing protection for those in distress. The construction of the self as a caregiver is structured around the answers to two questions: will I be a good mother? (= will I be able to protect this child?), and will I have a good child? (= will I want to protect this child?) (Solomon and George 1996). The goal of the caregiving system, therefore, is to keep the child close to the caregiver under conditions of threat, danger or distress.

> Subjectively, the role of caregiver, while a very powerful and compelling one, is not the only role the mother strives to fulfill. She may also be a worker, spouse, mother to other children, and a child to her own parents. Therefore, just as the infant must seek a dynamic balance between attachment and exploration, the parent must strike a balance between her need to protect and nurture the child and her need to pursue other goals. This sets the stage for psychological conflict within the mother and conflict between the parent and child. (Solomon and George 1996: 186)

In the manner of the AAI, researchers have developed an interview to assess internal models of caregiving. Mothers and fathers are asked to describe themselves as parents, the emotional quality of their relationship with their children, and perceived similarities and differences between themselves and their children. The experience and management of attachment-related issues (separations, distress, upsets, discipline and safety) are explored. Analysis of the interviews demonstrates four basic styles of information-processing and defensive exclusion associated with parents' representational models of caregiving:

1. a secure base (a balanced and flexible use of caregiving behaviour)
2. rejecting (deactivation of the caregiving system)

3. uncertain (defensive use of the caregiving system by splitting positive and negative evaluations of the child; unable to discuss and
   handle the two aspects at once)
4. helpless (disorganised caregiving).

It is worth emphasising at this point that the birth of a vulnerable,
demanding and lovable baby 'has enormous power to evoke caregiving behavior... mothers of varying attachment histories, including
very traumatic and disturbed ones, are very strongly motivated to
protect their young child' (Solomon and George 1996: 191). This has
important implications for when and how to work with parents who
feel that they are running into difficulty. The reality of the baby can
affect how mothers represent and model themselves and their baby.
Mothers unsure of their caring skills may gain in confidence if they
have a temperamentally responsive baby. On the other hand, a
temperamentally difficult baby, a baby who is ill or a child who picks
up his mother's anxiety and becomes distressed may undermine
confidence in the parenting role. Also, feeding into the character of a
mother's caregiving behaviour is the quality of support she receives
from her partner, her own parents, the family, the community and
society at large. These will, for better or worse, affect her views of
herself as a competent, caring, protective parent.

Attachment classification and practice

It is clearly not possible for field practitioners to carry out these attachment measurement procedures on a routine, daily basis; they remain the
tools of research psychologists. The laboratory rather than the home is
the usual setting. There may be occasional opportunities when practitioners might be able to refer a child or parent to a developmental
researcher for an assessment, but this will remain an exceptional event.
In contrast, however, practitioners have access to a much wider range of
knowledge about parents and their children than do researchers. Case
histories and information about past experiences are routinely available.
   Practitioners also have many opportunities to observe people
behaving, relating and coping in the natural settings of home, family,
school and neighbourhood. In particular, practitioners see children
and parents dealing with naturally occurring situations in which there
are attachment-related issues and experiences of distress. In many
cases, involvement with families will be spread over many months,

even years. The worker herself enters into emotionally charged relationships with mothers, fathers and children. Thus, social workers possess an extraordinarily rich, varied, detailed and unique picture of parents' and children's behaviour and relationships, which, although not collected in the systematic and standardised manner of the researcher, outbids the scientific enquiry in terms of depth, breadth, quantity and historical length.

These differences in knowledge acquisition lead to different procedures for determining parents' and children's attachment patterns and internal working models. The research scientist proceeds in the manner of a behavioural auditor or taxonomist. Specific behaviours and relationship features are first described and then classified. If a sufficient number of features associated with a particular attachment pattern are ticked as present, individuals and the character of their relationships are classified according to one of the four attachment types. It is rather like a biologist who classifies an animal according to its characteristics and behaviours. If the animal has four legs, teeth adapted to hunting, a tail and is carnivorous, it might be either a cat or a dog. But if the animal is observed also to have a supple, low slung body, a long tail that aids balance, sharp, retractable claws, a purr and nocturnal habits, it is likely to be a cat rather than a dog.

In contrast, the social worker accumulates information in the manner of a detective or a geological surveyor. Knowledge may crop up erratically, in patches, during a home visit, while watching the children play, from a file or in conversation with a teacher or health worker. Information pours in along a number of channels. The volume of knowledge quickly creates a psychological portrait of what seems to be happening. Past childhood experiences seem to make sense of the quality of the adult's current relationships. Parenting styles and children's behaviour appear to suggest links between the parents' anxieties and their child's emotional difficulties. Anger engendered in the social worker and the violence noted in the parents' marriage give an insight into how people feel and react when in close relationship with the parents. Pieced together and organised by an attachment-perspective, these myriad bits of knowledge gradually bring the overall psychosocial picture into focus. These emerging 'field pictures' can then be *matched* with the formal attachment portraits created by the developmental researchers. The social worker aims to achieve a working 'fit' between what she knows and sees, and the research evidence that defines the main attachment patterns and their associated behaviours.

Attachment patterns across the lifespan

One of the purposes of this book is to provide a detailed catalogue of the research evidence supporting each of the four basic attachment patterns, that is, the adaptive and maladaptive behaviours, relationship experiences, interpersonal styles and defensive strategies characteristic of secure, avoidant, ambivalent and disorganised attachments across the lifespan (Table 3.1 and Chapters 4–7). By developing a thorough understanding of the four attachment patterns and the psychological processes that underpin them, it is hoped that practitioners will develop a facility to analyse, assess and understand parents', children's and their own internal working models, attachment behaviours, personality types, defensive behaviours and relationship experiences.

The next four chapters present the research evidence for each of the four main attachment categories.

Table 3.1   Attachment behaviours and patterns across the lifespan

	Attachment type			
	Secure–autonomous	*Avoidant–dismissing*	*Ambivalent–preoccupied–entangled*	*Disorganised–unresolved*
Infancy	Secure	Insecure–avoidant	Insecure–ambivalent–resistant	Insecure–disorganised–disorientated
Toddlerhood–preschool–school age	Secure–optimal	Defended–disengaged	Dependent–deprived Coercive	Controlling–confused
Adolescence–adulthood	Autonomous–free to evaluate	Dismissing	Preoccupied–entangled–enmeshed	Unresolved loss/trauma–disorganised
Parenting style	Secure base	Rejecting	Uncertain	Helpless

4

Secure and autonomous patterns

The majority of children and adults in all cultures show secure and autonomous patterns of attachment behaviour. It is the modal style. In normal populations, we might typically expect to see around 55–65 per cent of people classified as secure and autonomous. In broad terms, 'felt security' finds both children and adults holding a positive view of the self, other people and close relationships. Possessed of a positive approach to social life, individuals are generally able to acknowledge and deal accurately, appropriately and effectively with strong feelings, including distress, anxiety and anger. The ability to make sense of both the self and others in relationships increases people's social competence.

It is not being suggested that secure individuals find life trouble free. Instead, their security is a measure of how they respond to life's ups and downs. To the extent that they can positively draw on a range of personal and social resources to cope with stress, individuals are able to retain an integrated view of both self and others. They can access and appraise the origin and character of their own and other people's feelings in such as a way as to preserve their self-esteem and autonomy. Also, being personally insightful, emotionally literate and socially fluent, secure people are viewed positively by others. The behaviours, relationship styles and personality characteristics associated with secure and autonomous patterns will be described across the lifespan.

Infancy

The inborn prosocial capacities of young infants evoke sensitive, responsive parenting. For example, the 'social smile' of babies acts as a positive stimulus to adults. As babies develop, they begin to use their smile preferentially with their attachment figures. Across cultures, a smiling baby tends to attract interest, promote social interaction and elicit positive responses from adults. It is also the case that attuned caregiving releases socially sophisticated behaviour in babies.

Mothers of secure infants are rated at the positive end of 'responsivity'. Most of the time, they are sensitive, accepting, cooperative, available, accessible and dependable. Mothers tend to be good at reading their children's signals. There is synchrony between mothers and their infants, involving well-timed, reciprocal, rewarding interactions. Communication of feelings, needs and wants is accurate. Parents have empathy. There is a sense of harmony. Mothers show a great deal of interest and fascination in their babies. They are, in Winnicott's wonderful phrase, 'good enough' parents.

Main (1995) recognises that, in such socio-emotionally synchronised relationships, infants begin to understand the consequences of both their own and their mother's behaviour. Mothers who are available, responsive and comforting generate a soothing, predictable environment. They help their infants to modulate strong states of arousal. This encourages babies to maintain maximum alertness. 'Put in attachment terms,' continues Crittenden (1992b: 580), 'when mothers are sensitively responsive, infants are freed from the disorganizing effects of intense emotional arousal and are able to explore their world.'

Clear interpersonal patterns begin to be perceived by infants that helps them to make sense of both their own and their mother's behaviour. The effect of such synchrony is to create a kind of interpersonal *scaffolding* that helps children to locate and support their growing understanding of their own and other people's emotions, mental states, behaviours and interactional styles.

The result of regularly experiencing such synchronised harmony is that children are able to access, acknowledge and integrate both their thoughts and the full range of their feelings. Cognition and affect support each other rather than exist in a state of conflict and confusion. Responsive, reciprocal parent–child relationships help infants to recognise, work out and understand:

- their own and other people's feelings
- the impact of their own feelings on their own behaviour
- how other people's behaviour affects their own feelings
- how their own feelings and behaviour seem to affect other people's feelings and behaviour.

Such understanding allows the child to acknowledge the power of feelings to affect behaviour.

This is the first step towards being able to *regulate* one's own emotions in ways that are socially appropriate and effective. In such ways, children become 'emotionally intelligent' (Goleman 1996). In addition, to the extent that other people feel that they know where they stand in relationship with others, communication becomes accurate and easy to manage. Social skills of this kind help to reduce interpersonal tension, confusion and difficulty. Relationships feel comfortable and relatively stress free. Benign interactional circles routinely form. The inability to regulate emotion leaves the individual at the mercy of strong feelings and confused thoughts.

Anger is perhaps the most potent attachment behaviour. The different patterns of attachment can be viewed at one level as strategies for managing anger. More secure children experience less anger over shorter periods of time than do insecure children. Carers tend to respond quickly to expressions of protest and anger, thus protecting their infants from an overlong exposure to unregulated distress. The babies' feelings of being emotionally overwhelmed and helpless are kept to a minimum.

Most of these ingredients are nicely captured in the way in which securely attached infants behave in the Strange Situation procedure (see Chapter 3). It will be remembered that the procedure is designed to induce mild and short-lived levels of stress in babies, typically aged between 12 and 18 months. Attached patterns become most pronounced under increased stress. Therefore, the way in which the infant reacts in the test, particularly the way he behaves upon reunion with his mother after the brief separation, indicates his internal working model. In turn, the model tells us how he is mentally representing his carer's emotional availability and his own self-worth.

STRANGE SITUATION

With the mother present, the infant immediately seeks out the toys. The child's play is active. From time to time, the baby shows the mother a toy, smiling and vocalising. When the mother exits, the child stops playing, shows distress, begins to protest and cry, and will often attempt to follow her out of the door. When the mother returns, the infant greets her eagerly, usually with arms outstretched. The mother typically picks up the child, offering comfort and reassurance. The baby is soon soothed and happily resumes play. The second separation sees further upset and protest. The appearance of the stranger fails to console the baby. The mother's second return again quickly helps the baby to recover equanimity. Exploratory play is soon re-established.

'What is most striking within this behavioral sequence', says Main (1995: 416), 'is the immediacy with which the baby's distress is terminated (he may cease crying immediately on seeing the mother), the comfort he takes in contact with her, and his readiness to return once again to play. The observer has witnessed what appears to be a miniature drama with a happy ending.' Mothers of securely attached infants therefore appear sensitive to their child's signals. They communicate and respond promptly and effectively. There is evidence of much cooperation between the two in which the mother provides gentle, well-timed, non-intrusive guidance. There is a fluid balance between attachment and exploration in the form of play.

Within such interactions, infants develop internal working models in which they experience others as emotionally available and dependable, particularly at times of need and arousal. There is a sense of 'basic trust' in their caregiver (Erikson 1968). Children experience themselves as lovable and worthy of care. They are the subject of interest and pleasure, concern and value to other people. Carers encourage children to explore their environment. As a result, they feel increasingly *autonomous*. They also recognise that they are able to do something about their distress themselves. Their behaviours bring about suitable responses from others. This implies that feelings can be accurately communicated and understood by others. Over time, sensitive caregiving encourages dialogue between infants and parents. This encourages children to develop emotional openness, understanding and fluency within their internal working model. The internal working models of securely attached children facilitate clear and direct communication in both present and future relationships. Within such relationships, young children also begin to recognise and understand both their own and other people's thoughts and feelings. Thus, the combination of receiving sensitive, attuned responses from others that help in the reduction of arousal, and the growing understanding of what affects one's own emotional states, enables children to regulate their own affect.

Within secure relationship patterns, both the self and other people are viewed positively. In exploration, children can rely on themselves but turn to others when the need arises. The result of such experiences and the expectations they create is that *self-esteem* and *self-efficacy* will be high. For all of us, there is a basic need to be viewed positively and to feel that we have some influence and control over our environment. Children who enjoy high self-esteem and feelings of personal effectiveness show the greatest *resilience* in the face of adversity. In other words, although securely attached children are least likely to experience sustained or severe social adversity, they are the ones most able to cope with stress. There is also evidence that infants who display difficult temperaments and innate 'negative emotionality' respond well to competent, sensitive parenting. Walden and Garber (1994: 428) report shifts between 3 and 9 months of age from negative emotionality to more positive emotionality if the children's parents are 'psychologically healthier', enjoy a stable partnership, interact harmoniously with their baby and have higher levels of engagement.

Toddlerhood and preschool age

Between 18 months and 4–5 years of age, children become mobile, learn to talk and become increasingly active in social relationships. Whereas in babyhood, emotional arousal and distress are dealt with behaviourally – crying, following and protesting – by toddlerhood, children also learn to deal with their feelings cognitively using language and mental processes. Within relationships, children learn to recognise links between behaviour and situations, and the emotions they cause. The more that children understand the nature and origin of their own and other people's emotional states, the more competent and socially adaptive will be their behaviour. The use of 'I', 'me' and self-descriptive utterances increases, indicating a growing sense of personal agency.

Emotional competence

With language, parents are able to help children to put names to different emotions. Emotion recognition is developmentally very important and helps to predict later social functioning. It also facilitates the regulation of affect. Securely attached children show good affect recognition. When presented with pictures of people with various emotional expressions on their faces, even quite young children can identify faces that are happy, sad, angry and frightened. In observational studies in which mothers are asked to read their children a story containing attachment-related issues (for example, the tale of the mummy owl and her three baby owls in which she flies off and leaves them to hunt for mice before eventually returning safe and well), there are plenty of opportunities for both mother and child to explore the feelings of sadness, anxiety and happiness associated with experiences of separation, availability and reunion. The identification and labelling of feelings in the story and links made with the child's own experience provide an *emotional scaffold* in which feelings can be recognised, understood and handled. Language provides children with the conceptual ability to make cognitive sense of and manage their own feelings. The more accurate that children's understanding of affect is, particularly in social contexts, the more emotionally competent they will be:

> Language is an important and potent tool that allows individuals to understand emotions... With the development of linguistic competence, children substantially increase their ability to communicate feelings to other persons, receive feedback about the appropriateness of their emotions, and obtain information about ways to manage emotional states. Moreover, the development of language can be influenced by emotions. (Walden and Garber 1994: 422)

Thus, the ability to recognise, discriminate and understand emotional states is associated with the capacity to regulate high arousal and distress. Children need to be able to talk about their feelings, to reflect on their emergent understanding of relationships and the interplay between the self and other people.

Saarni (1990) describes emotional competence as the successful negotiation of relationships in emotionally arousing situations. It is the ability to manage negative feelings in a socially and personally competent manner. Included in the capacity to like and be liked, and to be interpersonally successful, Saarni lists:

- an accurate awareness of one's own emotional state (including multiple emotions that occur and understanding possible biases in one's knowledge)
- the ability to read other's emotions
- the ability to label verbally and discuss emotion
- an empathic involvement in others' emotions
- recognition of the incongruences between an emotional expression and an inner state
- a knowledge of cultural display rules
- an understanding of unique personal information that aids in interpreting another's behaviour
- a knowledge of the impact of one's own behaviour on others
- the ability to self-regulate negative emotions
- an awareness of the contribution of genuine emotional expression to relationships
- self-satisfaction with one's emotional experience and behaviour.

Secure children show *flexibility* in both their experience and expression of feelings that allows them to access cognitively their own affective states, read social relationships accurately and respond adaptively.

Autonomy, exploration and play

Securely attached children also begin to show increasing independence. They can mentally represent their parents as emotionally available and thus become less concerned about their carers' actual physical presence. This allows them to play on their own or with peers for longer and longer periods without seeking parental involvement. For example, secure 4-year-olds play with their friends more harmoniously, more interactively and in a less controlling way than do their insecure peers. Children using secure strategies begin to consider the other person's perspective. They start to communicate and share their own thoughts, feelings and desires. Joint planning and negotiation become possible. Such experiences confirm children's feelings that the social world is intelligible, navigable and responsive.

The capacity to concentrate, solve problems and cope with frustration increases. Moreover, emotional competence seems positively to influence both problem-solving and learning behaviour. Pretend play, which requires an ability to imagine what it must be like and feel like to be someone or something else, becomes well established in securely attached children. Imaginative play is rich and increasingly complex. A sense of humour, and the ability to tease and deceive all require a sophisticated understanding of both one's own and other people's minds. The more that children are able to explore and experiment with their own and other people's thoughts and feelings, the greater will be their social understanding and relationship skills. For example, secure 4-year-olds show increased empathy. They are more inclined to support and offer comfort to a distressed sibling. Indeed, the more competent that children become in the business of social empathy, the more moral and thoughtful their behaviour appears to be. It also means that children begin to experience the more culturally based emotions such as guilt and shame, feelings that can further inhibit behaviour that is socially unacceptable.

The end result of children's growing ability to:

- recognise and make sense of their own and other people's feelings
- regulate their own affect

- assume other people's emotional availability
- develop good self-esteem
- feel autonomous, socially effective and competent

is a more integrated, balanced and flexible view of self. Crittenden (1995: 380) concludes that 'children's experience of evermore coherent integrations of information regarding the interface of external reality and their own behavior, beliefs, and feelings can be considered the basis of personal integrity'.

School age

The social and emotional skills acquired by secure school-age children are nicely illustrated by researchers using 'projective story-telling' to measure children's attachment behaviours. For example, George and Solomon (1996; Solomon *et al.* 1995), using dolls, invited 6-year-olds to act out and finish various stories in which there was an attachment-related issue. In one story, a monster appears at the children's bedtime; in another, the parents go away for the night, leaving the child with a babysitter. Secure children tell the story with imagination. They 'activate' their attachment behavioural system by deliberately introducing fears, dangers and anxieties. Burglars might break into the house or a fire might flare up while the children are making their supper. Parents and caregivers, however, are depicted as available, responsive and able to provide care and protection. In the nick of time, they come to the rescue and make everything better, and everyone lives happily ever after. Emotional tensions, conflicts and crises introduced into the narrative are successfully resolved.

Observations made of 6-year-old children in natural settings also see them inventing crises in their pretend play. Matters generally grow worse before children finally resolve the crisis. They enact the 'classic narrative structures' of all successful children's stories in which a crisis, often involving the loss of or separation from parents, descends on a child or group of children. Fears and dangers mount. The tension is resolved by the return of the parents, who banish fears, deal with dangers and bring everything back to normal with a happy ending.

'The manner in which secure children openly revealed their separation fears', observes George (1996: 415), 'suggested that they engaged in little or no defensive exclusion. Rather, fears were allowed to come to conscious awareness, integrated into the story, and resolved.' In other words, secure children have the confidence to acknowledge and the ability to understand and therefore handle difficult and anxiety-provoking emotions. Children who can acknowledge, accept and conceptualise (rather than avoid, deny, defensively split or misunderstand) distressing emotions such as fear and anger are better placed to manage and regulate emotional arousal.

School-age children's conduct and behaviour has been examined in the three main arenas in which they most often function: the family, and school and peer groups. The way in which children relate to their parents, siblings, peers and adult authority figures other than parents are key matters of interest to developmentalists and child welfare workers. Secure children appear to function reasonably well in each of these major settings.

Family life

In everyday relationships with their parents, children are reasonably cooperative as well as being compliant to parental directives. The quality of communication, responsiveness and interaction is good. Children are able to draw on undistorted, non-defended memories of previous relationship experiences and emotionally charged events. This helps them to represent reality with some accuracy. They are therefore less susceptible to emotional distortion. Their internal working models remain flexible; they are able to use a range of strategies to cope with the demands of social relationships and regulate affect. Moreover, secure children continue to learn from experience. Internal working models are constantly updated, revised and reorganised to increase the range of responses available to the individual. More fine-grained pictures can be painted of one's own and other people's emotions and behaviours. Secure children are less emotionally thrown by other people's anger or hostility.

Classroom behaviour and educational achievement

Secure children show less emotional dependence on their teachers (Sroufe 1989b). However, when they do experience difficulties, they are more likely to approach teachers in a positive, constructive fashion. They are also better behaved, more likely to follow school rules, more cooperative and easier to manage.

Bradley *et al.* (1988) showed that children who had enjoyed positive parental responsivity when they were aged 6 months behaved well at school when they were 10 years old. Similarly, children who had been given appropriate play materials and stimulus aged 2 years showed good academic achievement particularly in reading skills, when they reached 10 years of age. It is speculated that 2-year-old children who are supported and encouraged to explore and try out their burgeoning sensorimotor skills learn to how to control and handle their environment.

Peer relationships

Generally popular with their friends, secure children show good empathy, tend to be quickly included in group activities and show low levels of conflict in their play. Unlike the more extreme avoidant and ambivalent children, who are prone either to bully or to be bullied, secure children are less likely to be victimisers or victims.

By middle childhood, secure children show the following behaviours, capacities and abilities:

- a greater concentration at play
- more positive affect
- greater social competence
- greater resilience
- teachers treating them more matter-of-factly than either avoidant or ambivalent children
- skill at conflict resolution
- being neither victims or victimisers
- more competent behaviour with people with whom they have a secure attachment
- higher self-esteem
- lower fearfulness
- relatively few behavioural problems and lower likelihood of being referred to a mental health clinic.

Adolescence and adulthood

Attachment-related issues continue to affect adolescents and adults. The two basic types of adult attachment measure – the clinical interview (Main and Goldwyn 1984–94) and the self-report questionnaire (Hazan and Shaver 1987) – tap different aspects of the adolescent/adult make-up.

The AAI prompts people to reflect on and describe their attachment relationships in childhood. Individuals are invited to talk about their early childhood attachment-related memories and to evaluate them from their current adult perspective. Memories are sought which either support or contradict the general descriptions. Current relationships with parents and children are also described. Experiences of loss, separation and rejection, emotional upsets, hurts and sickness are discussed. The content of the interview therefore acts as an index of the way in which adults organise attachment-related thoughts, feelings and memories.

Secure adults appear able to access a wide range of childhood memories, both good and bad, and examine them in a rounded, realistic way. They are able to acknowledge and integrate painful experiences into their narrative. They are *free to evaluate* the full range of their attachment-related experiences, both past and present, hence the letter 'F' that is given to the 'secure' adult classification. To this extent, they are free of the distorting effects that accompany those who use a variety of defensive strategies to exclude difficult memories and handle current relationships. Individuals maintain a thoughtful balance about experiences, both good and bad. They recognise links between past and present experiences. They value close relationships. They suggest a solid, robust sense of self, able to withstand normal degrees of emotional buffeting. This adult classification is also referred to as the *secure–autonomous* pattern:

> A speaker's state of mind with respect to attachment is classified as secure–autonomous when – whether life history appears favorable or unfavorable – the presentation and evaluation of experiences is internally consistent, and responses are clear, relevant, and reasonably succinct. (Main 1996: 240)

Main is reminding us here that individuals who have experienced adversity, including abuse in their childhood, are not predestined to become insecure adults. Many maltreated children will have experiences or enjoy relationships that allow them to develop more flexible internal working models, the benefits of which allow them to reflect on and process negative as well as positive childhood memories (see also Pianta *et al.* 1996). Hilary's account of her own childhood abuse shows how she is able to appraise the experience in a full, balanced manner.

Hilary

Hilary was the only girl in a family of four children. Her father frequently worked away from home. Her mother had a very obsessive, controlling personality. She also had a great fascination with sexual matters. She insisted not only that her daughter scrubbed and washed herself thoroughly twice a day, but also that, after each bath, she stood naked in front of her mother and brothers for inspection. She talked a lot about men and sex with all her children. Hilary was sexually abused by one of her brothers from the age of 6 for a period of 4 years. At the time, she knew she could never go to her mother for protection; indeed, looking back on events, she now suspects that her mother was somehow indirectly encouraging the abuse. The brother also used physical violence to ensure his sister's silence. She left home as soon as she could to work residentially in a hotel. Although she had not achieved much success at school, she began attending college, where she performed well. At work, she was regularly promoted. Aged 20, she met a young heating engineer who was carrying out some work in the hotel. He was a very stable character who gave Hilary a lot of security. They eventually married. Although she was unable to mention her childhood traumas to him at first, after an outburst of tears and great upset, she finally told him her story. He was very understanding and offered great comfort. Hilary said this marked the beginning of her growing self-confidence, which enabled her to reflect on her very unhappy childhood in a way that, although painful, she felt was necessary if she were to function effectively.

Secure–autonomous adolescents and adults acknowledge the value and impact of attachment relationships. The influence of such relationships on personality development is recognised. They can tolerate imperfection in themselves, their parents and those with whom they are currently in close relationship, including their own children. When describing attachment experiences, they are able to provide the interviewer with specific, concrete examples. Their stories are coherent and reflective. They collaborate with the purposes of the interviewer. Accuracy and honesty often characterise the narrative.

The work of people such as Hazan and Shaver (1987), Bartholomew (1990) and Feeney *et al.* (1995) examines adult attachments using a self-report measure. Secure adults are defined as having a model of self that is positive, and a positive view of other people's availability. They identify with the following statements:

> I find it relatively easy to get close to others and am comfortable depending on them and having them depend on me. I don't often worry about being abandoned or about someone getting close to me. (Hazan and Shaver 1987)

> It is relatively easy for me to become emotionally close to others. I am comfortable depending on others and having others depend on me. I don't worry about being alone or having others not accept me. (Bartholomew 1990)

Feeney *et al.* (1995) see the secure adult using more integrating and compromising strategies. Within relationships with others, particularly those with whom they have an intimate relationship, there is reciprocity, much talk about personal experience (self-disclosure), negotiation and compromise, reflective and empathic listening, and cooperative problem-solving. Secure adults feel comfortable with closeness, enjoy good self-esteem, trust others and can develop a healthy dependence on those with whom they feel close. Channels of communication remain open.

When faced with a problem, conflict or difficulty, securely classified people approach matters positively. They show greater powers of concentration and patience. They remain constructively engaged with the problem rather than attempting to avoid it or becoming angry at its apparent intractability. Adults classified as secure are able to respond flexibly and adaptively to personal demands and stresses. They manage the need to be an autonomous individual and yet remain socially connected within close relationships in a balanced, constructive manner. It also must be remembered that there is a range of attachment styles even within the secure grouping, some 'reserved' types leaning towards mildly avoidant–dismissing patterns, and some socially and emotionally 'reactive' types shading towards the ambivalent–preoccupied response pattern (Crittenden 1997).

None of this to say that secure people will not experience stress. However, if they do face personal distress, their resilience is able to keep them positively orientated for longer. Also if they do seek help, for example from a counsellor or therapist, they are more likely to be helped than are more insecure people. Therapists are more able to engage with their ability to reflect and appraise on their own and other people's mental states:

> If attachment strategies direct how participants process distress-related memories in the AAI, they may also bias how individuals process distress cues in other settings. For the individual with a primary secure strategy, distress cues activate the attachment system and lead to active efforts to gain comfort or support from an attachment figure as part of an adaptive coping process. (Cole-Detke and Kobak 1996: 282–3)

Dozier (1990) also found that secure clients were more compliant with and responsive to treatment. There was less rejection of the treatment providers, leading to more openness and greater self-disclosure.

Parenthood

Secure–autonomous mothers provide more sensitive care. They acknowledge and accept both the positive and negative in their children's behaviour. In relationship with their children, they show more synchrony, responsiveness, involvement and warmth. They also provide more structure. Mothers who have been able to work through and resolve early aversive experiences are less likely to abuse their children. They represent a group of parents who break the intergenerational transmission of child abuse.

In effect, these mothers provide their children with a s*ecure base*. Their relationship with their children is that of a flexible, two-way, goal-corrected partnership. Parents' descriptions of themselves and their children are realistic (good and bad), although there is an overall emphasis on the positive. During infancy, when children need most care and protection, mothers are most alert, sensitive, responsive and available. With increasing age, parents are keen to help children to become more autonomous, tolerating a wider range of independent behaviours. Parents are able to achieve an age-appropriate balance over issues to do with the developmental tension between security and discipline, socialisation and individuality, exploration and safety, separation and comfort. Parents of secure children use disciplinary strategies that employ reciprocity (give and take), reasoning, negotiation and suggestion. Such techniques appear much more successful in helping children to achieve impulse control, compliance and self-reliance.

Conclusion

The secure, autonomous attachment style is the modal pattern. The psychosocial abilities it offers are highly functional in most social environments outside the family of origin. In broad terms, secure attachments provide protective experiences. The psychological skills and resiliences promoted by secure attachments are generally associated with good mental health. To this extent, the behaviours and skills sponsored by secure attachments act as a psychological benchmark against which the psychosocial characteristics associated with insecure attachments can be measured. In addition, in so far as the secure style implies social competence, resilience and mental health, it can also act as an intervention goal when working with children and parents whose attachment behaviours have been classified as insecure.

5

Avoidant, defended and dismissing patterns

In normal populations, we might expect between 15 and 23 per cent of people to show avoidant–dismissing patterns of attachment. It is a pattern distinctive of those who feel anxious in the presence of strong feelings, either in themselves or in other people. As a result, there is a slight wariness and nervousness about entering close relationships – not that intimacy is not desired; instead, it is viewed with caution or even, in extreme cases, some incomprehension. So, at times when greater intimacy is expected, such as marriage or parenthood, dismissing adults may experience increased unease and discomfort, or increase their detachment. 'Felt security' is achieved by an overreliance on the self and an underreliance on other people.

Of course, in many aspects of modern life, these personality characteristics can be highly functional. Jobs that value a willingness to become absorbed in abstract, practical or cognitive tasks appeal to those who find close personal relationships less than easy or not inherently attractive. Work involving computers, machines, figures, ideas, abstract concepts, and social isolation can feel both appealing and comfortable. In a sense, avoidant personality types fail to operate across the full range of socio-emotional experience. Theirs is a lopsided approach to social affairs, with a preference for the rational rather than the emotional, thought rather than feeling, cognition rather than affect, physical competence rather than social fluency.

The recognition that mildly insecure patterns do not equate with psychopathology once again needs to be emphasised. However, in the context of a book that concentrates on children whose developmental trajectories have taken a negative turn, we need to pay particular attention to the more dysfunctional aspects associated with each of the insecure patterns. In each of the three insecure patterns, particularly emphasis will be paid to the more extreme ends of the scale. There are increased developmental risks for all children who find themselves in insecure attachment relationships, but they are greatest for those who experience the most anxious versions. The types of risk, behaviour and relationship style associated with avoidant/dismissing patterns are distinctive and will be described across the main stages of the lifespan.

Infancy

Carers who feel agitated, distressed or hostile towards their babies pose their young children with a problem. When infants feel anxious and distressed, when their needs and states of emotional arousal are high, their attachment behavioural systems normally become activated. However, it is the infant's need, emotional arousal and distress that seems to cause the parents of avoidant babies particular difficulty. The more emotionally needy and demanding is the baby, the more distressed and rejecting becomes the caregiver. One way in which she attempts to deal with her child's feelings and her own agitation is to try to control the baby's affective states. She may attempt to define how her baby 'ought' to feel or what such feelings mean in a way that suit her needs rather than her child's.

For example, a crying baby may be told that he is not really distressed and that there is nothing to be upset about, even if the child is hurt, hungry or needs changing. It has also been observed that some carers 'correct' their child's feelings and memories, particularly if the parents feel threatened or distressed by their children's mental representations. This undermines children's confidence in their own perceptions. It also instils the notion into the young mind that there is only one right view of events; that shades of grey are troublesome and to be resisted. This 'intrusive' response is an attempt on the carer's part to control or suppress other people's expression of strong feelings that cause him or her considerable discomfort. Overall, then, the characteristic style of parents of infants classified as avoidant is a combination of distress, rebuff, rejection and hostility mixed with control, intrusion and overstimulation.

From the child's point of view, this means feelings that normally activate their attachment behaviour and which are designed to bring them into protective, caring proximity with the parent appear to produce the opposite effect. When faced with the infant's attachment needs, the mother or caregiver becomes emotionally less available and more psychologically distant. She withdraws when the child shows distress. In fact, her availability and responsiveness appear greatest when the baby is least distressed and aroused.

In behavioural terms, it seems that the baby's attachment behaviour is being 'punished' – the mother's responses are aversive. The result is that the infant's attachment behaviour and expression of negative affect are inhibited. They become 'deactivated', suppressed, falsified and subdued. If the child is to try to remain in protective proximity to the parent, it is better to downplay, or even psychologically disconnect, from feelings of upset, need and arousal. 'Inhibition of affective signals both has the predictable effect of reducing maternal rejection and anger and also teaches infants that expression of affect is counterproductive' (Crittenden 1995: 370). Avoidance, as a secondary attachment strategy, is attachment behaviour that is *organised* in relation to the set-goal of seeking some kind of psychological proximity to the carer. In spite of anxiety, children adapt their behaviour to that of their parents to ensure maximum availability under the circumstances. As long as children's internal working model and behaviour remain organised, they can maintain some kind of functional relationship with others.

The key elements of this adaptive defensive strategy can be seen in the Strange Situation.

STRANGE SITUATION

Once in the room, the baby begins immediately to play and explore but in a rather flat, unanimated, unemotional way. When the mother leaves the room, there is little evidence of protest or distress. The child remains with the stranger and continues to play in a rather perfunctory manner. This type of behaviour is maintained throughout the subsequent separation experiences. On both reunions, the infant does not make an obvious approach response to the parent. In many cases, the baby may even look away from her. The level of absorption in the toys increases. If the mother attempts to pick up the child, he or she may stiffen and turn away, but there is little outward sign of emotion. The child may point to the toy on the floor and indicate a wish to return to play. Once back on the floor, the child's attention returns to the room and the toys. Few signs of distress appear throughout the 20 minute procedure. 'The baby appears competent but affectless'. says Main (1995: 418).

The persistent attention given to the toys acts as a diversionary tactic. Such strategies help infants to minimise their attachment behaviours, which appear to distress their carers. Children restrict the communication of anger and upset. This is not to say that the child is not physio-logically experiencing distress and strong feelings (Spangler and Grossmann 1993). Instead, *the aroused feelings are not being expressed, accessed or acknowledged by the child.*

The picture painted, then, is one in which the child is not experi-encing synchronised, sensitive parenting. Mothers 'intrude' and stim-ulate their babies in ways that bear little relation to the child's actual state, needs or interests. In the home setting, mothers of avoidant chil-dren not only reject attachment behaviour but, in extreme cases, also appear averse to physical contact. In these cases, mothers say that they can barely bring themselves to touch their babies. This is a cause of great concern to them and is often a precursor to eventual rejection.

Defensively speaking, avoidant children feel unable to influence or control the caregiver. Emotional arousal in secure babies is normally regulated externally by the parent, who offers soothing care and comfort. Carers of avoidant children, however, psychologically remove themselves from emotionally laden encounters. The children of such carers therefore try to cope by 'shutting down' their affect from within. They attempt to regulate emotion by ignoring or denying it. Outside the parent–child relationship, this is not a developmentally constructive strategy. It cuts children off from the world of feeling and close relationships. They fail to learn about their own emotions and how these might relate to behaviour and the conduct of relationships. Indeed, the failure to display emotion may constrain the actual experi-ence of emotion (Main 1991). According to Crittenden (1995), avoidant infants learn to organise their behaviour without being able to interpret or use affective signals. Children who block the expres-sion or even experience of strong feelings are unable to use the infor-mation contained in affect to help them to organise their social behaviour within relationships. Individuals who block strong feelings appear detached, cold, false, socially gauche and even a little odd.

Avoidant children have therefore learned (cognitively) how to avoid hostile rejection but not how to elicit warm, accepting care-giving. They are able to make sense of what they know (cognition) but not how they feel (affect). 'Such infants are freed from the constraint of disorganizing emotions and, thus, may be able to interact with their environment. Consequently, their capacity for cognitive development may be enhanced whereas their experience with the inte-gration of cognition with affect is severely limited' (Crittenden 1992b: 581). This emphasis on the value of cognitive processes is further boosted by giving defensive preference to activation of the exploratory system (play, busyness and watchfulness and constructively acceptable behaviour). Exploration and behaving well appear to be more effective methods of maintaining proximity to the attachment figure than is showing feelings of distress.

Avoidant children's strategy also emphasises the value of the emotional control of both the self and others. Experience teaches the child that displays of distress and attempts to get close cause other people to withdraw. Therefore the most effective way to remain present in social situations and keep other people 'available' is to be undemanding and self-sufficient. In this sense, the child achieves a kind of 'felt security' – at least they know where they stand and how relationships seem to work.

Childhood

With the increasing capacity to handle matters symbolically, avoidant children of preschool age replace behavioural avoidance with *psychological inhibition*. As they age, avoidant children are less likely to seek emotional support from their carers. Their attachment style becomes more detached, cool, even socially correct, but the basic underlying style, according to Crittenden (1992a), remains one *defended* against affect. Children have learned that their carers feel more comfortable with activities and behaviours that are low in emotional content. Achievements and accomplishments are valued more than emotional closeness. Indeed, although parents may reject and devalue children's attachment needs, they may notice and praise their cognitive successes. Parental interest, approval and positive regard are given if children show things such as independence, task-competence, physical prowess or academic achievement.

Attention to objects rather than relationships is encouraged and practised. Competence in these areas brings about an inner sense of control (self-efficacy) and a feeling of positive self-regard. Positive self-regard is therefore conditional both on the suppression of anger and hurt, and on displays of self-reliance and achievement. Within such parent–child relationships lie the seeds of the need to achieve, perfectionism, workaholism and material success (Mayseless 1996: 217). Overall, children show cooperation and compliance but not a great deal of intimacy. However, although the desire to be self-sufficient is strong, the more extreme avoidant personalities can also exhibit hostility and antisocial behaviour. Such hostilities allow anger to be expressed and serve to keep others at bay (Mayseless 1996: 209).

The defended relationship, formed in the preschool years, continues into the school years. A variation on the infant Strange Situation procedure reveals the avoidant child's continued use of emotional inhibition. Within a clinical or laboratory setting, 6-year-old children and their parents are requested to cooperate in a number of activities (Main 1995: 425–6). During the tests, the parents and child are separated for about an hour, while both pursue different tasks. Upon reunion, avoidant children adopt various low-key, subtle responses. They might wander slowly away to seek a toy. Rather than be completely unresponsive (which may be interpreted as rude by parents and cause them to be angry), children are minimally responsive. They do just enough in the interaction to acknowledge the relationship but no more than is necessary. Their conversation is restricted. The children prefer to talk about things and objects, but even this kind of impersonal exchange is limited and undeveloped. Parents tend to take the conversational lead, asking factual-type questions that receive a factual-type response. There is a polite stiffness and formality to the talk.

In a study by Rosenberg (1984) of unstructured pretend, fantasy play, avoidant children seemed to act in a rather literal way. There was not much make-believe or use of the imagination. Play tended to be short, impoverished and without much elaboration. Relationship themes and the introduction of people's feelings were reported as being 'noticeably absent'. However, in a form of projective story-telling in which 6-year-old children were shown pictures depicting various parent–child separations, Main (1995: 431) reports that avoidant children did describe the child undergoing separation as probably feeling sad: 'He feels sad because he doesn't know if his mom will come back or his dad will come back.' What was distinctive of this group was their inability to come up with solutions or to become absorbed in the story. When asked what a child could 'do', these children said things like 'I don't know' or 'Run away', or they might even deny that an upsetting separation had occurred.

Similar observations have been made by Solomon *et al.* (1995). Using dolls to help them, 6-year-old children were invited to develop stories with an attachment-related issue. Some stories offered to the children involved monsters, while others began with the children being looked after for the night by a babysitter. In developing their stories, avoidant children did not fully activate their attachment behaviour. The events enacted did not threaten the children's safety. Not much happened in their stories; there was little raising of tension or introduction of imagined fear. In their stories, children simply watched television or ate meals. In the scenarios involving the return of parents, 'their reunion stories were characterized by psychological unavailability; most frequently family members sat down to watch TV or went immediately to bed... Their stories suggest that they 'immobilize' the attachment system by systematically scanning, sorting, and excluding fear, pain, and sadness from conscious awareness' (George 1996: 415).

Observations of avoidant 6-year-olds generally suggests the use of an internal working model in which others are not available but the self is strong, in control and not easily upset or affected. Displays of emotion imply weakness and vulnerability. The self in relationship with others therefore might be described as *insecure–invulnerable*. The use of bright but false affect continues as a way of keeping others involved, positively disposed and therefore psychologically available. Avoidant personalities attempt to modify their own behaviour as a way of defending against social rejection and withdrawal. In some cases, children may compulsively take on aspects of the parent's caregiving in a form of role reversal. If the parent is hostile, children can also become *compulsively compliant* (see also Chapter 7). There is an anxiety to 'do things right', to please, to overachieve. If the situation deteriorates, if other people, including parents, become unhappy, disapproving or rejecting, those with a defended–avoidant personality style feel responsible, unsettled, guilty or ashamed. They attempt to soothe the discontented, the unhappy and the hostile. The reverse is also the case – that when the child expresses negative feelings, they expect rejection. This is why they try to inhibit the expression of anger.

This constant reluctance to express, access or acknowledge emotion means that children's own affective states are not flexibly integrated with cognition in their internal working model. The result is that their own feelings in emotionally charged situations are not read well. Social competence becomes strained. Other people's emotional distress or dependency can be an irritation, a puzzle or a cause of upset. Bearing in mind that avoidant children have learned that the display of feelings brings rejection, hurt and pain, any breach of the defences of emotional denial, in the self or others, causes distress. The result can be an exaggerated, although often short-lived, loss of control in which anger and aggression, impatience and intolerance suddenly erupt.

Katie's avoidant strategy in relationship with her angry, with-holding mother illustrates many of the behavioural themes characteristic of the defended pattern.

Lorna and her daughter Katie (Gregory 1997)

Katie is 8 years old. She has two younger sisters, aged 6 and 1 year respectively. Katie's mother, Lorna, is 32 and currently living with Gary, who is the father of the youngest daughter. Lorna's father was in the army. She was the eldest of three children. Her parents separated when she was 6 years old. Lorna's own mother then began to drink heavily. She also met a new partner, but it was a stormy relationship. There is an unconfirmed suspicion that Lorna might have been sexually abused as a girl.

Lorna found herself having to look after her younger siblings while her mother went out working most of the day and early evenings. 'I never had a childhood,' said Lorna, 'I had to look after the little ones, take them to school, cook and clean. I would get into dreadful grief if the housework wasn't done.' There is a sense of great loss as Lorna describes these memories. She did not have any friends. As the children grew older, her younger sister became increasingly difficult to control. At first this worried Lorna – there was an incident in which her sister was visiting the house of an elderly male paedophile – but she learned to cope by 'cutting out such worries completely from her head'. Yet, in spite of these tough demands on her as a girl, Lorna still describes her mother in idealised terms – 'she was a good mother – I can't fault her'. The family culture was one of 'getting on with things, whatever'.

Lorna left home when she finished school. She lived in the same town as her mother but had little to do with her: 'She said she wanted to make a break.' Lorna got pregnant when she was 19 years old. She was not happy about the prospect of having a baby but did not want a termination. When Katie was a year old, Lorna suffered depression. She felt increasingly isolated. During Katie's second year, Lorna said that she began to feel increasingly distanced from her daughter – 'unconnected.' The more Katie placed demands on her mother, the more angry Lorna felt. She resented the restrictions on her life and career that having a baby entailed. She wanted to go to college. Again, she felt trapped with caring duties. A few years later, she met another man and once more had an unplanned pregnancy.

With the new baby, Katie's behaviour deteriorated. Katie had not been difficult to potty train, but she was beginning to be argumentative.

Lorna said she felt 'cold' towards Katie – 'I never liked her from the day she was born. She never fitted.' Lorna requested that Katie be looked after by foster carers. The social work response was to introduce support services into the home and keep Katie with her mother. Matters got worse when Katie reached the age of 6 years, the same age that Lorna had to start looking after herself as a child. Lorna said she felt no warmth for her; she did not even wish to touch her daughter. 'She found it very hard when Katie got upset because she didn't want to go anywhere near her.' The mother then threatened to strangle Katie. A child protection order was made, and Katie was placed on the child protection register. Katie was accommodated for 2 months. She appeared to everyone as a very unhappy little girl who seemed to keep all her worries to herself – 'under wraps'. For example, when she was 4 years old and at playgroup, she was very passive and wanted to hold the hand of the playgroup leader. However, at home she was aggressive, punching and kicking her sisters, and breaking toys.

'The first time I visited her at her home,' said the social worker, 'the mother kept the TV on. She kept her back to me, and she did a lot of shouting at the kids. I had arrived a little early and she more or less ignored me for the first five minutes. She said "You might as well come in then." Her body language was dismissive. When she spoke, she seemed to address the ether. It was a very clean and tidy house. She expressed the desire for her house to be unencumbered by children, muck and rubble. She wanted it to be a show house, and she was very cross that it couldn't be.' It was observed that, when Katie approached her mother, she would sidle up behind where mum was sitting and slowly lean against the shoulder of the chair. In this way, she was able to remain close to her mother but not in her sight. During the visit, Lorna never once turned round to acknowledge Katie, even though they were so close. The next appointment was at the clinic, but Lorna failed to turn up.

Lorna describes herself as a very strong person. She believed that life had taught her to be hard. 'You've got to be hard,' she said, 'or everybody's going to stamp all over you.' People, she said, seek her out because of her strength and sensible advice. Nevertheless, she felt very angry that everybody expected her to cope, but she felt she did not want to cope any longer but did not know how to stop. She wanted to have her own needs met. She had plans, ambitions. But everyone kept saying that she had to cope – look after the home, bring up the children, that mothers had to sacrifice themselves – and she felt 'furious'. She now suffered from bulimia, and, once again, was requesting

Katie's removal. Lorna knew that she was feeling anxious and depressed again. She had been to the library and borrowed a number of books on depression to see whether she could understand herself better.

Not long afterwards, Lorna ceased all social work contact, stopped her visits to the children's day centre and withdrew Katie from respite care.

School and peer group behaviour

In school, avoidantly classified children make few demands on teachers. They prefer to comply and even please in the presence of authority. A few become overachievers, placing great pressure on themselves to do well. In some cases, children may show perfectionist and compulsive tendencies. It has to be remembered that success in the physical environment or with cognitive behaviour has worked well for these children. Such behaviours has not threatened the availability of carers. An interest in things and ideas has also become an impersonal, non-emotional way of relating to people. Nevertheless, behind these responses there can be feelings of anxiety and tension, isolation and sadness, that can lead to flashes of aggression. Children who might behave as 'teacher's pet' in the classroom may display their anger as bullies when there are no powerful adults about, particularly if they have been abused at home. Also, to the extent that an understanding of emotions in the self aids empathy, some of the more disengaged avoidant children also lack social sensitivity. They have a poor understanding of the subtleties of interpersonal life. In milder forms, they can appear gauche, awkward and socially uncomfortable.

Just to add to the subtleties of this pattern, some children who have remained wary, alert and self-reliant may have learned to use their cognitive strengths to read and make very good sense of the way in which emotions affect relationships. It is in these children's interest to understand (intellectually) what is going on in other people's minds (but not their own). In a sense, they use their cognitive abilities to read external emotional events. To that extent, they may become skilled at handling social situations, but it tends to be an intellectual accomplishment rather than an exercise in emotional immersion. We see the beginnings of this in childhood, but for some avoidant styles, it becomes much more prominent in adulthood. Indeed, it can be the case that many people who go on to study relationships and conceptualise people's emotional life have reserved, defended tendencies. Study plays to their cognitive strengths, allows them to explore an area of life that they think is important but one with which they do not always find it easy to engage. The study of relationships and emotions has the added dividend of helping them to understand and experience the very thing that was not easily accessed as a child.

Adolescence and adulthood

The tendency to minimise the importance of attachments and the need for other people continues into adolescence and adult life. Attempts to maintain social independence and emotional self-reliance can still be recognised. Affect is downplayed or denied. If strong arousal of the emotions does occur, individuals find it difficult either to understand, process or regulate them. Internal working models that promote indifference to other people's views are based on the belief that others may not like them. Avoidant, defended patterns can range from being socially reserved to being compulsively self-reliant. Beyond this range, we begin to enter avoidant behaviours that are associated with maltreatment and disorganised attachment patterns (see Chapter 7).

The characteristics of the adult 'avoidant' pattern are picked up by the two adult attachment measures. The AAI recognises a group of people who tend to minimise the emotional effects that relationships, both past and present, have on them. In particular, there appears to be a systematic avoidance and dismissal of negative experiences and memories. Attachment-related information is avoided or even excluded from awareness. Experiences are cognitively processed without reference to or acknowledgement of any affective content. Their interview narrative can be terse and not always coherent:

> A speaker's state is classified as dismissing when Grice's maxim of quality is violated in that positive terms used to describe parents ('excellent mother, very normal relationship') are unsupported or actively contradicted ('I didn't tell her I broke my arm; she would have been really angry'). Such speakers often also violate quantity, in part by insisting on lack of memory. (Main 1996: 240)

The apparent detached attitude to relationships is described as disengaged or 'dismissing'. This adult attachment classification is therefore known the *dismissing* (Ds) pattern. When describing childhood memories of attachment-related issues, global statements are not backed by specific examples of either happy or painful memories.

Even if difficult experiences are recalled, any distress caused at the time is not acknowledged, nor does the memory appear to provoke much emotion during the interview. Individuals claim to be unaffected by adversity. Parents and carers are often 'idealised', being described as 'very good' or 'the best', even though the individual may later mention that a father was a 'severe disciplinarian' or a mother was 'not really a very warm person'. There are both contradictions in the narrative and a strange discrepancy between what is being described (emotionally laden) and its alleged emotional impact (very little). Overall, accounts tend to be on the short side, with the claim that the individual cannot remember much.

In terms of the defences, dismissing individuals use a minimising strategy in which they dismiss the importance of attachment (*derogation of attachment*) or the influence it has on them. The interview task itself demands some engagement with past, possibly anxiety-provoking memories. Thus, the dismissing interview response pattern can be seen as a kind of resistance to the task set. There is little distress evident in the narrative. The self is seen as strong, independent, separate and not troubled by feelings. Yet, in everyday life, the individual is not relaxed in the presence of either their own or other people's expressions of strong emotion. Such discomfort and awkwardness can make people appear socially detached, cold, inept or insincere.

Relationships, social interaction and affect regulation are often best managed via practical tasks. Alternatively, they might be dealt with cognitively and intellectually. 'Thoughts' rather than 'feelings' are used as a guide to behaviour. These strategies can often be quite successful, at least in their own terms. People may become experts about the workings of car engines or computers, and this knowledge provides a vehicle for communicating and engaging with fellow enthusiasts. However, when the same strategy and topic is employed with less interested people, social interaction is less successful. In general, when talking about achievements, memories and abilities, greater emphasis is placed on objects, activities and intellectual matters than on people, emotions and relationships.

There is a strong need to 'keep to the task'. By sticking to the job in hand, there is a sense of being in control. Anything or anyone that distracts the individual or frustrates what is being done will make those classified as dismissing feel agitated, anxious or angry. It is at such moments that aggressive behaviour is most likely to erupt. It is very upsetting to find that plans are being disrupted or achievements ignored. Allied with this outlook is a tendency to 'keep to the rules' and to get bothered when other people appear to 'break the rules', particularly if they appear to be getting away with something. The idea of 'something for nothing' is not acceptable; their own personal history has been one in which the reward of attention and response has been contingent on behaving in an acceptable manner. This links with the noted tendency towards compliance in close relationships seen within some types of dismissing attachment patterns. There can be, therefore, a heightened sense of justice and injustice, right and wrong, good and bad, that makes people rigid and sticklers for the rules.

The dismissing individual is also uncomfortable when there is a lack of focus or too many things are being asked of them. They like to see matters through to completion. Flitting between events, dropping one thing to take up another is not an attractive way of proceeding. When life gets too fragmented, busy or demanding, control of both the environment and their own feelings is in danger of being lost and anxiety levels rise. For the dismissing–defended personality, anxiety normally involves the deactivation of attachment behaviour and avoidance of the arousing stimulus. But, the usually non-arousing, deemotional world of tasks, intellect and activity is upset in the case of task overload or task dispersion. Here, the proliferation of tasks themselves becomes the actual cause of the anxiety. Arousal is therefore amplified. There is no escape, and strong feelings overwhelm the normally robust defences of denial, repression, intellectualisation and avoidance. This can be a very unsettling experience, leading to impatience and sudden loss of temper.

Using self-report measures of avoidant attachment behaviour, Bartholomew and Horowitz (1991) define the avoidant person's internal working model as one in which the self is seen as strong and positive, while others are viewed as unavailable and potentially rejecting. The willingness to disclose personal need and vulnerability is low. Dismissing adults are unlikely to seek social feedback. The self-description with which the individual identifies in Bartholomew's model states: 'I am comfortable without close emotional relationships. It is very important to me to feel independent and self-sufficient, and I prefer not to depend on others or have others depend on me.' Rather than depend on other people in times of difficulty, illness or setback, dismissing–avoidant personalities either try to deny that they are in a state of need or go it alone.

Although not necessarily competitive, there is a need to do well and achieve. This harks back to earlier experiences in which the child increased maternal proximity and acceptance by downplaying feelings and the need for an emotional relationship. Parental attention was most likely when the child was doing things well without a fuss. According to Feeney *et al.* (1995), there is, therefore, a moderate need for approval. Thus although there is broad view that the self has to be seen as independent and strong, it appears that the avoidant adult's 'attempts to maintain distance in their personal relationships might be, at least in part, anxiety driven' (Feeney *et al.* 1995: 142–3).

Crittenden (1992a, 1995) describes some 'defended' individuals as wanting to be liked and loved but doubting their lovability: they remain unsure of whether or not others like them. They therefore attempt to gain the approval and admiration of significant others. These individuals monitor both their own and the other's behaviour to ensure that whatever is being said or done is meeting with the other's approval; to be approved is to be liked. People can therefore become socially astute about other people's behaviour. This produces a 'chameleonlike' response to social situations. There is an anxiety to be accepted, not as one is but as the individual thinks others would like him or her to be. This produces a 'false' self. Indeed, there may not actually be a 'true' self with which to relate. The *anxiety* to be liked (and not rejected) means that the individual 'is' that which he or she thinks the other would perceive as most likeable. Individuals tend to respond to the needs of other people rather than their own attachment needs. All of this means that the individual becomes a keen and sensitive observer of how others might be seeing them. If they feel that the other's perceptions and evaluations are negative, they will modify their own behaviour in an attempt to shift the other person towards a more positive view. This strategy of monitoring and manipulating other people's reactions and perceptions also means that there is less insight into one's own emotional states – cognitive attention is directed outwards and not inwards.

Adult relationships

The anxiety that close relationships might potentially cause leads to a variety of defensive social behaviours, including emotional withholding and withdrawal, retention and non-sharing of knowledge, a stiff-upper lip, a reluctance to disclose information about oneself (feelings, whereabouts, other relationships, personal pursuits and activities) and a lack of emotional empathy when other people behave in a distressed manner. To control information helps people to feel in control. When other people express strong feelings or behave in a dependent way (feeling ill or being helpless), levels of anxiety and irritation increase. This might be dealt with by behaving in a variety of avoidant and dismissing ways, including withdrawal, intrusive control ('don't fuss; there's nothing to be upset about'), irritation, impatience and detachment. There is also a use of the force of reason and intellectual rigour to try to get other people to accept a preferred version of an emotionally charged event. Logic is employed to impose the 'correct' way to read feelings and relationship issues, an interpretation with which the dismissing personality feels more comfortable and in which their strength and reason remain intact.

Situations that might be expected to arouse feelings of distress therefore see people who are classified as dismissing–avoidant dampening down their attachment system. The overall style is one of emotional disengagement. They see neither themselves nor the other person as emotionally available at times of upset or conflict. Not surprisingly, they are not experienced as very supportive by partners at times of distress. Those on the receiving end of an avoidant partner's responses feel a lack of understanding, support and warmth. Dismissing individuals either minimise the need to feel upset or try to divert attention from the state of being distressed, partly as a result of the way in which they would try to deal with arousal in themselves and partly in an attempt to control and subdue the appearance of distress in others (Simpson *et al.* 1996: 900).

Physical health and illness

Although there is theoretical speculation that the different attachment patterns might have a bearing on the way in which illness is handled and expressed, few empirical studies have explored or tested the phenomenon. Some early work by Lewis *et al.* (1984) found that boys classified as insecure at 12 months had more somatic complaints at 6 years than did secure boys. In adults, Hazan and Shaver (1987, 1990) also reported that insecure individuals (both anxious and avoidant) described both more psychosomatic and more physical illnesses than did those classified as secure. Individuals showing dismissing attachment behaviours might be expected to resist acknowledging distress, preferring instead to be self-reliant, stoical and non-dependent in the face of illness. However, the inability to seek comfort from others at times of need may lead to psychological ill-health, which may in turn in turn produce physical symptoms. In a study of 93 first-year psychology students, Kotler *et al.* (1994) suggested that those with an avoidant attachment style coped with stress by trying to manage and suppress negative feelings rather than dealing with the source of stress directly. It is believed that emotional suppression can cause strain and tension leading to certain types of poor health, including tenseness, severe headaches and anxiety. John displays many behaviours typical of the avoidant/dimissing personality.

John

John is 43 years old and married to Tracey, who is 35 years old. They first met when she was 16 years old, and married 2 years later. John is thin and wiry. He chain-smokes rolled cigarettes. His father left his family when he was a baby, and he was raised by his mother as a lone parent until he was 9 years old. When he was 2 years old, he suffered some kind of infantile paralysis and was in hospital for 8 months. He was very ill with scarlet fever when he was 6 years old and again spent a short spell in hospital. His mother remarried a man who was in the army. The family then began to move around Europe a great deal. John describes his mother as a very loving person but is hazy about childhood details. He sees her as a very strong, purposeful woman: 'People didn't mess around with my mother.' The only word he can find to describe his relationship with his stepfather is 'respect'. When he was 16 years old, John left his parents in Germany to return to England.

As soon as John left school, he joined the Air Force as a mechanic and met Tracey. He was keen to do well at his job. 'When I used to get home, I was sometimes tired and sometimes I needed to study, but all Tracey wanted to do was "party". We used to row a lot. She'd go off in a huff.' Liam was born when John was 27 years old, but within 3 months of his birth, Tracey asked John to leave. 'I felt shattered, but I went.' He wanted to succeed in his job but felt that people did not appreciate his skills. John likes to do his work to a very high standard and feels agitated when either too much is asked of him or he is asked to leave one piece of work to go on to another. 'I like to know where I am. I like things ordered and under control, you know. I don't like it when people mess me around and I can't keep on top of the job.' John was always the first to volunteer if there was extra work to be done:

'I'm a workaholic.' Although he enjoyed both the life and the work in the Air Force, younger men kept being promoted over him. After 20 years, he decided to leave. He met up again with Tracey and they remarried, although by this time she had had two more sons.

John is proud of his attitude to work. 'Until now I've never been out of work. Even when I've been sick, I've forced myself to get well and go in. When I injured my leg quite badly, they told me I'd be off work for a year, but I was back on the job again 3 months later. The doctors were astonished that I was back to work so soon.' When he left the Air Force, he found a job as a mechanic repairing fleet lorries. This took him all over the country, and he liked both the travel, the busyness and the long hours. Eventually however, he was sacked: 'It was a set up; they wanted to get rid of me.' On a wet, cold day, John was near London fixing the engine of a broken-down lorry. 'I was underneath the engine, up to my ears in mud and grime fixing things up. The mobile phone rang just as I was sorting things out. The boss said, 'Stop that job and get over to Essex. There's an emergency I want you to see to.' I told him I was almost finished where I was, but he insisted. So I swore at him and told him it was ridiculous to leave a job that was nearly done. Well, for shouting and swearing at him over the phone, he sacked me. The real reason they got rid of me was that they wanted me to do more overtime on top of my travelling time, but I wasn't going to be ripped off like that.'

Now that he is at home and without a job, John is feeling very tense and agitated. He says that he was kept under strict discipline as a boy and that's how his own children and stepchildren should be treated. The two eldest boys show considerable behaviour problems ('They wind me up deliberately'), about which John feels there is nothing he can do. He is losing his temper more frequently and more violently. There are concerns that he has hit and bruised the boys. He copes either by going upstairs to play on the computer, or by going out and driving his car around for hours on end. He is now wondering whether it wouldn't be the best thing for all concerned if he simply just left the family: 'They'd probably be better off without me here. I can't stand all this upset and emotion and arguments.' He believes that he should be the 'breadwinner', and without the role he feels he is 'no use.'

Eating disorders

There is some speculation that eating disorders might be associated with lack of attention to or the inability to discriminate one's inner feelings and distress cues. A focus on dieting and the appearance of the body may provide a diversionary focus for distress-related cues.

In a study of 61 college women, Cole-Detke and Kobak (1996) identify what they believe to be different attachment strategies between those with symptoms of depression (more likely to be ambivalent–entangled–preoccupied) and of eating disorders (more likely to be avoidant–dismissing). The reporting of eating disorder symptoms was associated with denial or the minimisation of anger towards the parents, in contrast to depressives, who did report anger and feelings of hurt. Women with both types of disorder said that they did not feel confident in relationships. The group with eating disorders showed less cooperation and insight in the interview. The depressive women appeared preoccupied with unavailable, emotionally neglectful mothers. In contrast, 'eating disorder tendencies were uniquely associated with fathers who were emotionally unavailable as well as angry and critical of their daughters' (Cole-Detke and Kobak 1996: 286). Women with eating disorders *not* coupled with depression played down feelings of anger and vulnerability.

> Deactivating strategies evolve when individuals' models of parents lead them to assess the probability of gaining access to parents as low. However, because the goal of attaining access to an attachment figure is biologically prepared, disengagement efforts can never be entirely successful. Thus, disengagement efforts must continually redirect attention from attachment to other goals that allow more successful outcomes. In the case of eating disorder, the focus on appearance may serve a diversionary function by redirecting attention from attachment to more attainable goals such as changing one's appearance. Reports of eating disorder were uniquely associated with ratings of very poor relationships with fathers who were depicted as emotionally unavailable and highly critical of their daughters. Thus, participants may perceive the likelihood of gaining support in such relationships as very low. This is consistent with others' findings that women with bulimia recalled poor relationships with their fathers in particular and that these relationships were characterised by lack of paternal care or empathy and high paternal hostility, leaving their daughters to feel that they had failed to please their fathers. Thus, while daughters may disengage from efforts to gain comfort and support from their fathers, they may divert attention to appearance to make the self more acceptable. Ironically, these daughters may be trying to improve the father–daughter relationship by deactivating the attachment system and focusing on appearance... Finally, an externally orientated attentional set may heighten the individual's susceptibility to environmental influences such as sociocultural pressures. (Cole-Detke and Kobak 1996: 288)

This line of thinking receives some support from Fonagy *et al.* (1996: 28). In a study of psychiatric patients and a control group using the AAI, the researchers observed that those with an eating disorder tended to idealise their parents, echoing 'the clinical observation that participants with eating disorders are perfectionists whose eating disorder may stem from exaggerated standards that are also applied to parents.'

Drug and alcohol misuse

There is some research evidence emerging that dismissing strategies using 'derogation of attachment, absence of idealisation, and absence of preoccupying anger' (Allen *et al.* 1996: 258) are related to higher levels of hard drug use. This would make theoretical sense. If hard drug use is consistent with the notion of individuals developing symptoms that divert attention from distress and minimise the need for support, it might be expected that those classified as avoidant–dismissing might find hard drugs more attractive. The way in which drugs and alcohol are used by avoidant–dismissing and ambivalent–preoccupied types differ. Whereas those classified as preoccupied tend to overuse drugs and alcohol as a consequence of their need to be socially very involved and accepted, avoidant types – particularly those classified as disorganised–avoidant (see Chapter 7) – abuse substances to escape feelings and social anxieties.

Parenthood

When adults become parents, the character of their caregiving derives from their internal working model of attachment (George 1996). Models contain mental representations of both the self and others within relationships. These representations also guide the way in which parents perceive, emotionally experience and interact with their own children. Young children potentially pose great emotional as well physical demands on carers. We know that, when levels of feeling are raised within a relationship, the individual's characteristic ways of regulating affect are triggered. Affect regulation is closely bound up with the individual's attachment-related behaviour and the associated internal working model. Thus, the demands of young children are likely to activate the defensive strategies typically used by their carers at times of stress.

Carers who feel uncomfortable and anxious when faced with other people's distress and needs are unlikely to find it easy to be openly available and warmly responsive to the high demands made by babies. Dismissing parents, says Main (1995), find that the steady state of their mental representations of self (as strong and independent) and others (as rejecting and hostile) is easily upset by the emotional and proximity-seeking demands of babies. Their defensive response is to back off and withdraw from or control the source of emotional need and dependence. They may fail to perceive, interpret accurately or respond to those infant behaviours which threaten to disturb their established view of how to handle the self in close relationships. The baby's distress and dependency needs evoke feelings of anxiety in the parent. Anxiety triggers attachment behaviour, which in the case of the dismissing adult is dealt with by 'deactivating' the attachment system and withdrawing emotional availability. The baby experiences this as a behavioural 'punishment' in which normal attachment behaviour, instead of leading to increased proximity to and comfort from the attachment figure, actually leads to decreased proximity and raised anxiety.

Mrs Randall (Lieberman 1992: 560–1)

Mrs Randall perceives her 3-month-old son as 'spoiled'. She sees him as angrily demanding rather than simply hungry or distressed, and responds to him only after he becomes inconsolable and frantic. Mrs Randall remembers that as a child she was ridiculed and told to behave herself whenever she expressed a need. She cannot remember specific feelings... Mrs Randall sees herself in the present as a strong, 'no-nonsense' woman, and is conspicuously grateful to her parents for having taught her not to rely on others but only on herself. In her self-presentation, Mrs Randall does not acknowledge the quick, intense anger she feels when she thinks she is being ignored or intruded upon. This anger, rather than experienced as her own, is now projected on her baby whenever his crying triggers an unwelcome memory of her own childhood distress. It is possible that another reason for Mrs Randall's anger at her baby is that his wailing reminds her of her own fiercely disavowed vulnerability... we could begin to entertain the notion that this proudly self-reliant mother might feel secretly ashamed and disappointed for giving birth to a fussy, needy baby.

Over time, defensively, the only way for the baby to deal with this is to decrease his or her own attachment behaviour. This appears to be the best strategy if the carer is to be kept close and available. The carer is able to retain proximity and involvement much more comfortably if the baby is not expressing and exhibiting a high state of emotional arousal and need of her. Nevertheless, the caregiving style is essentially one of *rejection* of the child's attachment behaviour and emotional needs. There is a deactivation of the parent's caregiving system. This often means that children fail to receive adequate protection. Too much freedom and autonomy is given too young. In her studies, George (1996: 418) observes that:

> Most striking in the interviews with rejecting mothers was the exclusion of positive evaluations of themselves and their children. They emphasized the negative, portraying themselves and their children as unwilling and unworthy to participate in the relationship.

Caregiving that is rejecting is also insensitive. The carer is not acknowledging or responding to the baby's distress signals. The parent becomes involved with the baby either when it suits her or when she wants the child to deny the legitimacy of his or her own feelings. This latter response is designed to encourage the child not to show distress. It is therefore both intrusive and controlling: intrusive in the sense of instructing children how to define and understand their own experience, and controlling to the extent that it is an attempt to suppress behaviours in others that might cause anxiety and distress in one's self.

Mothers frequently say that they are not suited to be parents or caregivers. They feel uncomfortable with the maternal role. They will describe themselves as strict, tough, impatient or demanding (George 1996: 418). Children, too, are described as a pain, a chore, a nuisance, manipulative. They are criticised for not being very responsive, showing no pleasure in their relationship and generally being very unrewarding to the parent. Rejecting mothers emphasise their own perspectives. They are unwilling to acknowledge and handle their children's attachment needs. Even so, there is a good deal of intellectual recognition given to the importance of being a good mother. This may show itself in 'knowing the theory' and having the right equipment and toys – an idealised, stereotyped view of parenting. However, there is a gap between the ideal and the real. The feelings potentially provoked by the real child and the real demands of parenting are denied, forgotten and excluded:

This robust strategy protects the mother from having to confront details of past experience. It may be easier to maintain idealized abstractions of the past than of the present, however, because the mother's real-life daily interaction with her child threatens her attempts to suppress negative experiences, thwarting her defences. Despite efforts to minimize negative evaluations through stereotyping, these evaluations break through, leading ultimately to rejection of the child. (George and Solomon 1996: 210)

Crittenden (1992b) notes that mothers who are uncomfortable with emotion and resent their children's desire for comfort will provide them with a semantic interpretation that is unfavourable to children. For example, a child who has hurt himself and begins to cry might be told, 'You've not really hurt yourself. Don't cry. Don't be such a baby.' His mother is offering no emotional comfort or availability unless the child 'stops being a baby and ceases crying'. Semantically, the young child learns that to be a demanding baby is not a worthy state and to remain in a distressed condition is to have the self devalued by the parent. Equally, children cannot be a valued 'big boy' or 'big girl' unless they deny their feelings.

Simpson *et al.* (1996: 900) found that, compared with less avoidant mothers, mothers who scored higher on avoidant behaviours displayed less warmth and supportiveness toward their preschool children when teaching them new and difficult tasks. Other studies have suggested that the children of hostile, critical fathers (often associated with maltreatment; see Chapter 7) are at increased risk of showing externalising problem behaviour such as aggression at school, whereas children of detached, uninvolved fathers and preoccupied, anxious mothers are at greater risk of developing internalising, affective problem behaviours such as depression and moodiness (Cowan *et al.* 1996: 61).

Parents whose own childhood experiences were ones of hostile, intrusive rejection believe that physical harshness and fierce discipline are essential if their children are to meet their own high parental standards. Physical punishment is used to control and contain children's behaviour.

Sexually abusing families

Crittenden (1996) speculates that the motives behind parents who sexually abuse their children may differ depending on their attachment classification. There does not appear to be a unique set of symptoms associated with sexual abuse (Finkelhor 1990). Indeed, many of the long-term effects seem to be associated with variables above and beyond those of the abuse. Alexander (1992: 189) contends 'that long-term effects of sexual abuse, although obviously related to the specific nature of the abuse, are better understood according to a classification of the important attachment relationships concurrent with the abuse.'

In families in which members are emotionally disengaged, find it difficult to show their feelings, feel anxious about becoming emotionally close and are rigid about the rules that govern acceptable behaviour, interpersonal relationships are frustrating and troubling. There is distance, withdrawal and rejection between people:

> spousal relationships in such families might be one of distance, withdrawal and rejection. Sexual abuse might reflect a desperate attempt at a relationship... while, nevertheless, allowing the participants to remain psychologically distant and unavailable. If such a pattern exists, it would be likely that the perpetrators would highly condemn such behaviour and, like victimised children who forget the traumatising incident, the perpetrators might forget or deny their participation. To professionals, they would appear as incalcitrant, denying men who are willing to accept separation from their own families rather than admit their behavior and accept treatment. (Crittenden 1996: 165–6)

The case of Brad, who has been accused of sexually abusing his step-daughters, shows how fiercely held can be rational and defensive behaviours when the self is under close scrutiny.

Brad

Brad was raised by his mother and stepfather along with his four step-brothers and sisters. 'I had a happy childhood, I would say', recalls Brad. However, he also says elsewhere that he felt his mother was 'scarce' and 'not an emotional or physical type; she'd never give any of us cuddles'. On a number of occasions, his mother told him that if she had to choose between him and his stepfather, she wouldn't hesitate to choose his stepfather. Brad says that he did not discover that his stepfather was not in fact his real father until he was 15, and even then both his parents denied that this was the case. He was frightened of his stepfather, who was physically abusive, often beating and punching him with great violence. Brad reports many incidents in his childhood in which, although he was caught doing something wrong, he nevertheless claimed his innocence. He says that either he was unaware that what he was doing was wrong or the situation was misconstrued. For example, when he was 14 years old, a friend gave him some hash to smoke, except Brad says that he thought it was a menthol cigarette. They were caught, and Brad found himself in serious trouble. He goes to great lengths to convince the listener of his innocence and naïvety. The explanations are always elaborate, relentless and remorselessly reasonable. He left home when he was 16, spending some time in a children's home. With friends, Brad committed a large number of offences, including burglary, car theft and shoplifting. A number of offences included acts of violence. While in residential care, he sexually assaulted a female member of staff. He had a reputation for bullying women carers and would often make very suggestive sexual remarks. He was also arrested for making indecent assaults against girls in the neighbourhood. At the time, women said that they found him 'creepy' and 'very persistent'.

As an adult, Brad sees himself as something of a loner, adding that he prefers it that way. He believes himself to be a strong person but one who virtuously bottles up his feelings: 'I don't like to burden others with my worries.' He is also keen to impress people that he is someone who never loses his temper, even under great provocation.

He married his first wife, Debbie, 'honourably'. 'She fancied me, certainly and I suppose I thought it would be just a one night stand, but she got pregnant, even though she had told me that she was on the pill. I now realise that I married her for the wrong reason. I didn't love her and you should only marry for love. But I married because she was pregnant with the child and I wanted to do the right thing. I tried to make the relationship work, but she got very difficult with me.' Debbie, for her part, says that Brad 'overwhelmed' her and 'took control. Even when our relationship was over, he kept coming round every day pressuring me not to kick him out'.

Brad says that he is determined that his children should never go through what he went through as a child. 'It sounds crazy, but all the bad things that happened to me have made me a better person. I have sworn that I shall never abuse my children.' At the time he says this, he is separated from his first wife and children, including stepchildren. He has been accused of physically abusing his stepson and sexually abusing his stepdaughters. He vigorously denies these allegations. His campaign to prove his innocence has now lasted 2 years and remains intense. Brad tells an elaborate story about how one night he was trying to calm down his excitable stepson and his hand slipped and somehow the boy ended up with severe facial bruising. 'He jumped up suddenly and his face caught the corner of my elbow and I was so shocked at what happened because I could see my own father hitting me and I thought "Oh God, I'm becoming like him" even though, you know, it was just an accident. I was in tears, apologised profusely to Mikie and said that it would never happen again.'

Although the evidence that the young girls have been sexually abused is strong, Brad is absolutely adamant that it was not and could not possibly have been him. He felt that the most likely explanation was that, while the girls were in short term foster care, one of the foster carers' older sons must have carried out the abuse. 'They never did any of this sexualised behaviour before they went into these foster homes... Of course, like all fathers I played with my children. When they asked Suzie "Where did your daddy touch you?" she said her arms and legs and that I tickled her tummy and her bum. They are now trying to say that that was a kind of sexualised thing on my part. But I have tickled all my children like that at bathtime and bedtimes as part of a game to make them laugh, but there was no sexual motive of any kind in it... I am willing to take a lie detector test. I have seen whether I can take a truth drug to prove my innocence, but my solicitor says that no court will accept such evidence, so what can I do. I can have supervised contact at a place where there are other men, who, to be blunt, are a bunch of paedophiles and have actually been convicted by courts, all bar me and I feel as if I'm being accused as one of them.' Brad is currently researching the law on fathers' access and contact with their children, as well as what will count as evidence in a court of law. Social workers feel intimidated by him. His knowledge of what they can and cannot do is formidable. It is easy for social workers to find themselves trading facts, legal niceties and reason with him, only realising later that the central issues are quickly being lost.

Conclusion

In its milder forms, avoidant-type behaviour can be highly functional in many work and educational settings. Most difficulties are experienced in close, interpersonal relationships where the self is defended against the distress triggered by intimacy, dependence and disclosure. Defended and dismissing individuals can be quite hard to engage over emotionally demanding or challenging issues. They rely on cognitive manipulation of both their own and other people's emotional states, derogating feelings and using rational and intellectual ideas to side-step, brow-beat or deny attachment-related issues. Such encounters allow defended personality types to come across as plausible, reasonable and reassuring. Often, however, the other is left with a feeling of not having been fully engaged or being outwitted or kept at a slight distance. The defended personality is intrigued by and desirous of intimacy but feels more comfortable with autonomy. There is a struggle to keep the two in balance, an anxious kind of independence generally winning out.

Ambivalent, dependent and preoccupied patterns

Between 8 and 12 per cent of people in normal populations might expect to be classified as ambivalent–preoccupied. However, as with all three insecure groups, the proportions increase rapidly as researchers switch their attention to children and adults living in higher-risk psychosocial environments. When caregiving styles associated with this pattern also include maltreatment and severe neglect, we find a high number of children with problem behaviours.

The main characteristics of individuals classified as ambivalent include deep anxieties about the lovability and value of the self, and a troubled preoccupation with whether or not other people have sufficient interest in them to be emotionally available in times of need. The result is a personality type with low self-esteem coupled with a tendency to become emotionally entangled in close relationships. The general uncertainty felt by those classified as ambivalent makes them prone to separation anxiety. Whenever close relationships appear threatened or there is pressure to become more independent and self-directed (leaving home in late adolescence, a partner deciding to work in another part of the country), ambivalent–preoccupied personalities experience increased levels of stress and anxiety. They become fractious, fretful and clingy when the availability of close relationships feels in danger of being lost. 'Felt security' is achieved by maintaining a high level of involvement with other people. However, such involvement is also underpinned by an anxiety that unless attention to relationships is maintained, other people will lose interest.

Again, we have to remind ourselves that being classified as ambivalent and preoccupied is not the same as being psychopathologically diagnosed. In many situations, the personality characteristics shown by preoccupied types prove to be both appropriate and an asset. People who come alive in social gatherings contribute enormously to the success of conference networking, parties and celebrations. Those who like being centre stage can entertain and enliven others. Jobs that involve meeting, helping and becoming involved with the 'public' can be very appealing. Performers, event organisers and people who run pubs need to be outward-going. Individuals who make most of the social running can be a boon for those who are shy and reserved. And for those who see professions such as social work, foster care, counselling and nursing providing opportunities to get involved with people and pursue good causes on behalf of needy others, careers in these fields can look most attractive. None of this is to say that the majority of people who do such jobs would be classified as ambivalent and preoccupied. Instead, jobs perceived to be socially involved, people orientated, expressive and lively will have a particular appeal to those who feel more comfortable and react positively when there are people around, issues of need and dependency, and emotional involvement.

However, although the majority of people showing insecure organised attachment styles do not appear as behavioural or mental health problems, there are increased psychosocial risks associated with those placed in these categories. Only those at the extreme end of the spectrum are likely to appear in 'clinical' settings, where, as a result of social filtering, they will appear in high numbers. Whether or not an individual develops problematic behaviours will depend on the intensity of their insecurity or the stressfulness of their environment. In presenting the ambivalent pattern, we shall be concentrating on the more pronounced features typically found in parents and children seen by social and health workers. The types of risk, behaviour and relationship style associated with ambivalent/preoccupied patterns are distinctive and will be described across the main stages of the lifespan.

Infancy

Carers who are inconsistently sensitive to their baby's needs are experienced as unpredictably unresponsive. For children, their parents' emotional availability is experienced as erratic. Cooperation, synchrony and behavioural harmony are poor and irregular. Psychologically (but not necessarily physically), carers are *underinvolved* with their infants and so miss many of their distress signals. In this sense, babies might feel emotionally neglected. Both their physical needs and emotional states might go unnoticed for considerable periods of time. Although the baby is not rejected, not all of his or her behaviours are accepted. When young children who show ambivalent attachment patterns begin to explore and seek independence, their mothers feel uncomfortable. Autonomy shown by others, including their own children, implies a lack of need and love of them as carers. The carer's own psychological needs tend to govern the type of involvement that he or she has with the child. There is love for the child, but, as far as the infant is concerned, it is hard to win and in scarce supply.

The problem for the child, therefore, is to engage the attention and interest of a carer whose availability cannot be relied upon, particularly at times of distress. We know that when needs and levels of anxiety run high, children increase their attachment behaviour. Children whose mothers' emotional availability and general sensitivity are low therefore have to *raise their level of attachment behaviour* in order to gain attention. They have to break through the parent's lack of responsiveness by increasing attachment behaviours such as crying, clinging, following, making constant demands, shouting and tugging. Mothers are usually physically present, often in a rather passive, sedentary fashion, but it seems difficult to arouse their interest or stimulate them into giving care and attention. Their involvement and interest remain unreliable and unpredictable. Inconsistent mothers are sometimes comforting, sometimes angry and sometimes ineffective (Belsky and Cassidy 1994). Because of such uncertainties, 'the ambivalent individual is prone to separation anxiety and tends to be clinging while manifesting unresolved anger directed at the caregiver' (Mayseless 1996: 209).

Eventually, however, with persistence and heightened attachment behaviour, children expect some kind of response. A biscuit may be handed over, a place on mother's lap won. 'Here, have a candy if that will shut you up!' might yell an exasperated parent. At other times, the baby's difficult, whining and demanding behaviour might provoke a more aggressive response. The mother might shout or slap her young child.

In behavioural terms, maternal responses that are erratic and unpredictable are tantamount to putting the baby on an intermittent reinforcement schedule. As parents, they are 'non-contingently' responsive. That is, the carer's more responsive behaviours bear no direct relation to the behaviour of the child. The child can therefore establish no connection between what he or she does and the response of the mother other than that increased activation of attachment behaviour seems to provoke a reaction sooner or later. This reinforces the child's persistence. The strategy of *maximising* attachment behaviour therefore works well with inconsistent, erratically available parents. Yelling, following, clinging, pleading and having temper tantrums are eventually rewarded with attention.

Thus, the infant's anxiety that the carer might not be available at times of distress is reduced by the child *organising* a defensive strategy that increases – or *hyperactivates* – their attachment behaviour. This achieves a secondary *felt security*. That is, by keeping one's attachment system operating at full, one's behaviour is organised in such a way as to keep an inconsistent caregiver maximally available. Her availability is never going to be high, but the strategy is designed to glean the most out of an otherwise thin caregiving and protective emotional prospect.

A key feature of this strategy is that because carers are inconsistent, children are unable to make predictions. This means that they are unable to organise their behaviour on the basis of *mentally* predicting their caregiver's responsiveness. In other words, *cognition* fails them (Crittenden 1997). There is no obvious pattern to their carer's responsive behaviours. Not having been exposed to a regular social environment, children have not learned how to think about what works best in terms of gaining other people's interest and attention. Other people's promises, words and explanations are inherently unreliable and unpredictable, whatever they might say. It is therefore better to rely on behaviour that is primarily *emotional* and *affective*. This is why it feels safer to keep attachment behaviour operating at maximum most of the time. Such a strategy also means that children experience an association between (a) feelings of need and desire, and (b) feelings of anger, uncertainty, resentment and anxiety aroused when their attachment behaviour is activated. Sudden switches between these feelings of need and anger, desire and resentment, take place in attachment-saturated encounters. There is also confusion between feeling needy and feeling angry, so that the experience of one seems to imply the other.

Within such caregiving relationships, infants experience the self as not of sufficient interest or worth to command automatic love and care. Although the infant, with great effort, does manage to provoke other people into making a response, interactionally speaking the young child does not experience himself or herself as socially very effective. There is a sense of uncertainty and anxiety that the self is neither valued nor liked. This can lead to feelings of doubt, despair and inadequacy. Feelings of worthlessness and depression are particularly heightened when carers are physically absent. Increasing attachment behaviour is pointless without the physical presence of the attachment figure. When attachment behaviour is switched off, there is a sense of emptiness. Cognition, reflection, task preoccupation and thought have never loomed large in these children's psychological repertoire, so when they are removed from people or people decide to absent themselves from them, their normally hyperactivated affective state is redundant, and they are left feeling dull, worthless and full of despair. Within the child's internal working model, the expectation of other people is that they will not be interested or routinely available. However, intimacy (being in close relationship) is preferred to autonomy (experienced as not being in close relationship).

We also need to remind ourselves that the attachment system and exploratory system are mutually exclusive: when one is switched on, the other is off. Children who organise their behaviour around a highly activated attachment strategy therefore do so at the expense of exploration. This means that much of their time and energy is spent keeping other people available by crying, fussing, being fretful, complaining, following and seeking attention. There is an angry *preoccupation* with whether or not other people are interested, involved and responsive. There is little energy left over for constructive play, task accomplishment, curiosity and exploration of the environment, either physically, socially or intellectually. Again, this means that cognition loses out to emotion in children's build-up of experience. It is, in fact, possible to split the ambivalent group into those infants who are actively and openly *angry* with their carers (C1) and those who are passive, but nevertheless intensely *preoccupied* with and *dependent* on their carers (C2).

In both cases, children show great distress at the prospect and actual experience of separation. Upon reunion, ambivalent children may approach the carer with anger while at the same time demanding attention (hence their *ambivalence*). They seek proximity but doubt and *resist* comfort. There is thus a mixture of approach and resist behaviours that include distress and aggression, need and rejection, clinging and fighting. In contrast to children classified as avoidant who focus on the environment, those classified as ambivalent–resistant focus insistently and relentlessly on the caregiver. Most of these behaviours can be identified during the Strange Situation procedure:

> The baby may be fretful shortly following room entrance. He either fails entirely to engage in the toys, sitting passively by mother's feet (sub category C2), or else he may engage in some activity with the toys, while interrupting that activity frequently with fussing or with fretful returns to mother (C1). In either case, he seems preoccupied with his mother even prior to her leave-taking; he is fearful or angrily resistant towards the stranger; and he exhibits

great distress on each separation. If he falls in Ainsworth's actively angry sub category (C1), he may seek the mother directly on room entrance, like a secure baby. After that, however, he will alternate bids for proximity with expressions of angry rejection, perhaps displaying tantrum behaviour. If he falls in Ainsworth's passive sub-category of Strange Situation behavior (C2), he may barely raise his arms in greeting, appearing too distressed or incompetent to approach. Signs of resistance to the mother will then also be weak, but the baby will be unable to terminate his distress by the end of the episode. (Main 1995: 419)

Children classified as ambivalent are therefore dominated by affect. They find it difficult to regulate their emotions. As a result, they exclude much external information and cognitive experience about people and relationships, learning little about the social world (including themselves) and the way it works. They depend entirely on their attachment figure to help them to regulate their arousal. However, children's constant demands frustrate others, wearing them out and leading to exasperation and even abandonment. Anxious, hyperactivated attachment behaviour can therefore adversely affect interpersonal relationships.

Although infants classified as ambivalent may not experience hostile, abusive parenting, if they do suffer maltreatment it is more likely to be a case of *neglect* (both physical and emotional), perhaps combined with parental exasperation and aggression.

Childhood

Once children leave infancy, and presuming they continue to experience a broadly neglectful, underinvolved style of parenting, the basic pattern of interpersonal relationships remains the same. Children now, of course, are mobile and can talk. This adds two new behaviours to their hyperactivated attachment repertoire. They can physically follow their carer. And they can shout and scream verbal demands at their mothers and fathers to pay attention and become involved. They can also complain about being ignored and treated unfairly. The result is an increase in noise, attention-seeking behaviour and dependence, and an unwillingness to be soothed and placated for any length of time.

Although these strategies are likely to provoke parents into making erratic responses, they are equally likely to make them cross. It can also result in them threatening to abandon the relationship. Carers convey the message that the child cannot take their emotional avail-ability for granted. This threatened loss of the attachment figure further raises children's anxiety and in turn further increases their attachment behaviour. Relationships remain charged with a loud emotional content. Threats of separation and the loss of availability by parents are countered by children showing increased distress, anger and dependency.

A slightly different developmental trajectory is followed in cases where there is *severe physical neglect*, typical of parents whose caring skills are very limited. Young children may lapse into a passive, depressed dependence. They become listless, apathetic and develop-mentally delayed. They often are isolated during occasions of free play with other children. Speech is poor. Crittenden (1996) observes that, as the children become more passive, they offer less impetus to their parents to become engaged. A cycle of decreasing stimulation is created. They appear to represent both themselves and others mentally as helpless. Their general lack of competence can even suggest depression. Although most severely neglected children continue in this rather dull, passive mode, a few, as they grow older, display frantic, desperate behaviour in an attempt to provoke some kind of stimulation. Their hyperactivity is without focus.

Although the parents of ambivalently classified children cope reasonably well with them as dependent babies, they become increas-ingly flustered as their children become older, more active and demanding. Family life is characterised by a preoccupation with other people's availability. Threats and counter-threats about who cares and who does not, who loves and who does not, are constantly traded. Each member is intent on ensuring that his or her own needs are heard and met. The result is family life with little structure, few rules, high levels of impulsivity and much disorder. Relationships feel emotion-ally *enmeshed* and *entangled*. Severely neglectful parents often respond with outbursts of frustration and anger when situations become overwhelming. Crittenden (1996) continues her observations by noting that, unlike the aggression shown in other families, violence in neglectful families is unpredictable and diffuse. Situations can quickly escalate and explode. Children never quite know where they are with their parents.

In projective story-telling tests, ambivalent children find it difficult simultaneously to acknowledge and deal with happy and unhappy events, and other people's availability and non-availability. For example, in a story in which parents might leave children with their grandmother while they go away for the night, ambivalent preschoolers 'split' the emotions associated with this attachment-related issue so that the anxiety-provoking elements are kept out of play. In their parents' absence, the children in the story play in a very busy, happy fashion. Upon the return of their parents, children demonstrate a confused reaction in which the family's reintegration is delayed. Anxiety is handled by separating positive and negative affect, allowing only one at a time to be at the forefront of feeling. In George and Solomon's work: 'Negative feelings resulting from separation fears were acknowledged yet kept separate as the children attempted to divert their attention to positive events. Even upon reunion these children were uncertain as to how to integrate disconnected fears, sadness, and pain with the happiness that surrounded the parents' return home' (George 1996: 415–16).

Crittenden (1995: 386) offers a conceptual underpinning to these kinds of observation. The parents of profoundly ambivalent children 'act out' rather than try to explain their feelings. Children's experience of emotions is immediate and not mediated by language or conceptual understanding. They develop 'episodic models' of what do in highly arousing and conflictual circumstances. Highly charged emotional 'episodes' of interaction from the past are used to guide behaviour in present situations of arousal and distress. Situations in which there is great need or distress trigger an immediate emotional reaction, with little thought or reflection.

Parents, too, are poor at helping their children to name and differentiate their feelings. This limits children's conceptual, semantic and *cognitive* understanding of their own and other people's feelings, and how feelings are linked to behaviour. Without such 'emotional, social and semantic scaffolding', children find it difficult to recognise, regulate and handle affect. The children therefore feel uneasy and unfamiliar with those who deal with emotional conflict by the use of rational, thought-based arguments. Better to respond to anxiety using affectively driven behaviours than thought and reflection. Reason and words can never be trusted. These children experience few semantic guides on how to behave. Parents' words are seen as inconsistent, misleading and confusing. Parents who lie, trick, fail to keep promises and mislead their children in attempts to control them increase doubts about the reliability of cognition. 'You just play with your sister; I'll be back in a minute', says a mother who does not come home until late evening.

Thus, rational explanations by other people of their behaviours and feelings are disregarded. Much of the potential knowledge and under-standing about one's own and other people's behaviour in relationships is therefore ignored. Internal working models become heavily biased towards the processing of affect. The individual's ability or willingness to make intellectual sense of what is going on is limited. Lack of cognitive reflection reduces people's options of how best to behave in demanding social situations. Ambivalent children tend to have one major mode of response – emotional acting out. Sticking to feelings, displayed at high intensity, leads to the most familiar outcome.

Lies by caregivers also mean that children are unable to negotiate a goal-corrected partnership. Prospects of separation (and return) require information and plans to be shared openly and honestly. When this does not take place, or promises are broken, trust breaks down. For ambivalent children, attachment-related issues can therefore quickly lead to conflict. Separations and absences, no matter how short they are said to be, are not tolerated. Promises about not being long are not trusted. Separation issues generally provoke anger and protest. Shared cognitive understanding becomes increasingly diffi-cult. The only reliable way to provoke involvement is to run relation-ships on an emotional rather than a cognitive agenda.

Coercive strategies

By the time that ambivalent children reach the age of 3 or 4 years, they begin to develop strategies that allow them a slight increase in the control of their social environment. Their interpersonal experience remains one in which there is an underlying uncertainty about other people's emotional availability. However, they evolve refinements in the way in which their hyperactivated attachment system is deployed, known as *coercive* strategies:

> In the preschool years, children become capable of discerning intuitively the predictable effects of their resistant and passive behavior. On the basis of this awareness, they may organize their behavior around a strategy of alternatively threatening their attachment figures into compliance with their wishes with angry behavior and bribing them into compliance with disarming (for example, charmingly seductive) behavior. They use evidence of maternal feelings of guilt and anger to regulate their shifts in behavior pattern from threatening to disarming and the reverse. Their strategy, in other words, becomes *coercive*.
> (Crittenden 1992b: 583)

> Moreover, because changing caregiver's behavior satisfies children's desires, there is the appearance that attachment figures are responsible for children's feelings. Consequently, coercive children tend to blame others for their problems. (Crittenden 1995: 375)

Coy, disarming behaviour is activated by children when their parents appear in danger of becoming angry and aggressive. It is an attempt to disarm, placate and emotionally seduce the other person, often using helpless, babyish and vulnerable speech and behaviour. These *submissive* behaviours represent attempts to control the other person's threatening responses. Helplessness and infantile behaviour are attempts to evoke a protective, nurturing response from others and thus reduce their aggression. On the other hand, if the other person is viewed as uncertain and unresponsive, children display behaviours that are demanding, angry and threatening.

It is this combined use of threatening and disarming behaviours that comprise the *coercive* strategy, designed to keep the other actively and demonstratively involved at all times. Not to be involved, not to be in a heightened state of responsiveness, is experienced as loss and abandonment. Most coercive children are therefore preoccupied and overinvolved with their attachment figures. They fail to learn constructive interactional skills. They find it difficult to be self-reliant. Their insistent, whining demands wear out the interest and responsivity of others, who are finally driven away. This abandonment by the other confirms the internal working model that represents other people as ultimately unreliable and uninterested.

A common variation on the coercive style is to secure other people's availability by the use of socially acceptable helpless and dependent behaviours. These might include feeling unwell in some general, unspecified way or being very picky about food. 'All of these function to force adults to cater to children without the child's having to make reasoned arguments for the attention' (Crittenden 1995: 395). Thus, children begin to develop a more organised strategy in the face of inconsistent, unpredictable parenting that relies on a constant switching between loud, threatening behaviour when responsiveness is unforthcoming, and coy, disarming behaviour when parents are about to explode with anger. Parents begin to feel increasingly *frustrated*, *manipulated* and *not in control*. They see themselves as victims of their children's intensifying demands and difficult behaviour. They feel despair, anger and uncertainty. At this point, they also begin to complain to partners, teachers and child welfare agents about the unmanagability of their children.

Ambivalent children's prolonged and high-intensity use of strong feelings means that they lose the ability to differentiate between emotions. Ironically, too, strategies that involve the frequent use of full-volume anger result in anger losing much of its communicative power. For both parents and children, outbursts of extreme anger are just as likely to occur over minor events (the loss of a sock) as they are over major upsets (the loss of a partner).

Generally, children classified as ambivalent show poor levels of concentration. They are easily distracted, moving quickly from one activity to another. Tasks are abandoned in order to provoke attention from others who are present. Children are restless and attention seeking. It seems more important for them to generate an environment that is much higher in emotional content than in practical, task-orientated or cognitive purpose. This often means that they are exasperating children with whom to work. Relationships quickly break down as the bias is always towards the affective side of whatever is taking place. The ambivalent child is more concerned about the other person's emotional availability ('Do you like me?', 'Do you prefer her to me?', 'If you love me, you'll do what I want to do', 'Will you be my best friend and play with no-one else?'). The result is that, along with other insecure children, those classified as ambivalent are often unpopular with their peers. They experience more conflict, dissatisfaction and disharmony in close relationships, with a greater likelihood of outbursts of aggression, impulsivity and frustration.

Experiences of failed peer relationships simply confirm the accuracy of ambivalent children's internal working model. They fail to see connections between their own and other people's feelings and behaviours. Unable to take the other person's perspective, they accept no responsibility for their contribution to the outcome of relationships. Failures are always the fault of others, who are seen as depriving, denying, punishing and unloving. Children see themselves as perpetual victims. They are more likely to be bullied than bully. They see themselves as blameless. Arguments and difficulties are other people's fault. But the basic, underlying plea is 'Why won't you love me?' Within their internal working model, the self is viewed as unworthy of love, ineffective and incompetent. Feelings of anxiety, uncertainty and dissatisfaction are therefore experienced in most close relationships.

These needy interactions can be seen in Simon's relationship with his mother, Maggie. She feels that she can no longer control him, while Simon feels angry and confused about her emotional inconsistency and unavailability.

Simon

Simon, aged 14, lives with his mother, Maggie, his half-brother Christopher aged 11, and his stepfather, Jim, who is the father of neither of the boys and is 10 years older than Maggie. Simon's mother is finding Simon's aggressive, confrontational, argumentative behaviour more and more upsetting. She says that he has rejected her and shows no respect. With increasing frequency, she says that she cannot handle him and would like him removed. The family social worker has said, 'Maggie states that Simon is mad and needs psychiatric help. Simon on the other hand states that his mother is mad and that she needs psychiatric help.' There has been a long history of Maggie saying that she cannot cope with Simon. On previous occasions, he has either been looked after by his maternal grandmother or placed with foster carers. When Maggie was living with Christopher's father, who was a very violent man, there were unproven suspicions that Simon had occasionally been subjected to physical abuse by his stepfather. Simon remembers him with fear and hatred. During her stormy relationship with Christopher's father, Maggie twice took an overdose, once when he said he was going to leave her, and again when she found out that he was having an affair with the next-door neighbour.

The police are called in regularly to sort out violent arguments between Simon and his mother. They punch each other. Simon smashes furniture and attacks his younger brother, who he says 'winds' him up deliberately to get him into trouble. On one occasion, after there had been physical aggression between mother and son, Simon barricaded himself into the loft. The incident was triggered by a minor disagreement over a slice of cake, which quickly escalated into serious physical violence and destructive behaviour. His mother called the police and had him arrested. Another incident witnessed Maggie chasing Simon around the house with a breadknife threatening to kill him. Simon has also been suspended from school on a number of occasions for attacking other children, and on one occasion a member of staff. When matters are feeling particularly out of hand, Maggie is in contact with her social worker on a daily basis.

When he is feeling sad, Simon says that his mum is very important to him, but at other times he says that she is 'a pain in the backside – she never listens. She gives me hassle all the time and it drives me mental.' He seems very mixed up about how he feels about her – at one level he wants everything to be warm and nice, at another he is very angry and says he hates his mother: 'She relies too much on other people to do things for her. I don't trust her.' He has very low self-esteem and has been judged to be depressed. Thoughts of suicide have crossed his mind, but he says that he hasn't 'the guts' to do it. He has few friends, but desperately wants to be liked. He says he hates his brother. The future worries him – it seems bleak and friendless. He wishes that his mum and birth-father had never split up when he was a baby, that he had more friends, that his mother's back pains would get better and that she were more available and less dependent on others. But he adds fatalistically: 'But it's life. You talk about these things, but they won't ever happen.'

Maggie is always complaining, both officially and unofficially, that no-one is doing anything to help and that everyone is failing both Simon and herself. Everyone seems to blame everyone else. Each family member behaves as if they feel deprived of love, attention and understanding. Maggie's husband says he now wants a divorce. Simon taunts her continually. In a recent desperate telephone call to her social worker, Maggie said, 'If you don't do something, I shall commit suicide!' and then slammed the phone down. She says that she is 34 years old but feels 104 and is 'sinking fast'. She has severe back problems, which she claims incapacitate her, although those close to her are not so sure that she is as debilitated as much as she says. Everything she says or does seems to have a 'very dramatic, theatrical' quality to it. Everyone's behaviour seems exaggerated, 'as if to get a response'. Family life is described by Maggie as either 'paradise' or 'total hell'. With some pride, Maggie decided to name their home 'The Mad House' and had a plaque specially made. The family live in a small two-bedroomed bungalow. She runs an animal sanctuary. In the house at any one time are typically a dozen dogs, several cats and an assortment of parrots and budgerigars. 'I trust animals more than people', she has said. 'They have more love to give than human beings.'

Peer relationships

The general preoccupation with other people's availability and relationships means that coercive children constantly seek social interaction. They use displays of affectivity to attract attention to themselves. They feel most alive in the company of others, particularly when the action is lively and charged. There is an attraction to being in gangs, especially those which push social boundaries to the limit. The gang is a potentially permanently available, responsive group. Within groups, ambivalent–coercive children will display much attention-seeking behaviour. They show off, act silly, behave immaturely and do not know when to stop or sense when enough is enough. Relationships within the gang can rapidly switch between the seductive and the quarrelsome (Crittenden 1995). Threats of leaving and abandonment are used to try to control people's availability.

There are also strong feelings of jealousy and possessiveness. Issues of best friends, who likes who and attempts to make friendships exclusive mean that relationships are experienced as stressful and conflictual. Children find it difficult to share close friends and readily feel unloved. They regularly go into a sulk or embrace the role of victim. Feeling picked on is a constant complaint. As other people's inconsistent emotional responsivity has caused these children to feel distress and anxiety in the first place, other people are always blamed by ambivalent children for making them feel upset, angry or hurt. It is other people who are expected to change if things are to improve. If others fail to respond or offer emotional acceptance, resentments are stored, grudges held and hostilities raised.

School

Low levels of concentration, the need for attention, the claim to be helpless and the inability to work independently mean that children classified as ambivalent, more particularly those seen as coercive, quickly become known to teachers. Most of their attention is spent on relationships and other people's emotional availability, leaving little time or wish to attend to academic matters.

In a study of 10–11-year-old children from materially poor families attending a summer day camp, Urban et al. (1991) observed that children with insecure attachment histories were rated as more dependent, less socially competent, less ego-resilient and more likely to want to interact with camp counsellors than were children with a secure attachment history. Children with ambivalent classifications were most likely to evoke support and nurturing from adults, although they were less likely to have made a friend than were more secure children (Elicker *et al.* 1992).

Coercive strategies, neglect and abuse

In extreme cases of parental uncertainty, agitation, anger and distress, children often exaggerate one of the component parts of the coercive strategy. Thus, in maltreating, neglectful or highly chaotic families, coercion can be stretched by children so that either *aggression* or *help-lessness* become dominant. Aggression represents the angry approach response heightened to the level of *threat* – the coercive–aggressive pattern of 'attack and punish' designed to provoke a response and gain attention. Helplessness represents the emotional 'need' and desire component exaggerated to the level of extreme passivity – the coercive–helpless pattern employed to elicit care and protection.

Coercive–aggressive patterns

The raised demands of ambivalent children are readily experienced by parents as criticism of their caregiving abilities. As a result, parents' feelings of uncertainty and failure, ineffectiveness and unworthiness, increase. These anxieties activate their own attachment needs, reducing their ability to respond, offer support and provide cognitive guidance. Parents who experience anxiety when faced with their children's growing independence find themselves trying to deal with mounting behaviour and control problems. When distressed, the parents' own attachment style comes into play. They react to their children's loud and uncontrollable behaviour in one of three typical ways:

- displays of anger, aggression and abuse
- threats of abandonment and emotional withholding
- moods of collapsed despair in which they feel depressed, unloved, helpless and ineffective.

Distress causes ambivalent children to communicate their anxieties quickly and urgently. However, they fail to develop cognitive models that allow them to take the perspective of the other. This means that they are unable to compromise, negotiate, reflect and jointly plan in a goal-corrected fashion between their desires and those of adults. Behaviours to the mutual advantage of both parent and child cannot be agreed.

Although feelings of anger are acknowledged, they are not controlled. Anger and bossiness is used to punish other people for being emotionally unavailable, denying and unresponsive. Conduct disorders therefore include angry, threatening, fearful and acting out behaviours. Pleading, placatory, seductive behaviours only appear when the other person either threatens to abandon the relationship or becomes dangerously angry.

> Unfortunately, when displays of affect are so exaggerated that they are not easily terminated, children may become preoccupied with the display. In such cases, children may become too distraught to communicate anything specific regarding the cause of distress or may so frustrate caregivers that attachment figures lash out in anger or withdraw assistance. In such cases, children not only create risk to themselves, they also fail to learn to monitor others' affect... the intensity of the display of affect is both so emotionally arousing and so cognitively distracting that coercive children often lose sight of the true problem (that is, being safe and feeling secure). This preoccupation can interfere with their generating, or even noticing, alternative solutions. (Crittenden 1992a: 221, 230)

In turn, parents also try to use coercive, cajoling behaviours with their increasingly difficult children. They may threaten their children with their own availability by talk of abandonment ('If you don't behave, I'll leave you/kill myself'). There are frequent, sentimental expressions of love for their children as well as constant enquiries about whether their children love them. Anxiety makes parents behave unpredictably. When both children and parents are using coercive behaviours, the result is relationships that are loud, volatile, conflictual and emotionally exaggerated. There are rapid swings between love and hate, intimacy and anger, giving and denying. There are lots of dramatic comings and goings.

Coercive children, in contrast to avoidant–defended children, 'are likely to demand immediate gratification as a substitute for true comfort; consequently, they may exhibit impatience, eating disorders tied to excessive intake, and immaturity. In addition, they may use risk-taking behavior that cannot fail to elicit protective attention, for example, careless hyperactivity, extreme refusal to eat, toleration of violent relationships. Irrational risk taking also implies disbelief in the contingencies that usually link events, a pattern first established in infancy with inconsistent parental responsiveness' (Crittenden 1995: 394). Many children referred to the psychological services fit the coercive pattern of attachment and mental functioning.

Coercive children are generally attention-seeking and socially disruptive, behaviours that are particularly problematic in the context of school. They veer between being aggressively demanding and helplessly pathetic, both behaviours designed to provoke attention from others depending on whether they are being perceived as unresponsive or angry. With age, particularly during adolescence and early adulthood, these conduct disorders can escalate into delinquency and violence. Threatening, 'in-your-face' behaviours increase. Other people are blamed for slights, upsets, setbacks, failures and difficulties. Crittenden (1995, 1997) describes a sequence of escalating coercive strategies, the milder of which are practised by nearly all children in the preschool years at some time, the stronger taking both children and adults into the area of psychopathology:

Threatening/Disarming
↓
Aggressive/Helpless
↓
Punitive/Seductive
↓
Menacing/Paranoid

Some children, depending on whether their caregiver is experienced predominantly as either uncertain or abusive, may begin to overdevelop one half of one of the above four coercive strategies in an attempt to maintain the other's involvement. Some extremely aggressive children, for example, may become preoccupied with retribution and revenge against those whom they feel have offended them (Crittenden 1997). Feeling paranoid about other people who are perceived as 'having it in for them' is matched by feelings of menace, revenge and attack.

Kevin's mother, Julie, is anxious and uncertain in her role as caregiver. She feels that she cannot manage Kevin. They have heated battles in which there is much shouting and screaming. Kevin switches between aggression and sadness. His mother, teachers and social worker feel exhausted in their dealings with him.

Julie and her son, Kevin (Gregory 1997)

Family life is characterised by a high degree of enmeshment and aggression. Kevin's behaviour is becoming increasingly coercive, with a growing level of anger and aggression. However, there are also undercurrents of disorganisation in Kevins behaviour, and unresolved feelings of trauma and loss in his mother (see Chapter 7).

Kevin is aged 11 years. His mother, Julie, now 30 years old, feels that he is getting beyond her control. His anger and aggression towards her and his two younger brothers, Paul (8 years) and Ethan (5 years), are increasing. Kevin is also showing violent behaviour at school. He winds people up and then lashes out. When adults try to talk to him about his behaviour, he tries to deflect the conversation – he'll claim to have a pain in his elbow, or he'll complain his pen isn't working. He cannot keep still. He constantly fidgets, fiddles and moves restlessly about, twisting and turning.

Julie has a violent relationship with the boys' father, Tony. They met when she was 19 and he was 18. Along with her children, she has spent long periods of time in women's refuges. Many social workers and other health and welfare agencies have been involved with the family over the years, mainly over concerns that the children have been witnessing Tony's violence towards their mother. The parents are currently living apart, although Tony has a house in a nearby street and continues to visit. A longed-for baby girl was born when Kevin was aged 6 years, but she suffered a cot death when she was 10 months old. Julie and Tony cannot talk about the loss, but Julie does talk a lot to Kevin about when his baby sister died.

When he was a boy, Tony was sexually abused by a relative. Julie describes him as like a child. She says that with Tony she really has four children not three. He wants 'totally to possess' Julie. He gets very jealous. He wants to know where she has been, who she has seen, who has visited the house. If he convinces himself that she has talked to another man, he becomes very angry and agitated. Julie feels trapped.

Julie talks a great deal, and her social worker says that she is constantly 'losing the thread of what she is saying as she gets caught up in her own anxiety. She'll stand there with her head in her hands, shaking her head, saying that she doesn't remember what she was saying.' She feels that her life is a muddle but that there is nothing that she can do about it. Seeing beyond today seems impossible for Julie. The emotional temperature is always high. Everything is dramatic. Things are said to be either dreadful or wonderful.

Julie suffers many aches and pains in her chest and joints. She also suffers from migraines, cramps and breathlessness. 'I nearly always see her in the kitchen', says her social worker. 'She's wandering up and down, picking things up then putting them down. A couple of times, she's reached up to get something from a wall cupboard in what seems to be a very awkward fashion. She twists her body, then she has a 'spasm'. Then she'll start to limp and complain that she can't move her leg because she's in dreadful pain. All these psychosomatic illnesses have been investigated by doctors – X-rays, blood test, you name it, she's had it – but never anything the matter.' Julie has also received counselling.

Julie says that her mum has a temper but that she is also 'very caring'. Her mother still lives locally and they are in almost daily contact. Julie continues to need approval and emotional attention from her mother, but she feels that she does not receive it. In fact, the relation-ship between them is 'antagonistic'. The social worker still sees Julie as being needy and 'child-like' with her mother. 'All Julie feels she gets from her mother is criticism.'

Although Julie talks a great deal, professionals find it quite hard to get a clear picture of what is going on. Even so, those who work with her initially find her appealing. 'It's almost as if when you go in you are the only one who has ever been there. If you are young and naïve, you might be quite seduced by that, because she engages you very actively and she makes you feel important. That you are the worker she wants to talk to. She downplays previous workers. It would be easy to be seduced into thinking that because you have such a good relationship with her that you are the only one she will be helped by. It's very hard to leave when you visit. She'll be talking to you as you're getting in the car, saying "Oh! Yes, and another thing."' Julie can also cause professionals to feel much exasperation. For example, it was very frustrating to discover that, on her return from the refuge, it was not long before she allowed Tony back, although the relationship inevitably broke down in a very short space of time. 'I was feeling more and more cross with her', explained the social worker. 'It felt as if I wasn't getting anywhere with her. There was an injunction on Tony not to visit the house and then one of the kids would let slip that he'd spent the night there and then they had a big bust up and he'd kicked her shins. It made me wonder what the hell I was doing there.' However, when social workers feel that they have had enough of 'being messed around', she 'gets the message'. When she felt there was danger of losing the contact and 'saw the service disappearing over the horizon, she suddenly frogmarched Kevin back with more problems'. Professionals feel that Julie 'sucks' them in to meet her needs rather than Kevin's. She wants constant reassurance that she is being a good mother. 'I do feel sympathy for her. It's a funny mixture because I feel sympathetic but sometimes I feel punitive towards her. She is very needy and I feel that she could totally subsume me.'

Julie experiences uncertainty and ambivalence in her role as carer. She is always telling the children how much she loves them, that she is only doing things that they do not like because she loves them. 'She's in a constant dialogue with the children, explaining what she's doing in an attempt to overcome her fear of being perceived as a bad mother or somebody who doesn't protect her kids. She constantly feels blamed.' There is much blurring of parent–child boundaries and levels of enmeshment are high. Kevin is privy to all his mother's thoughts and feelings. Kevin also appears to have many strong feelings but 'he doesn't know where to direct them or when to stop, like being angry. He's angry about all sorts of things. About being the oldest, because he has most of the responsibility. Because he has to be a man for his mum, that he has to listen to all her thought and feelings. His younger brothers go to bed and then there's a conspiracy between Mum and Kevin that if he goes to bed, he can then get up later when the others are asleep and he can be 'cosy' with Mum downstairs. She can then talk to him with her stream of consciousness stuff.'

Kevin has a vivid, violent fantasy life (also see Chapter 7 on disorganised patterns that are punitive and fearful): 'He said that there was a massacre in his school playground and he felled this chap who was wielding an axe. Nobody else noticed that this massacre was going on. He had rugby tackled the axeman, a complete stranger, and had become a hero.'

In another session the social worker learned that one of Kevin's wishes was that his mum and dad would stop fighting. 'He describes how he sits upstairs with his hands over his ears and his head on his knees when his mum is being beaten up. He wants all that to stop.'

Coercive–helpless patterns

In severely neglecting, highly underinvolved families, there is a pervasive air of incompetence, fatalism and depression. Family life is often structured around the mother and her children. There are few rules, blurred generational boundaries and little impulse control. Poverty is common. Children with parents who have learning difficulties appear at particularly increased risk (Crittenden 1996). Levels of attunement and responsiveness between family members tend to be low. Carers lack an understanding of their children's needs, particularly for stimulation and interaction. Although, with age and increased locomotion, some young children begin to react hyperactively in an attempt to provoke some kind of stimulation, many others become apathetic and increasingly listless.

Children adopting very submissive, disgruntled ambivalent patterns appear to have given up on the twin-pronged character of the coercive strategy. Displays of heightened attachment behaviour, including anger and emotional demands, only seem to make otherwise underinvolved caregivers feel more helpless and frustrated, and even more likely to withdraw from the relationship. Children are therefore left with attachment behaviours that emphasise their helplessness, vulnerability, passivity, fear and incompetence. Teachers may be inclined to nurture them and tolerate their high dependency. Helpless, fatalistic children may even court victimisation. It is also not uncommon for them to display and exaggerate illnesses and vague, rather generalised physical upsets that demand adult attention (Crittenden 1995: 395). Extreme pickiness over food is common.

However, the absence of anger in these children tends not to alert others to their strong emotional needs or motivate them to respond (Crittenden 1992a: 221). The result is that such children are left preoccupied with trying to regain their attachment figures but are unable to risk more than disgruntled, pouty facial expressions and a general air of dissatisfaction and vulnerability. Inhibition is said to be present when children fail to initiate or respond to social interactions across a range of relationships. There is a lack of demonstrable affection, which may be coupled with excessive dependence or clinginess. In this pattern, children show an exaggerated suppression of exploration. They are hesitant to approach, touch and play with objects. They withdraw from social interaction with unfamiliar people (Lieberman and Pawl 1988: 333). Smiling and other displays of affect are highly restricted.

Some helpless, inhibited children have caregivers who are gratified by their children's dependence and discourage autonomy and exploration by either withdrawing emotionally or punishing displays of independence. 'These children are likely to equate exploration... with maternal emotional unavailability and lack of protection' (Lieberman and Pawl 1988: 334).

Adolescence and adulthood

Without major changes taking place in children's psychosocial environment, the coercive pattern is likely to be maintained into adolescence and adulthood. Adults whose ability to regulate their own aroused emotions is low experience higher levels of distress and poor social functioning in close and intimate relationships.

In adolescence, the more extreme coercive behavioural strategies become increasingly disruptive, attention-seeking and difficult to control. Antisocial behaviour, conflict, control problems, impulsivity, poor concentration and poor staying power increase. Preoccupied adolescents often become a problem for both parents and teachers. A growing sense of unfairness and injustice means that their level of whining and complaining increases. Life is lived at a heightened pitch of dissatisfaction and anger. Feelings of guilt and personal responsibility are largely absent. Parents and peers are subjected to intimidation to make them respond and provide. Individuals learn little about how relationships work or how the self contributes to the content of interpersonal life, even though those with hyperactivating strategies remain preoccupied and deeply entangled with other people's availability and emotional interest.

These characteristics are picked up in the AAI. Adults are judged *preoccupied–entangled–enmeshed* (E pattern) when they exhibit a confused, angry or passive preoccupation with attachment figures in particular and relationships in general. When recalling childhood memories, adults showing the preoccupied pattern become easily absorbed by issues of love and hate that they believe characterise all their close relationships. They appear overly involved in family relationships and emotional conflict, both past and present. Anger surfaces as people talk about who was loved and not loved, in favour and not in favour, who was emotionally withholding and who was emotionally giving. Often the same person can, at different times during the story, be all good or all bad, all loving or all denying. Many feel that they never met parental expectations. There appears to be a struggle between anger with and a desire for approval from parents. However, these positive and negative feelings fail to become integrated into the same rounded, realistically evaluated picture. Uncertainty and ambivalence about other people therefore saturate accounts. There is not a strong sense of self as separate from and independent of others. Individuals tends to see themselves in terms of other people's reactions. Moods go up and down depending on the emotional climate in which individuals feel themselves to be.

In the AAI, the manner of speech often contains clichés ('We had a love/hate relationship') or is childish. Although many, often overly long, descriptions are offered about childhood experiences, they are confused and ambiguous. There is little self-reflection or ability to step back and evaluate behaviour and experiences.

Attachment issues are 'maximised' and given great prominence in the interview. The characteristic combinations of anger and passivity, need and deprivation, love and hate, flow through the recollections. The anger and anxiety surrounding other people's emotional availability seems not to have been resolved. Indeed, strong feelings, particularly those of anger, appear to be the main organising themes when talking about people and relationships. Individuals remain caught up in the emotionality of relationships and appear unable to move beyond them. So, even when talking about current relationships with their parents, preoccupied speakers, although describing them positively, nevertheless intersperse the account with many examples in which love was withheld and anger was felt.

Hazan and Shaver (1987), using self-report measures, classify adults as preoccupied if they agree with the following statement:

> I find that others are reluctant to get as close as I would I like. I often worry that my partner doesn't really love me or won't want to stay with me. I want to merge completely with another person, and this desire sometimes scares people away.

This confirms the individual's use of an internal working model in which the self is viewed negatively and with high-dependency needs, and others are viewed positively inasmuch their attention and interest is eagerly sought. The result is overdependence on others. To be involved is to feel wanted. Thus, although there is a constant urge to be in relationships, the continued availability or reliability of others cannot be trusted or taken for granted. A good deal of emotional energy is spent on keeping other people involved, responsive and attentive, achieved by keeping attachment behaviours running at high intensity. There is a need to be emotionally close, but to be dependent on someone who may hurt you by abandoning you is also fraught with anxiety: 'I need you, but I can't trust you.' The other person's emotional availability and continued presence can never be taken for granted; loss, separation and abandonment are constantly feared.

There is a general feeling of being emotionally deprived. The interactional agenda therefore revolves around the giving and withholding of love and affection.

Profound ambivalence about one's anxious dependence on and preoccupation with others leads to relationships being characterised by conflict, jealousy, possessiveness and uncertainty. The pervasive fear is one of being emotionally abandoned. So long as life is busy, full, involved and exaggerated, the feeling is that the self is, after all, relevant and worthy of interest. However, if the individual is abandoned or ignored, the self feels empty. Also, as people with an insecure, ambivalent history are often likely to form relationships with other people who are also insecure, the result is a partnership that is full of upset, drama and argument. The presentation of problems to others becomes increasingly exaggerated in attempts to hold their attention and force their involvement (Crittenden 1995).

The intense emotional demands made on others by anxious, insecure people can become so wearing that they soon exhaust partners and friends as well as the health and welfare professionals with whom they are involved (Lopez 1995: 410).

In relationships, 'ambivalent' men often need to control the money, worried that if their partners have financial freedom, sexual licence may not be far behind. In many cases, it is not unusual for these deep feelings of insecurity and jealousy to lead male partners to be very possessive. They forbid their wives to go out on their own except for the most mundane reasons. They come home and want to know who their partners have seen and to whom they have spoken, what was said and why. The constant fear is that their partners will leave them. The result is behaviours by the anxious partner that are aggressive, restricting and dependent, all suggesting a high reluctance to let go. At other times, however, when things are going well and there is much togetherness, enmeshed sentimentality spills over into acts of exaggerated generosity. There is the giving of 'over-the-top' presents, declarations of love and devotion, a general flood of feeling and coy, disarming, babyish talk. These two extremes are yet another reminder of the coercive way in which relationships are played. These rapid switches of strongly expressed positive and negative feelings, threat and seduction, regularly lead to rows and *conflict* in which one or the other partner threatens to leave the relationship:

one woman, when explaining why she did not wish for a separation, announced with a note of triumph in her voice that her husband had threatened he would come to 'get her' if she moved out. He needed her too, she insisted. In most of these marriages, it was found, each party was apt to stress how much the other needed them, while disclaiming their own need for the partner. By need, of course, they meant desire for a caregiving figure. What they dreaded most was loneliness. (Mattinson and Sinclair 1979: 121)

Defensive behaviours

The preoccupied individual appears to operate in one of two mutually exclusive modes. Either everything and everyone is wonderful, loving and giving, or everything and everyone is hateful, denying and wilfully cruel. This represents a form of *defensive splitting*. Preoccupied individuals have problems simultaneously acknowledging and handling feelings of desire and anger. At any one time, people and things are either all good or all bad, all-giving or all-denying. It is difficult to integrate contrasting feelings within the same strategy or see and *accept* the other person as a complex blend of good points and bad that require different responses at different times. The individual therefore copes with emotional conflict and confusion by acknowledging and reacting to only one of the contradictory feelings. This one feeling alone then guides behaviour at any particular time. For example, one minute the other person (who might be a social worker) is treated as wonderful and the 'best', while the next she is angrily dismissed as hostile and depriving. In general, feelings are *acted out* rather than contained.

Mental health

Insecure attachment patterns are overrepresented in clinical samples (van IJzendoorn and Bakermans-Kranenburg 1996). Low self-esteem and low self-efficacy are highly associated with depression. In a study by Cole-Detke and Kobak (1996: 286), preoccupied women who reported feeling depressed also played up feelings of anger as well as emphasising their vulnerability. Rates of reported symptoms, whether of minor illnesses, mental health problems or relationship difficulties, tend to be highest for those classified as preoccupied–entangled. Symptoms are used as distress signals (to elicit care and involvement). High symptomatology also suggests that those using a hyperactivating attachment strategy may become 'overly preoccupied with their own shortcomings, focus excessively on attachment relationships, and fail to develop a more active or instrumental form of coping that results in increased autonomy and competence. This pattern may create a strong bias toward perceiving distress as an inner-directed problem involving low self-esteem, chronic negative affect, and feelings of hopelessness' (Cole-Detke and Kobak 1996: 287).

People classified as preoccupied–entangled also show higher rates of mood disorder, borderline personality disorder and anxiety. They experience problems with low self-esteem and intimate relationships (Kobak and Sceery 1988; Dozier and Lee 1995; Pianta *et al.* 1996; Rosenstein and Horowitz 1996). Strategies relying on the maximisation of attachment behaviour in which signals of distress are increased aim to draw in an otherwise inconsistent and unreliable attachment figure who may be a parent or a partner, a social worker or a doctor. Negative affects therefore become exaggerated.

Fonagy *et al.* (1996) found that 75 per cent of individuals diagnosed with a borderline personality disorder (intense, demanding interpersonal relationships, emotional instability, impulsiveness, lack of control over anger, a fear of real or imagined abandonment and chronic feelings of emptiness) were classified as preoccupied. Interviews established that the vast majority of patients had very disturbed childhood histories. They experienced their parents as less loving and more neglecting. The researchers observed that not only was the capacity of preoccupied types to 'self-reflect' low, but the ability to understand other people's mental states was also poor. This leaves them highly vulnerable to interpersonal stress. These attention-seeking patterns of behaviour are shown by Barry.

Barry

Aged 42, married and a father of four, Barry has been known to both the mental health services as a patient and the child welfare services as the father of a 9-year-old boy with behaviour problems. Barry currently suffers sleep disturbance, depression, anger and financial worries. He says he feels a high degree of hopelessness. In the past, he has attended both anger and anxiety management groups (with little apparent success). Several years ago, he fell down the stairs and injured his back. He said he was pushed by a relative and is demanding compensation.

Although Barry now walks with a stick and says he is in constant pain, medical examinations have failed to find the cause of the problem.

Barry is also one of four children. He describes his childhood as very unhappy. There was a lot of violence and conflict in the home, especially between his parents. His father, he says, was 'tyrannical'. Although he mentions that his mother was a very loving person, he describes several episodes when she 'disappeared' for several weeks, leaving the children to be looked after by short-term foster carers. Nevertheless, Barry stayed at home until he was 26 years old, when his parents 'kicked him out'.

Immediately after leaving home, he met and married his wife, Linda. They have four children living. Their first child suffered a cot death. The family currently live 'in a permanent state of crisis and chaos'. There are mounting financial debts. His behaviour is impulsive. When he feels particularly distressed, he 'self-harms' – takes an overdose, falls over and further damages himself. Barry is very dissatisfied with most of the professionals with whom he is in almost daily contact – social workers, doctors, mental health workers, disability workers, benefits officers and lawyers (over his compensation). He seems to be in conflict with a large number of people who he believes are intent on denying him his rights, his money, their interest, their understanding or their compassion. 'They're all useless'. he says. The only one who really understands him, he believes, is his wife, 'and she'll never let me down because she knows how much I need her'. Even so, the marriage is troubled by conflict and crisis. Several times over the past year, Linda has taken the children and herself off to her mother's house after a particularly stormy row. Barry immediately feels contrite and rescues the situation by crying, abjectly apologising and begging forgiveness. Linda then returns home. The most recent incident required the children to be looked after by foster carers after both Linda and Barry, in a pact, took an overdose of his pills for depression. He telephoned the emergency services and they were both admitted to hospital for an overnight stay. The social worker says that Barry 'lacks insight'.

Parenthood

The fear of losing the attention and interest of other people typically drives the anxious individual into close relationships that are formed young, quickly and often without discrimination. In high-risk groups, children, too, are often likely to arrive, sometimes in quantity and quick succession, while their mothers are young and in and out of different relationships.

The ambivalent personality is basically attention-seeking. There is a need to 'make things happen'. It *feels* better to be at the centre of emotional turmoil than outside social relationships altogether. Loneliness is greatly feared, and much emotional energy might be spent in warding it off. Hyperactivating the attachment system represents an attempt to force people into responding. There is a need to keep interactions alive and active – quietness and passivity are interpreted as a lack of interest, love or concern. The emotional demands and heightened quality of relationships are therefore designed to keep the fear of being rejected at bay.

Social workers who become involved with parents and children with such personalities find that their clients' lives are full of problems and crises. Households are disorganised. Generational boundaries are blurred. The family's emotional life is entangled. Everyone wants to know what everyone else is feeling and doing – who is being moody, who prefers who, who is being unfair. Routines and structures are largely absent. Children, extended family, friends, neighbours and pets wander in and out of the home. There is never a dull moment. Dramas are a daily occurrence. Attempts at suicide, accident-prone children, quarrels followed by theatrical walk-outs, rows with neighbours, aggressive behaviour at the benefits office, attention-seeking by heavy drinking at the pub, feeling constantly unwell, abandoning the children at the door of social services, crying copiously in the presence of a sympathetic other – all serve to keep a potentially unresponsive world involved. The abandonment of others, whether partners or children, is used coercively in attempts to control the behaviour of other people in order to ensure their continued presence (Mattinson and Sinclair 1979).

Once children are no longer babies (that is, not totally dependent), they are said by their 'ambivalent' parents to be impossible to control. A threatened loss of love is constantly used in attempts to discipline, disclaim or disconfirm children's feelings and behaviours: 'You made me ill', 'If I die it will be your fault', 'I wish I had never given birth to you', 'If you carry on like that I shall kill myself.' Such threats compromise children's ability to understand and handle feelings of distress.

Parents with ambivalent personalities feel a degree of helplessness and unlovability meaning that their own needs and emotions tend to dominate their dealings with their own children. This makes them insensitive, unpredictable parents who are poor at reading their children's needs and distress signals. They deprive their children of the very warmth, attention and responsiveness that they crave themselves. There is a general psychological underinvolvement. They discourage autonomy in their children (independence implies freedom, unavailability, a denial of love and a loss of the relationship).

Unlike dismissing–rejecting mothers, preoccupied–uncertain mothers feel that being a carer and being in relationship with a child who needs them is important. Most anxious adults, believes Crittenden (1992b), approach parenthood with the expectation that, finally, they will experience the kind of closeness and intimacy for which they long. The birth of children reawakens old desires. 'In other words, after a history of failed relationships, they will find hope in the birth of children' (Crittenden 1992b: 590). But, in the event, most children of severely insecure parents fail to convey contentment. In the case of ambivalent parents, their children are tetchy, demanding and fretful. They soon become a disappointment to their parents, and parenthood itself soon becomes a stressful business. Mothers and fathers are left confused, angry and bitter. Even though they are now parents, nothing seems to have changed. They have doubts about their fitness to care for others. Other people, who now include their own children, continue to be experienced as difficult and unresponsive.

Solomon and George (1996) describe the defensive style of ambivalent mothers as 'cognitive disconnection'. Their caregiving style is *uncertain*. They are not sure about how they feel and how they should react. When initially talking about their children in the research interviews, parents describe their children in very positive terms – perfect, clever, honest, fair, sensitive. Parenting was a pleasure and relationships are wonderful. During the later stages of the 'caregiving' interview, however, children are described as demanding and difficult, immature and angry. Integrating and dealing with both the positive and negative aspects of children, the parent–child relationship and their own feelings as parents prove difficult and cause feelings of doubt and uncertainty about what is going on, why people do what they do and what should be done about it. Limited protection is provided. Mothers do not always recognise dangers, remain unsure when it is appropriate to intervene and help, and generally behave in a neglectful way.

Inevitably, caregiving is described with some ambivalence. Parents will speak glowingly and lovingly about their children one moment, only to express anger, hostility and hate a short while later. Discussing the findings of their own research, George and Solomon (1996: 211) offer the following explanation:

> In contrast to the defensive exclusion through deactivation, cognitive disconnection allows the caregiving system to remain activated. We believe that if these mothers were unable to disconnect and separate negative affect from the child, they would be forced to acknowledge their feelings of rejection. Unable to reject the child, they (and their child) were left feeling uncertain.

Tracey is the mother of four children. At the moment, she feels 'stressed out'. At various times during the interview with her, she describes her children as either 'wonderful and talented' or 'uncontrollable and ungrateful'. She talks about all her significant relationships with a high level of ambivalence.

Tracey and her family

Tracey is 35 years old. She is the mother of four children: Liam aged 14 years, Sean 11 years, Paul 7 years and Maria 1 year. She lives with John, who is the father of Liam and Maria. The parents are having major behavioural problems with both Liam and Sean. Over the past year, Liam has become more aggressive. Recent incidents include smashing a telephone kiosk, setting fire to a telephone kiosk and then threatening to attack the police and fire officers with a javelin when they arrived; showing very aggressive and violent behaviour towards Sean, including threatening to kill him; and getting into arguments and violent confrontations with his mother, threatening her with a knife on one occasion. At school, he is prone to violent outbursts and has to be removed from the class before he will calm down. He cannot stand being teased. Liam has few, if any, friends. He says he hates Sean and on one occasion was prowling round the house with a length of rope saying that he was going to strangle his brother and then hang him when he returned home. Tracey said that Liam was out of her control and demanded his immediate removal. Liam is currently living in a special residential unit. He wants to return home, but he knows that when he is there, his feelings seem to get out of his and other people's control. This confuses and upsets him. A lot of his anger is directed at his mother, but he remains entangled with her moods, feelings and responses.

While Liam's behaviour is aggressive and confused, his brother Sean's behaviour appears more underhand and deviant, although he has smashed his hand through a window and been excluded from school for fighting. Sean has stolen money from his parents, including his father's credit card. He has run away from home, gone missing for a night and stolen property from buildings. In conversation, Sean says he is worried that his mother will run away and leave them. 'I love her, but I don't think she loves me.' Like his brother, he does not appear to have any close friends. He says he does not trust anyone. He has a fear that he will lose control of himself and get into violent fights. He feels that family life is out of control and that anything might happen. He shows signs of depression.

Tracey chain-smokes and is slightly overweight. The house is cluttered and untidy. For example, the breadknife recently went missing and was eventually found a week later under a pile of the baby's clothes that were waiting to be washed. When the social worker arrives for a visit, Tracey does not get up to answer the door but shouts to the worker to let herself in. The atmosphere in the house is always hot, enclosed, and stuffy. The curtains often remain closed all day. The family has three cats and a dog.

Tracey is the next to the youngest of five children. Throughout her childhood, she felt that her mother preferred her brothers and sisters, which she says hurt. 'There were times when I felt that I didn't belong; that perhaps I might have been adopted.' She says she has a 'love/hate relationship' with her eldest brother. She became very ill with encephalitis when she was aged 5 years. The family were in Singapore at the time, and she was flown back to England. She was in hospital 5 months, during which time she did not see her mother. 'My heart stopped beating 3 times and each time they had to resuscitate me from near death.' She felt she got on best with her mother when, as a little girl, she was 'very, very ill'. When she was 14, her father left the Air Force and, together with her mother, ran a pub. Her parents quarrelled a lot, and Tracey said she felt increasingly anxious that they would split up. Even so, Tracey said that she loved the pub life: 'I'd run one tomorrow if I could.'

Her feelings about her parents still betray much ambivalence, uncertainty and preoccupation. 'My mother is a very loving, very caring person... She has always seemed more for my brothers and sister than me. I'm always rowing with her; she doesn't care.' 'My relationship with my dad was fun-loving. I've always felt closer to him than my mum. I felt he was more loving... When I was about 17 my dad told me that when I was 18, he'd kick me out of the house, so I left anyway and went to live with my boyfriend.'

Tracey has low self-esteem and says that she suffers depression and a variety of minor ailments. She is still anxious to please her parents and worries that, if she has lost their approval, they will not love her. This also makes her feel angry and resentful, particularly if she puts herself out for them and they show no gratitude. Tracey likes to describe her self as 'a flat volcano'. 'Underneath I've got all this anger.' Periodically, she explodes, particularly with her mother. Tracey talks a lot about her parents and how much she loves them. She telephones them every day. She feels that she is too easy-going with the children. 'Sean winds me up the easiest. He just sits there and laughs. If I say anything to him, he laughs at me and I hate that. It makes me feel as if I'm inadequate, not doing my job right. He gets me furious. He's a sod.' Tracey, with no sense of irony, says that she loves Liam, particularly now that he is in fact in care and not living at home: 'I do love him. When he phones I tell him how much I love him and miss him.'

As a teenager, Tracey says she was 'very naughty'. She gave birth to Liam when she was 19, but 3 months later left John, the father. After a series of violent relationships and two more pregnancies, Tracey and John remarried. The couple argue a great deal. All the family members feel that Tracey makes heavy emotional demands on them that no-one seems able to satisfy. They react either by being aggressive or upset, or they leave.

van IJzendoorn and Bakermans-Kranenburg (1996: 15) found that insecure parents were overrepresented in clinical samples of disturbed children. In a group of parents of clinical children on a three-way coding, only 14 per cent of parents were classified as autonomous, whereas 45 per cent were classified as preoccupied–entangled and 41 per cent dismissing–avoidant.

Social workers are easily drawn into the family's dynamics. The pressure to take sides – 'love me, don't love them' – is constant. As long as the social worker is accepting, giving and perceived to be non-critical, she is 'seduced': 'You're wonderful, the best social worker I've ever had; much better than the last one who was rubbish.' As soon as she is perceived to be withholding, unavailable or taking someone else's point of view, however, she will be angrily rejected as 'useless, hateful', someone who must never visit the home again. Social workers, like others, are likely to be seen as either for them or against them, all-giving or all-denying. Maintaining a balanced, rounded view can be emotionally quite difficult for professionals. It feels good to be wanted but bad to be on the receiving end of other people's 'unreasonable' anger. The result can be that workers feel emotionally confused, tossed about and worn out. This can cause feelings of anger. There is an increasing reluctance to be available: physically, practically and emotionally. Mattinson and Sinclair (1979) describe the social worker's experience of these two positions as feeling like either a 'sucker' or a 'bastard'. The parent's behavioural strategy with either partner or professional remains coercive: disarming and seductive when needs are being met, threatening, demanding and aggressive when availability seems uncertain.

Neglectful parents

Although physical and emotional neglect are suffered by many insecure children, there is a higher incidence among those whose parents are classified as severely preoccupied and ambivalent. The parenting style is one of uncertainty and incompetence. Parents often have a poor educational track record, and many also have learning difficulties (Crittenden 1996; see also Schofield 1996). Matters are made much worse when families live in poverty, there are frequent house moves, and there are large numbers of children and relatively few adults. Competition for attention among the children is therefore high, and adult availability is low. Men often bear only a tangential relationship to the lives of neglectful families, dipping in and out in a confused, often volatile fashion (Cicchetti and Toth 1995b; Crittenden 1996). Maternal grandmothers, on the other hand, are typically extensively involved. They exist as continuing significant emotional presences for mothers and often live close by.

The confusion, noise and chaos of family life engenders feelings of helplessness and inadequacy in mothers, most of whom appear to be depressed. The various combinations of tiredness, financial stress, poor accommodation, depression, flat affect, a lack of education, learning difficulties and physical neglect are frequently observed by child protection agents. The parents provide low psychological availability for their children. In these depressed, unstimulating families, interaction tends to be lifeless, brief and negative. The internal working model of both parents and children is one of helplessness and powerlessness. Both oneself and other people seem unable to do anything to meet needs or bring about change. Putting any effort into achieving goals feels futile. Luck and fate ('if it's meant to happen, it will happen') says Crittenden (1996), become the main way of explaining things. There is a general air of lethargy and passivity, emptiness and depression:

> In sum, neglectful families appear to experience very attenuated interpersonal relationships. Men are distanced from the mother–child core of the family, interaction and affective involvement between adults and children is minimal, and relationships with friends are limited in quantity and intensity. On the other hand, there is an element of enmeshment in neglectful families, with multigenerational family units blending and maintaining proximity, continuity, and functional unity over time. (Crittenden 1996: 163)

As neglected children progress through school, they increase their withdrawal from and avoidance of their peers. According to Cicchetti and Toth (1995a: 551), this social withdrawal may be an active strategy of avoidance rather than merely a passive orientation toward peer interaction. In any event, it leads to increasing isolation and peer rejection.

Sexually abusing parents

In enmeshed families, where generational and emotional boundaries are blurred, members maintain a constant anxiety about relationships and the availability of others. The fear of emotional abandonment and not being accepted is ever-present. Other people are felt to be unfair, depriving and denying, while the self is experienced as fair, put-upon and victimised. Crittenden (1995: 165) speculates that, in these families, sexual activity reflects a desire for affection and involvement whether with spouse or children – an 'unsoothable anxiety'. According to Crittenden, sexually abusing men in such families, whose sexual inhibitions are further lowered by drugs or alcohol, are likely to admit their abuse but claim that the child invited it and enjoyed it, and that it was loving. However, unlike disorganised–avoidant sexual abusers (see Chapter 5), they are also likely to admit remorse and will readily insist that it will not happen again. The greater fear is to lose family membership, so such men will agree to do whatever is asked in order to maintain contact with their partners and children.

Conclusion

Insecure, coercive individuals cannot take for granted other people's interest and emotional availability. This leads to an anxious preoccupation with relationships. However, the demanding behaviours associated with concerns about being loved and wanted tend to wear other people out. Emotional manipulation and issues of dependency place great strains on others. This can result in the other wanting to abandon the relationship, thus confirming the dependent individual's fear that other people cannot be taken for granted. Feelings of self-worth and effectiveness remain low. Practitioners have to be aware of the feelings that 'ambivalent' people engender in themselves and others. The tempation is to give up on the anxious, coercive, dependent client by closing the case. Lack of attention, however, merely leads to an increase in attachment behaviour. Consistent, balanced and accurate responses generally pay 'long term' dividends, with the emphasis on 'long-term'. These are not easy cases with which to stay involved. Practitioners need good support and understanding from their own agency if they are to maintain the emotional and intellectual resources necessary to 'stick with' demanding and enmeshed families.

7

Disorganised, controlling and unresolved patterns

The insecure disorganised attachment pattern is associated with those who have suffered and failed to resolve losses and traumas. The traumas vary widely from physical abuse to being parented by someone suffering a serious psychiatric illness or alcohol addiction. The disorganised pattern is frequently met by those working with behaviourally very disturbed children. Perhaps a little confusing at first sight, the disorganised–unresolved classification can be superimposed on one of the three organised attachment patterns of secure, avoidant and ambivalent, whichever 'best fits'. This is meant to suggest that, when the individual is not immediately caught up in their fear and distress, an underpinning 'organised' attachment style operates. However, at times of stress and emotional low points, the disorganised interactional pattern predominates, adversely affecting relationships and the ability to cope.

Individuals displaying disorganised and unresolved attachment patterns can be very hard to understand and even more difficult to help, yet they constitute the hard core of most clinical and welfare caseloads. The behaviours, relationship styles and personality characteristics associated with disorganised–unresolved attachment patterns will be described throughout the lifespan from infancy to adulthood.

Infancy

Insecurely attached children classified as either avoidant or ambivalent do manage to organise elements of their attachment behaviour in order to gain proximity to their attachment figure. This they do by either deactivating or hyperactivating their attachment behaviour. However, insecurely attached infants classified as *disorganised*, as the name implies, develop *no organised behavioural strategy* for regulating their affect, achieving proximity or gaining care and protection. Their defensive strategies collapse. They have no way of adapting their attachment behaviour to the caregiving relationship in which they find themselves. Main and Solomon (1990) were the first to recognise and characterise this fourth attachment pattern in previously unclassifiable video tapes of infants in the Strange Situation. In a meta-analysis, van IJzendoorn (1995) concluded that 15 per cent of all young children in normal populations were being classified as disorganised.

Infants are classified as disorganised–disorientated if, in the presence of their parent, their behaviour seems to lack an effective proximity-seeking strategy (Main 1995: 424). These behaviours, broadly divided into apprehension, confusion (contradictory approach and avoidance behaviours) and trances (freezing), only appear to make sense if they are seen as reflecting children's fear and disorientation in the relationship with their carer.

Disorganisation and disorientation of attachment behaviour arises when the infant has been alarmed by *the parent* rather than the external situation. Unpredictable, scary, violent or deeply puzzling behaviour by the caregiver leads the infant to be either *afraid of* or *afraid for* the caregiver. The child is therefore faced with an irresolvable paradox. The parent frightens the child. Fear raises distress and anxiety, which activates attachment behaviour whose purpose is to get the child into close and safe proximity with the carer. But the carer is the *source* of the fear and distress. Conflict behaviour therefore results because the source of security for the infant is also the source of fear. If the child attempts to approach the carer for comfort and attention (the case with secure and ambivalent patterns), anxiety increases further. If the child tries to shift attention away from the parent (the case with the avoidant pattern) or flee, this also fails to reduce the parent's rejecting/hostile/intrusive behaviour. Increasing emotional or physical distance also raises anxiety.

In other words, whatever attachment behaviours the child tries, unlike any of the three organised patterns, anxiety and distress continue to rise and threaten to overwhelm the infant. The experience is highly distressing. There is a profound sense of fear and helplessness. The internal working model achieved by these children represents the self, others and relationships chaotically and incoherently. There appear to be no organised rules based on experience that are available to predict and guide attachment behaviour, achieve affect regulation and increase felt security. Thus, when early care includes maltreatment:

children adapt not only behaviorally to shield themselves from further trauma, but also their internal working models proceed representationally to defend the developing self in ways that have unfortunate effects for subsequent emotional regulation and relationship development. (McCrone *et al*. 1994: 99–100)

Disorganised attachment patterns are particularly likely when parents:

- have unresolved losses or have themselves suffered traumatic experiences, including childhood abuse (Ainsworth and Eichberg 1991)
- have serious affective disorders, including depression (DeMulder and Radke-Yarrow 1991; Radke-Yarrow 1991)
- are active alcoholics (O'Connor *et al*. 1987) or heavy users of hard drugs
- are maltreating (Carlson *et al*. 1989).

Maltreated infants

It is therefore not surprising that the majority (typically around 80 per cent) of maltreated infants are classified as *disorganised* or *disorientated* (the D pattern) in their attachment behaviour. However, by no means all 'disorganised' children have been maltreated.

Care that is severely unresponsive or traumatic is likely to see children developing models or representations of themselves as unworthy and bad, and others as unavailable, frightening and exploitative. The more children lack confidence in the availability of care and protection provided by the other, the more prone they will be to experience intense or chronic fear (Bowlby 1973, 1980).

Ainsworth and Wittig (1969) have also demonstrated that maltreated children *do* form selective attachments to their caregivers, although they are much more likely to be insecure than those of non-maltreated children (Crittenden 1985). Parents who have suffered neglect in their own childhoods but *not* violence or abuse are much less likely to have children who develop disorganised attachment patterns (Lyons-Ruth and Block 1996). The more severe the history of violence and abuse in parents' own childhoods, the more *hostile* and *intrusive* appears to be their interaction with their children. In addition, the more disorganised the attachment, the more aggressive is children's behaviour likely to be in later childhood.

Maltreating carers communicate to their babies that 'I do not understand you', 'I am not able to hear you' or 'Your signals are not meaningful or important.' Children develop a deep lack of confidence in the caregiver's ability to provide protection, safety, love, comfort and attention. As a result, they develop intense or chronic fears and emotions that threaten to swamp their whole being. In the face of physical abuse, fear predominates over anger. As infants, the only options appear to be helpless thrashing about, turning around in circles in distress, psychologically opting out (not 'being there', becoming trance-like or 'freezing'), identifying with the source of the fear (seeing the self as evil, dangerous and bad) or becoming self-absorbed in closed feedback behaviours that at least remain under the control of the self (rhythmic rocking, head-banging, covering the face with the hands or biting the self).

Parents with unresolved traumas

Parents who appear frightened, alarmed or profoundly unavailable and unresponsive (through drink, drugs, depression or psychosis) present their young children with behaviours that appear to have *no comprehensible relationship* to ongoing events in the immediate environment (Main 1996). The parent's unresolved fears and traumas are transmitted through their own scary or scared behaviour. In this sense, parents with unresolved internal fears are also experienced by children as frightening, similar to parents who are physically violent and abusive. Behaviourally, in both cases there is nothing that children can do; they have no attachment strategy to decrease anxiety, gain emotional proximity, experience understanding or increase felt security. In such relationships, infants (Main 1995):

- are unable to identify the source of alarm
- may develop unexplained fears and phobias on this basis
- and may possibly even identify the *self* as the source of the alarm

particularly if they are exposed to flight or retreat behaviour by the parent (for example, parents who become trance-like or back away).

Frightening/frightened parental behaviours may therefore create vulnerabilities in the child's development of the concept of self, which is seen as inexplicably powerful yet somehow bad or dangerous in terms of its apparent disturbing effect on others. There is nothing present in the environment that seems to explain the parent's behaviour, other than the child him- or herself. The feeling arises that perhaps they are responsible for the frightening or frightened state of their attachment figure. Such experiences produce vulnerabilities, anxieties and phobias that appear untraceable. Children get the idea that close, dependent relationships are the source of fear. Attachment experiences precipitate catastrophic fantasies, often violent in nature with much talk of death, lurking dangers and powerful supernatural forces.

Long-term prospective studies of infants classified as disorganised or disorientated are finding that they are at a highly increased risk of developing aggressive behaviours, mental disorders, school behaviour problems and other psychopathologies (Greenberg *et al.* 1991; Solomon *et al.* 1995; Lyons-Ruth 1996; Main 1996: 239).

Childhood

As children enter toddlerhood, the different types of fear-inducing care create different attachment dilemmas. The underlying, shared experience of all disorganised children remains one of fear, distress and anxiety in their caregiving relationship, resulting in the initial lack or collapse of a consistent strategy for organising responses to the need for comfort and security when under stress (Lyons-Ruth 1996: 76). However, children's continued attempts to deal with the fear will vary over time depending on whether the caregiver is abusive or severely depressed, seriously neglectful or psychologically traumatised, or various combinations of all of these.

In all disorganised types, children experience themselves fundamentally as unworthy of care, and their caregivers as unavailable to provide care and protection. Attachment needs cannot be met within the relationship. There is the diffuse *fear* in children that they will be abandoned, destroyed by aggression or overwhelmed by affect. Thus, close relationships in general begin to evoke feelings of fear as well as anger (the other in the relationship being perceived as unavailable to help children to cope with and understand their distress). In defensive attempts to deal with heightened anxiety and attachment-related issues, children begin unconsciously to exclude certain perceptions and experiences. This means that they are not fully, realistically or appropriately engaged with either their own or other people's emotional states.

In the first year or two of life, prior to language acquisition, children's experiences of fear and distress are laid down in memories in a form that remains difficult to access consciously or semantically. Situations that evoke 'memories' of these early fears and anxieties are 'felt' rather than 'thought'. Laid down in non-linguistic memory systems, it is difficult to articulate or access early traumatic memories of loss and abuse (LeDoux 1998). Such feelings remain powerful but hard to regulate. There is the ever-present feeling that one will be overwhelmed and swept away by turbulent emotions. One way of dealing with them defensively is to exclude them from consciousness or deny them. Thus, some children deny danger or their own fear, or they do not acknowledge a parent's failure to love or provide protection. This denies distress in the immediate situation but, as a distortion of reality, it fails to help children to learn accurately about themselves and others. This restricts the flow of information both within the internal working model and between the self and others:

> The pain, distress, shame and feelings of helpless rage associated with experiences of abuse may create mental barriers to reliving these unresolvable agonies; such barriers can prevent individuals from recalling them. The outcome may be both inexplicable shifts in behavior and failure of individuals to learn to control their behavior when highly aroused. (Crittenden 1996: 160–1)

However, as children enter the preschool years, the totally disorganised attachment response proves psychologically difficult to sustain without complete mental breakdown. A degree of developmental reorganisation begins to take place (Lyons-Ruth 1996: 68). Children attempt to organise their behaviour in various ways to try to increase predictability in what seems to be a frighteningly unpredictable social environment. In effect, they try to exert control over the disturbing elements in their environment (this includes most relationships). Hence older disorganised children are often labelled as *controlling*. However, their mental representations of attachment-related experiences remain disorganised. It is no surprise, therefore, that most distress-related issues continue to trigger confused, unintegrated, angry and often violent behaviour.

So, by the age of 4 or 5, although children may still show disorganised attachment behaviour in situations of distress, they also begin to develop more organised attachment strategies. The organisation achieved will depend on the prevailing character of the relationship with their caregiver (who may be hostile, intrusive, rejecting, neglecting or unavailable). In the case of children who suffer some form of maltreatment or severe insecurity, the disorganised (D) pattern will therefore be accompanied by a 'best-fitting' organised pattern of avoidant, ambivalent or, in milder cases, even secure attachment.

Crittenden (1992a) also argues that many children who are classified as disorganised in fact show an underlying logic (that is, organisation) in their behaviour as they attempt to adapt to the adverse peculiarities of the relationship with their caregiver. However, she equates the *disorganised–controlling* pattern, in which children show either excessive *caregiving* or *compliant* behaviours, with a subtype of the avoidant–defended pattern, albeit at the far end of the avoidant spectrum (see Chapter 5). Crittenden also prefers to see the disorganised–controlling pattern, in which children behave *punitively* towards their carer, as an extreme but logical extension of the ambivalent–coercive–aggressive pattern. We have followed her line of thinking to a point and consider the coercive–aggressive strategy in Chapter 6 as a version of childhood ambivalent patterns that takes place within caregiving systems that are very uncertain, emotionally inconsistent and often violent.

Some children fail to develop selective attachments altogether, and although, strictly speaking, we should not classify them as 'disorganised', children showing these *non-attached* patterns often develop very disturbed behaviours and disorders of attachment. For convenience, these non-attached groups will also be considered in this chapter.

It will be apparent, then, that attachment behaviours in disturbed and abusive caregiving relationships are complex. They are still in the process of being explored and worked out. There are difficult conceptual issues in which confusions and overlaps between maltreatment, disorganised attachments and disordered attachments easily occur. Although there is broad agreement about some of the main features, similar symptoms and behaviours are being classified slightly differently by different researchers (for example, see Crittenden 1992a, 1992b, 1997; Zeanah and Emde 1994; Lyons-Ruth 1996; Zeanah 1996). The following disorganised–controlling attachment types and subtypes represent a raw, provisional attempt to confound the various classifications developed by a number of the key authors in the field. There is much behavioural and conceptual overlap between the groups, but they serve to highlight the major features of the disorganised–controlling and non-attachment attachment patterns:

1. *Disorganised–controlling ('best-fitting' avoidant or defended) patterns*
   - punitive–aggressive–fearful
   - compulsive caregiving (parental role inversion)
   - compulsive compliance.

2. *Non-attachment patterns*
   - inhibited
   - disinhibited.

Disorganised–controlling patterns

For at least three different reasons, the parents of disorganised–controlling children fail to meet their children's attachment needs:

- The carer's own attachment needs are so dominant and pressing.
- The carer reacts violently and abusively to other people's distress and attachment-related behaviour.
- The carer may react in a frightened manner, for example parents who have an unresolved trauma with regard to some childhood attachment or loss, a condition often associated with depression.

By trying to meet their parents' attachment needs rather than their own, children may retain a level of safe proximity and involvement. However, in order to achieve this, children have to strongly deactivate their own attachment needs.

Controlling behaviours, or 'parenting the parent', represent various forms of *role reversal,* children being either caregiving or punitive towards their parents. In effect, these children attempt to 'solve' the 'irresolvable' paradox presented by their frightening, frightened or anxious parents by stepping into or identifying with aspects of the caregiver's role (Main 1995: 433). If parents are traumatised, they may well accept their children's attempts to control the caregiving relationship.

Mayseless (1996: 211) provides an interesting discussion of the role reversal phenomenon. She describes the emergence of such organised adaptations to frightening and helpless caregiving as the 'disorganised-turning-into-controlling' pattern. Other people are seen by children as either irresponsible or potentially dangerous and in need of constant watchfulness. The self is seen as competent and in control, but one's own attachment needs are neither acknowledged nor met. For example, caregivers in violent relationships whose attachment needs remain unsatisfied may turn to their children rather than adults for care and attention. The child's own attachment needs are either ignored or simply not met. The only way the child can gain closeness to the parent is by trying to cater to the parent's needs for comfort and reassurance.

Burkett (1991) found that many women abused as children relied more on their children to provide them with emotional support. In practice, it is difficult for very young children realistically to provide their parents with comfort and care. 'Further,' adds Mayseless (1996: 211), 'some of the ways in which the parents may convey their own need to be nurtured may be aggressive, frightening, or incomprehensible to the child. Since they do not understand the conditions under which they can gain proximity and contact, infants react in a disorganized, disorientated manner.' It is only when children reach 3–4 years of age that they begin to grasp what it is their parents want. In terms of an increasingly goal-corrected partnership in which the child is having to make most of the adjustments, it becomes possible to identify what the parent needs and how those needs might be met. To the extent that children are able to get this right (parenting the parent), they increase their parent's physical availability.

Various disorganised–controlling patterns, in which children avoid and suppress their own attachment needs, can be identified, each representing an attempt by the child to reorganise attachment behaviour in the context of a caregiving relationship that is experienced as frightened, frightening or neglectful. Some of these strategies represent attempts to increase parental proximity and availability. Others represent attempts to keep fearful experiences out of consciousness by denying the danger and assuming control, often in an aggressive, startled manner. Three *controlling* subgroups might be recognised (see also Crittenden 1992a; Zeanah 1996):

- compulsive compliance
- compulsive caregiving (role inversion or parenting the parent)
- aggressive–fearful.

The controlling punitive, compulsive caregiving and compliant types are defined as 'best-fit' avoidant (or defended) attachment patterns because they represent attempts to maintain access without intimacy. Compliant children are particularly vigilant and wary of their parents' moods and behaviours, enabling them to anticipate, and possibly diffuse, anger and aggression. Children have learned that being open and explicit about their true thoughts and feelings leads to rejection, disregard or assault. The full extent of their need to feel protected and loved therefore cannot be expressed. They have to deny certain feelings and distort their thoughts and perceptions to gain proximity. Children, by denying their own needs, attempt to behave in ways of which they think their parents would approve. Although they are good at reading other people's moods, these children are very poor at recognising and acknowledging the nature and origin of their own feelings of arousal. They therefore lack interpersonal congruence and empathy.

Compulsive compliant patterns

Many children of maltreating, abusive parents learn to *inhibit* displays of feeling that seem to anger their carers and provoke rejection. In other words, by controlling the expression of their own feelings, children are also taking responsibility for trying to regulate their parents' behaviour. The *compulsive compliant* pattern is therefore one in which children become very submissive in order to remain involved and acceptable to the caregiver. Defended children become responsible for managing their own protection and feelings (see also Chapter 5). Children sense that the only way in which they are able to gain acceptance and closeness to their parents is to adopt behaviour that is totally submissive and compliant (Crittenden 1992a). The intensive efforts to do everything right and not get on the wrong side of their parents may be, according to Crittenden (1995: 378), the basis of compulsive behaviours. However, when not in the presence of the feared parent, children can show considerable anger and aggression. Cut off from acknowledging their own affect, these children might show little remorse or any willingness to change their behaviour.

As children grow older, they may resort to being falsely bright and cheerful in attempts to keep on the right side of a withdrawn or hostile parent. This group of avoidant children become skilled at interpreting social signals, covering their true feelings and meeting the demands of others. Indeed, they might become socially adept, although exchanges remain clever rather than warm and personal. Their strategy remains one of defence, but one in which they attempt to influence and control the feelings and perceptions of others (particularly those directed at them) through altering their own behaviour. Wary compliance can be shown from a very young age, as the case of Rebecca shows.

Rebecca (Lieberman 1992: 566)

Rebecca is a toddler who lives with her mother in a small flat. The two of them are alone together all day. They sleep in the same bed. Mrs Hermann has multiple phobias and rarely leaves her apartment. She sees the world as a dangerous place. She says of Rebecca, 'She is the only thing I have in the world. I need to protect her very well because she is very vulnerable. I could not live without her.' The mother grows alarmed if Rebecca attempts to explore. When her daughter does get angry with her, Mrs Hermann retorts, 'You don't love me, that's why you do that.' Rebecca is a subdued girl. She adapts to her mother's message that she needs her to remain dependent and constricted to keep her mother's love. 'At home, she spends long periods of time on her mother's lap. Her favorite activities are those that keep her close to her mother, such as looking at books together.' In new situations, Rebecca is very cautious and takes a while before she will play with unfamiliar toys. 'When she does, she keeps nervous visual tabs on her mother, as if checking to see whether or not she is permitted to play. The mother's face remains blank with no signs of pleasure or approval.' The little girl does not respond to the social invitations of other children or adults. She therefore has few friends. In Ogden's (1982: 16) words, the parent conveys the message to the child: 'If you are not what I need you to be, you don't exist for me.'

Parents who are physically abusive towards their children generally have problems *initiating* and *managing* relationships in a constructive manner. Issues of control are extremely important to parents whose behaviour towards their children is intrusive, hostile and threatening. Family life is often characterised by violence. In a review of the research, Crittenden (1996) reports that abusive families interact less frequently and more negatively than do non-abusive families. Both parents and children often cover feelings of hostility with falsely pleasant behaviour. For example, although abused children may be compliant with teachers, they bully their peers. Abusive mothers may be aggressive with their babies but submissive to partners and plausible to social workers.

Discrepancies between communications (smiling followed by a smack or love mixed with violence) mean that both adults and children do not trust what people say and what they are liable to do (a mismatch between semantics and behaviour). It becomes easier to separate the behavioural and semantic memory systems, one based on what has physically happened, the other based on what was said (particularly by parents) to have happened. The result can be that violent carers talk quite calmly and positively about how to parent without recognising how this conflicts with their own highly aroused and abusive style of childrearing.

Compulsive caregiving (role inversion or parenting the parent)

Compulsive caregiving, as Bowlby (1980) described it, witnesses individuals tending to repress their own needs and instead care for others as a way of retaining emotional involvement with them. Children from low-risk backgrounds classified as disorganised typically develop a 'controlling' strategy in which they try to take over responsibility for the quality of the caregiving relationship. Although infants are soothed by their mothers' presence, they nevertheless show unusual signs of hesitation, apprehension and confusion (Lyons-Ruth 1996: 68). Milder cases rarely appear as maltreated children, but they may cause welfare agencies some concern. The parents typically have unresolved losses and traumas from their own childhoods. These include experiences such as the death of or abandonment by their mother, sexual abuse and physical abuse. Non-abusing parents who are alcoholics or substance abusers might also suffer periods when they appear unaccountably distant and unavailable. In less mild cases, violent but helpless parents can also engender role reversal in their children, many of whom might have suffered abuse and yet display anxious concern over their parent's needs and behaviour.

As parents, the presence and needs of their own children is an unconscious reminder of their unresolved traumas and the attachment-related anxieties surrounding them. The child may therefore cause the parent emotional distress for reasons that are apparent to neither the parent nor the child. It is the parent's own attachment needs that come to the fore when the child attempts to display attachment behaviours. The only way the child can increase parental proximity and availability is to try to comfort and care for the parent. Children therefore suppress their own attachment needs and reverse the direction of the caregiving relationship. A distressed parent is emotionally unavailable.

> Distressing the parent results in guilt and fear of abandonment by the child. To achieve and maintain closeness to the parent, to avoid passivity and helplessness, the child must offer rather than solicit care; must not expect to receive help in containing and processing anxiety but, on the contrary, must give such assistance. Later on, such children may appear very self-sufficient and choose a partner who is as needy as was the parent. This role-reversal restricts the child's development, with the inevitable degree of failure increasing guilt and lowering self-esteem. The emotional unavailability of the parent produces an experience of acute and chronic loss. The capacity to ask for care is suppressed, but the need remains strong and unassuaged. (Barnett and Parker 1998: 147–8)

Therefore, parents who appear frightened, withdrawn or unresponsive for no apparent reason can cause children to become *afraid for* the parent. The child fears being unable to arouse their carer more than they fear rejection. The only way for the child to secure proximity is to reverse roles and care for the parent. The children's behaviour can appear overbright, cheerful and very solicitous. There is a false, exaggerated, *brittle* quality to much of the children's determined lightheartedness – a loud, overpitched laugh, an overplayed bid to be independent. Nevertheless, anger and anxiety over the attachment figure's lack of availability and responsiveness underpin these overly positive behaviours. Caroline shows a number of behaviours typical of compulsive caregiving.

Caroline (Lieberman 1992: 565)

Caroline is 18 months old. She lives with her mother, who is chronically depressed. The mother describes the household as 'noxious to the soul'. She cannot tolerate the idea that her depression is affecting Caroline. She says: 'Caroline is the only one who makes me laugh.' It is observed that Caroline silently enacts the role of a clown. 'She disappears into her room and comes out wearing increasingly more preposterous costumes. Caroline makes her mother laugh, but she herself never laughs... As this pattern becomes better established, it further consolidates the child's maladaptive perceptions of self, others, and emotional relationships.'

The strategy of role reversal can easily generalise so that compulsive caregiving is activated whenever the individual feels anxious about (and responsible for) another person's distress. The concept of *co-dependency* is often associated with compulsive caregiving, the need to be needed and 'women who love too much', in the telling words of Norwood (1985). In the adult version, people become involved with needy, dependent others (alcoholics, addicts, abusers and depressives), but always in the role of giving care (professionally as well as person-ally), never receiving it. The individual's self-esteem is low, depres-sion is common, eating disorders are not unusual, and compulsive behaviours are frequent. However, anger generally lies just beneath the surface and can occasionally erupt in acts of aggression and violence, particularly when the individual's own pressing unmet needs burst through the self-imposed restraint. It is not being in a relationship that raises the individual's anxiety. The individual's fear is that she will fall into a 'terrific emptiness because she feels she could not exist alone' (Kasl 1989: 31). When the caregiving behaviours fail to sustain a close relationship, individuals quickly collapse, their strength suddenly disappearing as they enter a phase of hopelessness and depression.

Aggressive–fearful

The world of the maltreated disorganised child is frightening and unpredictable. Children continue to find it difficult to work out a clear relationship between their own behaviour and the way in which their parents are likely to respond. They suffer abuse, neglect and repeated emotional (and often physical) abandonment. They experience repeated changes of carer. For the young mind, these are catastrophic experiences in which the very self seems at the point of psychological disintegration (as fear and helplessness flood the consciousness) or physical annihilation (as the protective caregiver has either been lost or, just as alarmingly, is the actual source of the danger). Nothing that the child does seems able to stop, reduce or regularise the trauma. Disorganised children therefore show a great deal of contradictory, confused attachment behaviour. They remain in a state of conflict and apprehension about whether or not to approach the caregiver. Confused mixtures of ambivalent and avoidant, coercive and defended behaviours might be seen.

The disturbed developmental pathways taken by maltreated children classified as 'controlling–aggressive' or 'controlling–punitive' witness a range of highly antisocial and maladaptive behaviours. In diagnostic terms, these behaviours are sometimes classified as 'reactive attachment disorders', particularly by therapists working with fostered and adopted children who have pre-placement histories of abuse, neglect and multiple placements. Behaviours typical of children classified as aggressive, disorganised–controlling or controlling–punitive include:

- superficial and charming behaviour with strangers
- proneness to act grandiosely and make extravagant claims
- restlessness: a constant need for stimulation and activity that often leads to antisocial behaviours
- a dislike of being touched and held
- a lack of affection and bossiness with carers
- high levels of resentment
- high levels of anger, rage and even violence towards female carers, oppositional behaviours and the constant blaming of others
- if the children are placed for adoption, often acting as if their new carers (particularly adoptive mothers) were responsible for their past abuse and hurt; this can be puzzling and hurtful for new carers
- little eye contact
- few smiles, a poor sense of humour and a lack of playing
- coercive, demanding behaviour
- 'crazy', obvious lying and using manipulative lying to get what they want
- early sexual activity
- stealing and conduct disorders
- abnormal eating patterns (gorging, stealing food, hoarding or refusing to eat, particularly in presence of other family members), these eating problems reflecting early failures of nurturing and repeated experiences of hunger and physical neglect
- poor impulse control
- a high breakage rate of toys and objects, and a tendency to trash rooms when in a temper
- poor peer relations
- a lack of conscience and moral sensibilities
- aggressive towards their peers, including the sexual abuse of other children
- cruelty to animals
- a preoccupation with fire, blood, gore and weapons, often expressed in violent drawings
- self-neglect and poor personal hygiene.

The origins of these behaviours is said to lie in early childhood when children might normally expect to develop trust in the availability of others to provide comfort and care. However, carers who violate this trust by being abusive or unavailable (psychologically or physically) fail to provide children with comfort at times of high emotional arousal and need, either because they are the cause of the fear or because they are absent. Children therefore remain in a state of high arousal, distress and rage, an experience that is frightening and disturbing. These aggressive behaviours can be exacerbated by subjecting the young child to multiple moves and frequent changes of carer. In abusive homes, children may reach the point of high arousal, but their attachment behaviour then provokes an aggressive, violent response by their caregiver:

> Injury at the height of arousal is an effect – it's just the wrong effect. Abuse becomes gratification, and the child believes that he has the power to arouse others and cause them to act out anger and abuse. He begins to trust his power and control, and not that of others. Eventually he learns to lose his fear, and may learn not to feel physical pain. The final outcome is that he learns he can trust no-one except himself to gratify his needs. And that is a dangerous lesson. Because he trusts no one, he never learns to identify with other people and cannot develop compassion, empathy, love, or any of the other positive emotions that result from interaction. In fact, the only way he learns to interact with others is through aggression and violence. (Keck and Kupecky 1995: 47)

Anger begins to feel strong. Children know where they stand with anger; they know what to expect. Other people nearly always respond to anger:

> They either disengage and flee or engage and fight. If the child has orchestrated the angry interaction, either response may be acceptable to him because he no longer feels vulnerable. On the contrary, he feels consumed with power. After all, if a four-year-old can get an adult to act like a four-year-old, that's quite an accomplishment. (Keck and Kupecky 1995: 51)

For children, these various frightening and uncontrollable states are psychologically unsustainable. Young children have to try to introduce some predictability, understanding and control into their dangerous, painful, unpredictable world. The solutions to their problem begin to define the way in which they cognitively represent themselves and other people in their emerging internal working models. Seemingly, the only predictable element in the abusive parent–child relationship is the child him- or herself. Therefore children begin to feel that the only route to feeling remotely safe, physically and psychologically, is *to take control of the self, other people and the situations in which they find themselves.* Adults who try to provide care simply cannot be trusted. Physical and psychological survival appears to depend on being vigilant and wary, and going it alone. Close caregiving relationships in which children might normally expect to feel safe and trusting have resulted in abuse and feelings of fear, distress and hurt. For maltreated children, closeness to others spells danger. Intimacy therefore has to be resisted. An overlay of an avoidant strategy begins to develop in an attempt to disengage from the fearful consequences of expressing attachment needs in a violent, dangerous or frightening relationship with the caregiver. Children attempt to 'care' for and protect themselves by making sure that no-one tries to 'care' for them, as care by others has always led to trauma and threats to their very survival.

The controlling–punitive category has many similarities with Crittenden's coercive–controlling pattern in which children begin to emphasise the threatening–punitive–aggressive component of their coercive ambivalent strategy, dropping the coy/disarming mode altogether (see Chapter 6). Children, typically with a history of rejection and hostile abuse, attempt to assert some control of the distressing relationship with the caregiver by taking those role characteristics of the parent that are aggressive and punitive. Children become bossy. They are derogatory about their parents, constantly making remarks designed to ridicule, belittle and humiliate. They quickly show annoyance and anger, and attempt to punish their parents. In a sense, they attempt to defend themselves against the deep confusion and distress created by carers who are unpredictably angry and violent by 'identifying with the aggressor'. If you become the aggressor, even though you are likely to receive further rejection and hostility, at least there is a sense of knowing where you are in the relationship. However, the result is that most relationships (with parents, peers and teachers) are anticipated as hostile and rejecting, with the result that children make increasing use of their controlling–aggressive strategy as a defensive manoeuvre to keep the other in place and at an emotional distance.

Zeanah (1996: 48) describes a similar subgroup, which he terms *disordered attachment with self-endangerment.* This subgroup includes children who are reckless and accident prone. They fail to use their attachment figure as a secure base, moving away without checking back with their caregivers when their attachment system ought to be aroused. 'Recklessness and accident-proneness can be interpreted as the predominance of exploration at the expense of attachment behavior... Children showing this pattern may be developing counterphobic defenses against anxiety in the sense that they attempt to manage their uncertainty over the mother's availability as a protector by taking off on their own and courting danger, rather than seeking protection from a source they perceive as unreliable' (Lieberman and Pawl 1988: 333). Denying, excluding or disconnecting from feelings of distress, despair and fear is a defence against weakness and vulnerability. Thus, children deny danger: fearful situations are approached recklessly and with impunity.

In early toddlerhood, controlling–avoidant strategies help to achieve a perverse predictability that to the outsider might seem bizarre and self-destructive. Rhythmic rocking, head-banging, hair-pulling, trance-like states and self-mutilation are typical examples of such self-referential controlling behaviours. Children become locked into a closed loop of experience that is predictable and under their control. Such behaviours allow children to disconnect from the outside world, which they have found to be dangerous and unpredictable.

There is, then, an anxious need by many maltreated and traumatised children to be in control of events and other people in order to feel safe. Food might be hoarded to meet the anxiety of hunger. A child might lie extensively in an attempt to preclude hostile reactions by others. Anger might be expressed in destructive or cruel ways. The fear might be kept at bay by keeping others at a distance. If they are not in control, experience has taught these children that terrible things happen – feelings overwhelm the mind, distress mounts and the self falls apart. If these children suffer trauma and confusion from a very early age, many begin to show disturbed, aggressive behaviour even as young as 3 or 4. The case of Jack illustrates many features of this behavioural response.

Jack

Jack lived with his mother, Jenny, for the first 6 years of his life. There is a history of problem behaviour, Jenny finding Jack increasingly difficult to handle. 'By the time he was three', says his mother, 'he was completely wild.' On a number of occasions, Jack was looked after by foster carers, but he always returned to the care of his mother after a few weeks or so.

During his sixth year, Jack was excluded from school. He was becoming increasingly aggressive with other children and teachers, a pattern also shown by his older brother, Tom, when he was Jack's age. Jack's school work was poor; he lacked concentration. Tom was often very violent and abusive towards Jack, punching him and stubbing cigarettes out on his skin. The previous year, Jack had poked out his brother's pet rabbit's eyes before strangling the animal to death. After that incident, he was placed with foster carers. Over the following months, he was gradually reintroduced to his mother, eventually returning home full time. More recently, Jack's behaviour has become even more violent, uncontrolled and aggressive with both adults and peers. When asked to draw, his pictures are full of violence and frightening events. For example, he drew a monster eating a little boy, which Jack said represented his dad devouring him. At school, he would describe lurid imaginary scenes in which there was a great deal of blood, injury and unresolved violence.

Jack's mother, Jenny, was the younger of two girls, the children of an army officer. The family moved around the world a great deal when she was young. 'I felt unloved as a child. I seemed to be very naughty all the time. None of the other children ever liked me... I felt I was a bad person.' Jenny describes her mother as distant, uninterested and unloving, and sometimes verbally cruel. 'She once told me that I wasn't my father's child, which I don't think is true. But it stuck at the back of my mind... Now I can't bear her near me or touching me.' She was frightened of her father, who was very rigid and aggressive. Both parents went out socialising a lot, drinking heavily and leaving Jenny to her own devices. She said she learned to cope on her own, never to make a fuss, no matter how hurt or upset she felt. 'I don't ever remember being ill.' Her elder sister suffered severe eczema and asthma. She was a very quite, withdrawn, compliant girl. When Jenny was 8 years old, her father and some of his army friends sexually abused her on numerous occasions. 'My mother knew and when I told her, her exact words were "Well it happens to little girls." I've never forgiven her for that.' Jenny now wonders whether her mother was sexually abused as a girl.

Aged 10 years, Jenny says that she had a 'breakdown'. She was placed on medication but then sent off to boarding school. Her parents separated. 'When I was home, I could hear my mother crying and I used think it was all my fault. But at the same time I wanted to go and kill her because I couldn't bear to hear her crying.' By the time she was 13, Jenny was seriously bulimic: 'I used to make myself sick all the while. I lost a lot of weight and got very ill. I then went on to alcohol.' She was asked to leave her school. At 16, Jenny left home. She also started taking hard drugs. She began to steal, break into houses, shoplift and commit fraud to pay for her habits. The men with whom she became involved were alcoholics, drug addicts and violent. By this time Jenny, too, was an alcoholic. The father of her two sons was particularly violent, knocking out her teeth and breaking her nose.

Throughout Jack's first 6 years, Jenny was often found either completely drunk or drugged while her son was in her care. Jack and Tom witnessed a great deal of extreme violence by their father against Jenny. It is less clear whether their father was physically abusive to the boys, although it seems highly likely that he was. Certainly, Jack was physically abused by his older brother and possibly by his mother. Jenny said that she felt worried that she might harm Jack in some significant but unspecified way. Her own well-being improves when she is no longer responsible for his care. When Jack is not living with her, Jenny says that she feels relieved and less anxious.

When he was 6 years old, Jack physically attacked his teachers, classmates and the headteacher. He also seriously vandalised an office. His subsequent exclusion from school and very aggressive behaviour towards his mother resulted in his being placed once again in foster care. At first, he seemed to settle well, and both social worker and foster parents felt very optimistic, thinking that this might evolve into a long-term placement. The foster carers ran a small farm. A couple of months later, however, Jack's behaviour deteriorated. He attacked some of the farm animals, including head-butting a goat! He attacked his younger foster sister. Eventually, the foster carers demanded his instant removal; they said that they couldn't cope a minute longer with his considerable aggression and complete uncontrollability. In his desperation, the foster father had been driven to punish Jack in an increasingly severe fashion, including locking him in a pig-pen. Two further short-term periods of being looked after by foster parents were finally followed by placement in special therapeutic residential care. For each placement, the initial view was that Jack had settled well, and people began making optimistic statements about his improved behaviour, but about 6–8 weeks later, his highly disturbed behaviour returned with increased intensity. For example, while driving Jack in her car, a foster carer was puzzled when a lorry driver repeatedly pointed to the back of her vehicle. Only when she turned round did she see Jack with his trousers down masturbating against the window.

As we have seen, it appears to many aggressive 'controlling' children that, in relationship with their carers, it is they, as children, who by their very presence seem to 'cause' other people to become angry, violent, very frightened or, in the case of parents who are depressed or alcoholic, in need of care themselves. Children begin to see the self as strong and powerful, but also dangerous and bad in terms of how they seem to affect others. In their presence, other people seem to behave in ways that appear frightening, dramatic and violent.

Representations of the self therefore have two distinct dimensions:

- The young self is seen as powerful and bad in terms of its apparent effect on others (violent and uncontrollable things seeming to happen when the child is around).
- The self is defensively represented as strong and invulnerable so that these frightening and dangerous forces can be attacked or ignored or even denied.

Indeed, as children's behaviour grows worse, it is not unusual to hear birth parents describe their difficult children as evil monsters or 'mental head cases'. Children, too, will often depict themselves as 'evil creatures' or as some form of dangerous, invincible force that cannot be defeated no matter what frightening and threatening things might take place. Seeing the self as in total control, invulnerable and inaccessible to the outside world represents an extreme attempt to deal with an interpersonal life that constantly seems to threaten violence and annihilation, both physical and psychological. If the self is not in complete control, the child feels that terrible things might happen. Crises will escalate. Helplessness and rage will consume consciousness. The strange, often frightening world of many of these children is recognised in the case of Joe. As is frequently shown in their drawings and their imagination, children like Joe see themselves as both the source of dangerous forces and also the potential victim of those self-same forces.

Joe

Joe, aged 7, has been punched and badly bruised on a number of occasions by his mother. She is in a violent relationship with her partner. Joe's behaviour at school has deteriorated, with an increasing number of aggressive assaults on classmates and uncontrollable class-room behaviour. He refuses to be told what to do by his mother and now by his female teachers. He has a deep fascination with and addiction to violent, bloody films. He is afraid to go to sleep at night in case he is attacked by a monster in his bedroom. He once told his teacher he wanted to die. Joe says he has an invisible 10 ft bear who follows him about. This bear is very big and frightening and might attack anybody who tries to attack Joe. Joe said that even he was scared of the bear, but the creature wouldn't go away.

Projective story-telling techniques vividly capture the various ways in which disorganised children try to deal with raised anxiety and attachment-related issues. Disorganised children find it very difficult to resolve attachment-related distress in whatever form it appears. Main identifies five responses to the invitation to complete attachment-related, distress–affected stories or engage in pretend play (Main 1995):

1. a refusal to respond and participate (children telling impoverished stories in which all negative feelings are excluded)
2. an enactment of fearful, disorganised, catastrophic fantasy, with no resolution of the crises
3. fearful silences and whispering, an inability to speak and sitting in frozen silence
4. inexplicable fear and a complete inability to engage with the story and play
5. mysterious agents appear who control what is going on ('invisible, unknown actors').

Children who do respond are asked to develop stories in which an accident might happen, a scary event take place or parents go away for the night. Disorganised children tell overelaborate stories in which extreme catastrophes occur without warning. Crises escalate and rapidly spin out of control. Dangerous events or people appear, vanquished only to reappear. The children seem unable to keep fearful events at bay for but a moment before they return. They are helpless in the face of danger. The tension, distress and conflict are never resolved. Parents fail to provide protection and safety. George

(1996: 416) describes the results of her own tests using the following techniques:

> Their stories depicted parents and other adult figures as frightened, frightening, chaotic or helpless. Dangerous events (for example, the family car raging out of control, or an abusive babysitter or parent) were left unresolved. Adults who potentially might have been of help were depicted as physically or psychologically unavailable or abusive. Children frequently were depicted as helpless to get assistance from others, to control their behaviour, or the events surrounding them. Some children, for example, were thrown in jail or beaten. In some instances, the child's only recourse was to keep secrets or hide. Stories often ended in chaos and disintegration of the self and the family.

The children are unable to use any organised strategy to handle their extreme attachment-related anxiety. They feel vulnerable. 'Flooded by pain, anger, fear, and distress, their representational models become dysregulated; they are left feeling helpless and out of control' (George 1996: 416). The fear of *feeling out of control* is a constant theme in the experiences, behaviours and models displayed by children classified as disorganised.

Defensively, ways of trying to deal with these overwhelming feelings include *projection* of the blame onto others; becoming aggressive with irrelevant, non-responsible figures (mistreating animals or abusing the self while idealising parents); and becoming absorbed, preoccupied and compulsively obsessed with minor activities as a way of excluding thinking about strong, angry feelings (obsessions, compulsions and hypochondria). Each of these defences is an attempt to exclude arousing, contradictory information from consciousness. Children appear to project past frightening, violent events into new situations, especially into those where there is some ambiguity. This has serious implications for these children's conduct in social situations in which they might feel confused, distressed or incompetent.

These attachment/distress-related behaviours leave little time for exploration or social learning. Maltreated children show less novelty-seeking and pretend play. They are less cognitively competent (Cicchetti *et al.* 1989). These children, especially those with conduct disorders, also exhibit reading problems and 'verbal deficits' (Lyons-Ruth 1996: 69). Children who are not provided with the words and concepts to recognise and understand their feelings (emotional scaffolding) are those who find it difficult to regulate affect.

The poverty of interpersonal exchanges, particularly in the case of children whose mothers are depressed, means that children are exposed to fewer words to aid them in identifying, conceptualising and discriminating their feelings and other mental states. Depressed mothers also spend more time with their children in 'negative affective states' that lack stimulation and interpersonal synchrony (Walden and Garber 1994). Beeghly and Cicchetti (1994) found that children who had experienced severe neglect and abuse used less internal state language and talked less about their own thoughts, feelings and actions than did non-maltreated toddlers. They were also less able to differentiate between different feelings (for example, being confused between their feelings of sadness, anger and fear). Their range of feelings also appeared limited and rather blunted. The knock-on effect of these limits was the inability of many maltreated children to differentiate, label and understand emotional expressions in other people.

Lack of 'emotional scaffolding' means that it is hard to distinguish, understand and control emotions both in the self and others. Feelings of anger and need become confused, so that to experience one might be to display the other. Fear, rage, distress and sadness also become muddled and undifferentiated. The result is social confusion and incompetence that results in further aggression, withdrawal or both. Disorganised children therefore tend to misunderstand and mis-play many social situations, further adding to their distress, mistrust and sudden displays of intense rage and anger. All attachment-related issues, including distress in others, seem to lead to arousal, agitation and aggression, with the result that parents and other children can be attacked, often with great rage and violence.

Holmes (1997: 239) sees abused children growing up in a world in which their feelings and the meaning they try to give to traumatic experiences are discounted and obliterated by their carers. However, children are still dependent on their abusers and will often show quite pronounced attachment behaviour. This indicates attachment without intimacy. 'By destroying the child's autonomy, the abuser also destroys the possibility of intimacy' (Holmes 1997: 239). The more that these children are frightened, the more they cling to their attachment figures. Abused children are also likely to deny the hostile, negative feelings and the mental representations that their attachment figures hold of them as children. To accept such feelings and representations is to have to face the painful, disorganising fact that your carer, whom you love and on whom you have to depend, has 'malevolent intentions' towards you.

Dean *et al.* (1986), working with maltreated children aged between 6 and 14 years of age, noted that they reported that parents were justified in treating children punitively and unkindly because children deserved to be punished. The children also described how they tried to please their parents with kindness even though the parents remained unresponsive. 'Perhaps as an attempt to resolve contradictions between models of self and others, older maltreated children (9–14) appeared to adopt a 'perfect-parent – worthless-child' model' (McCrone *et al.* 1994: 104–5).

The case of Luke illustrates how a young child reacts and tries to cope with a mother whose behaviour is unpredictable, very unreliable and often scary. In attempts to bring some certainty into his chaotic life, Luke behaves in an increasingly controlling and punitive manner.

Luke

Luke, aged 10 years, has two younger half brothers, Christopher (8 years) and Michael (aged 6 years). He also has an elder half sister, Lisa, aged 13, who is living with foster carers. His mother, Alison, now 30 years old, constantly experiences problems with the two older boys and her responsibilities as a caregiver.

Alison had a disturbed childhood. Her mother left the family and went to live in America with her new boyfriend when Alison was 2 years old. Her father then married Linda. They had two children. Linda, Alison's stepmother, was also looking after two boys who were the children of her sister who had died. Alison saw little of her father as a girl. 'My dad was just never there, but I loved him dearly... I don't speak to him these days; haven't done for about the last 3 years I suppose.' Alison said that she hated her stepmother and her stepmother hated her: 'I'm still terrified of her. There was no love or caring. We all lived in constant fear. I thought she was a very strong person, a clever person, very manipulative, very controlling. I feel sick if I ever go anywhere near her house. But I love her.' The stepmother ran the family home with great strictness, fear and physical abuse. 'I looked after myself most of the time', remembered Alison. 'I started running away when I was about 8. I used to pray not to wake up in the morning. My sister was hospitalised a few times. We were all on the 'at risk' register. We all missed school a lot of times because of the bruise marks on us.' Alison was also sexually abused by her stepbrothers.

By the time Alison reached her early teens, she was seen as a very difficult child. She was a school non-attender, sexually very active, promiscuous and 'totally out of control'. She was placed in foster care. When she was 16 years old, she was heavily into drugs, theft and prostitution. 'I felt the world owed me a living and I was going to have it.' At 17 years, Alison gave birth to Lisa, whom she eventually placed in the care of Linda, her stepmother. 'I thought it easiest if I let Linda take over. She wanted to look after Lisa. I felt I owed her to her.' Lisa was physically and emotionally abused while in the care of Linda, her maternal stepgrandmother, and sexually abused by her uncle and his friend, thus more or less repeating Alison's own childhood experiences in the care of Linda. Lisa was eventually removed and placed with foster carers.

Alison next formed a relationship with Nigel and gave birth to Luke. Nigel is not Luke's father but the boy does not know this. The marriage was volatile and violent, with repeated episodes of Nigel walking out. There were significant financial problems. Major quarrels with the neighbours erupted. The family was evicted twice. Alison made suicidal gestures on a number of occasions, one in the presence of Luke. When he was 6 years old, he found his mother comatose with a note pinned to her chest that read: 'By the time you read this, I will be dead.' The marriage to Nigel eventually broke down.

By the time Luke started school, he was described as 'a very disturbed, angry little boy'. He was placed in temporary foster care, with a view to a permanent placement. However, through her work for an 'escort agency', Alison began a relationship with a client, Dave, 23 years her senior. They led an extravagant lifestyle, going on expensive holidays and spending a good deal of money. Dave encouraged Alison to demand all three boys back out of foster care, a plan that eventually succeeded. Alison kept telling the boys that they were not to love their foster carers, who, she said, were trying to take them away from their mummy. The result was that the foster placements broke down.

Upon their return, Dave was unable to control the boys, particularly Luke, who was being blamed for many of the family's problems. Luke suffered a good deal of physical abuse at the hands of his mother's partner. Dave's heavy drinking got worse, his business collapsed and he had a breakdown and was admitted to psychiatric hospital. The family found itself homeless and entered a homeless families hostel. When all her other supports break down, Alison appeals to social workers for help. 'When things are in crisis – I think she's a crisis junky – we get urgent phone calls every day', said her social worker.

In between times, she either fights or evades social workers. In her needy phases, social workers are 'the good guys'. Her current worker said, 'When she needs us, I'm the best social worker she's ever had. She said her previous worker was no good. Alison said how nice it was at last to have a social worker who had a heart, who had a soul!' Alison wonders why her relationships with men always turn violent. She thinks she might have a strange, bad power that 'turns' people. 'What is it about me that seems to change these people. They seem alright to begin with. It's as if I must do something to make them turn.'

When Luke was 8 years old, he began to worry a great deal about his mother. His teachers described him a 'sad, angry, nervous little boy who often seemed more frightened than depressed. Sometimes he'd totally withdraw and we couldn't reach him.' He would try to defend her against some of her more violent partners, actually taking a knife out and threatening to kill one man, saying, 'You are not going to hurt my mummy.' Alison felt that she tried too hard to be a good mother, desperately trying not to be like her own stepmother. 'I often ended up letting Luke look after me.' His child psychiatrist said that he was 'a child who thinks he's omnipotent'. He also started stealing, lying and bullying other children, often in an aggressive manner. 'He bullied his younger brother. Like, he would pierce his brother's feet with a needle while he was asleep.' His school work deteriorated. His mother found him impossible to control. His caring behaviour towards her was becoming increasingly angry and punitive. 'He won't accept being controlled by Alison any more. He says that if his mum can't cope he will be thrown out.'

Once again, Luke was placed in foster care. But only 2 days after he joined his new family, he fell off his bike, which he'd been riding in an extremely careless way, and hit his head on a concrete bollard, fracturing his skull. Luke spent several weeks in hospital, where he was seriously ill. Alison visited him daily. The hospital staff thought she was 'wonderful'. Partly on the basis of this allegedly devoted behaviour, Luke was once more discharged to his mother's care.

In summary, children classified as disorganised and controlling, aggressive and defended, punitive and fearful:

- *avoid* closeness in relationships (intimacy implying fear and danger)
- *control* rather than be controlled (because they fear remaining at the mercy of an unpredictable, dangerous world)

● defensively exclude and deny hostile, distressing and frightening experiences – this includes assuming a self that is seen as *powerful, aggressive, invulnerable* and *punitive*, able to attack and keep dangerous, threatening forces at bay, forces that cannot be allowed to intrude or have any frightening effect on the self, forces that must be kept under control or even annihilated.

Peer relationships

In children aged 4–6 years old, the most powerful predictors of hostile, aggressive behaviour towards peers is an infant attachment classification of disorganised–disorientated (Lyons-Ruth *et al.* 1993). In addition, if during the second year mothers also perceive their children to be difficult, the risk of the children showing major externalising, aggressive problem behaviours by the time they start school aged 5 years increases even further (Shaw *et al.* 1996). It appears, therefore, that the profound conflict, fear and disorganisation shown by many maltreated children in their attachment behaviour, coupled with parents who are highly critical of their children as toddlers and whose own relationships are characterised by conflict, places children at a high risk of later social maladaptation.

Rothbaum and Weisz (1994) have also observed that both parents and abused children attribute hostile, negative qualities to each other. Indeed, across all relationships, both parents and children attribute hostile intentions to others, particularly in ambiguous, provocative situations. Maltreated children do appear more alert to, distracted by and rapidly aroused in the presence of conflict, violence and upset between parents or among peers. Alessandri (1991) observed that maltreating mothers interacted less with their children and used fewer verbal and physical strategies to guide their children's attention. Disorganised children show a very low propensity to initiate social interaction or indeed respond constructively to interactions initiated by others.

Physically abused children in particular tend to be both verbally and physically aggressive with their peers (Rogosch *et al.* 1995: 592). In contrast, other maltreated children withdraw socially from and actively avoid their peers. The least socially competent children are both aggressive and withdrawn (Rogosch and Cicchetti 1994). These conflicted aggressive–withdrawing, 'approach–avoidance', ambivalent–avoidant (A–C) responses might also affect the way in which disorganised children respond to new relationships. Withdrawal is often an active strategy used as a way of avoiding the stress and confusion of social interaction (Mueller and Silverman 1989).

Not surprisingly, many maltreated children are not popular with their peers. They tend to be unhappy children who rarely laugh or smile. They can be rigid and inflexible in both their thinking and their behaviour. They typically attack whatever or whoever causes them distress. Additionally, they lack empathy.

Conduct disorders, school behaviour and educational performance
Before they begin school, many maltreated children classified as disorganised show behaviours diagnosed as oppositional defiant disorder (ODD). ODD includes such behaviours as non-compliance towards authority figures, tantrums and being argumentative and provocative. Not as severe or antisocial as conduct disorder, which includes behaviours such as fighting, truancy, stealing and fire-setting, most children who develop severe conduct disorders in later childhood have a history of ODD. Thus, (a) the identification of ODD, (b) disorganised attachment patterns, and (c) hostile, critical, low-warmth parenting places preschool children at a high risk of developing major conduct disorders and social maladaptation by the time they are of school age.

Cicchetti and Toth (1995a: 552–4) note that adaptation to school, including integration into the peer group and a successful approach to academic tasks, is related to future adjustment. Maltreated children find the school environment particularly difficult. They easily get into trouble, which leads teachers to use more controlling strategies, further undermining the development of self-motivation. Physically abused children are aggressive, non-compliant, prone to acting out and function poorly on cognitive tasks. Neglected children are poor on cognitive tasks, anxious, inattentive and most likely to say that they are unable to understand their work. They lack initiative and are heavily dependent on teachers for help, approval and encouragement. They rely on external cues rather than on their own inner resources and motivation. 'It is not surprising that children who have been maltreated are at extremely high risk for failure at school' (Cicchetti and Toth 1995a: 552).

Sexual abuse
A number of researchers have shown that the negative consequences of sexual abuse interact in complex ways with other types of maltreat-

ment, including emotional abuse, physical abuse, psychological abuse and neglect (Crittenden 1996; Toth and Cicchetti 1996). Children classified as secure, avoidant, ambivalent and disorganised will show different behavioural reactions and proceed along different developmental trajectories in response to sexual abuse.

The most frequently observed psychological consequences of children being sexually abused and classified as disorganised in their attachment status include feeling depressed, uncertain and socially less competent. There is confusion about how to handle the self in relationships. In those cases of sexual abuse in which children had a secure attachment with a carer, fewer clinical symptoms are observed. The trauma of the abuse is still considerable, but the children's ability to achieve psychological recovery appears greater.

> Thus, the present findings provide an interesting view on the sequelae of childhood sexual abuse and may be helpful in accounting for the varied outcomes that have been described in childhood victims of sexual abuse. Outcome for these children is likely to be a function of the perpetrator of the abuse and of the protection or lack thereof that the sexually abused child perceives from their primary caregiver. (Toth and Cicchetti 1996: 39)

If traumas are also mixed up with sexual abuse, children become even more confused about the nature and expression of intimacy. Feelings of love, need, arousal, intimacy, hurt, fear and guilt form a disturbing psychological cocktail leading to behaviours that are often sexualised, including the sexual abuse of other children. There is growing evidence that many sexually abused children go on as children and adults to abuse other children (Vizard *et al.* 1995). Although not all sexually abused children become sexual abusers, most sexual abusers have suffered either sexual abuse, physical abuse or both in their childhoods.

When children's attachment figures become sexually active with them, attachment relationships become confused and sexualised. Love, sex and closeness in relationship become mixed with fears of pain, rejection and abandonment. This makes the conduct of all close relationships problematic for these children. To form relationships with others implies sex, yet intimacy inevitably arouses fear, distress and anger.

Young perpetrators are both victims and abusers. They have a relentless, angry desire to sexually abuse others. Childhood trauma and the resulting pathological impact on development finds these children engulfed with aggressive, destructive forces that include the urge to abuse others and, in many cases, to commit suicide. Feelings of depression, anxiety and low self-esteem are common. Conflicts can occur over gender identity. Some abused children show dysfunctional sexual development. Many have very poor relationships with their peers. Woods (1997: 380) gives the example of 18-year-old Gary.

Gary

Gary, 18, who had abused many children, spent his first few sessions rocking and drawing stereotyped pictures of cars. He said, 'I can't talk about what they [his parents] did to me because it makes me so angry that I will have to do it to someone else... If I tell you [those] thoughts then you would either hit me or get rid of me.' And, after a short pause, he said, 'In fact you should get rid of me; I should be killed and then everyone could forget me.'

Non-attached patterns

Some environments prevent young children forming selective attachment relationships. Residential institutions may (or may not) provide infants with reasonable physical care, but they experience many and frequent changes of carer (shifts and new jobs). This means that there is little point in children investing in any particular relationship. Similarly, infants looked after by streams of temporary carers (mothers, grandmothers, foster parents and friends of the parents) for short periods also fail to develop selective attachments. Yet other children may be so severely neglected physically and emotionally by their parents or carers that, during any one day, they are largely left to their own devices and receive very little contact with adults. Parents with serious drug or alcohol addictions may, to all intents and purposes, be unavailable for large tracts of most days. So, for example, non-attached children do not consistently turn to a specific person for help when they are sick, hurt or hungry.

Long-term behavioural sequelae include: problems recognising and interpreting bodily sensations; problems understanding cause and effect relations, including a good notion of time and time-keeping; intellectual impairment; poor concentration and attentional problems;

hyperactivity; significant educational problems; poor peer and social relationships; and difficulties feeling secure or committed to others in close relationships, including developing attachments with new carers.

Lack of close warm, reciprocal relationships during the first 1 or 2 years of life deprives the brain of critical social and emotional experiences during a phase of rapid and sensitive neuronal reorganisation. As a result, the brain's hard neuronal wiring is adversely affected, leaving many who are maltreated with long-term, possibly permanent neurological damage and cognitive processing dysfunctions. Severe emotional deprivation can literally result in the brain failing to establish neuronal connections that help children to recognise and process emotional, social and relationship stimuli.

Zeanah (1996: 48) recognises two types of non-attachment:

- the emotionally withdrawn (non-attached inhibited)
- the indiscriminately social (non-attached disinhibited).

Non-attached children with *inhibition* show emotional withdrawal. They rarely smile. They appear to have little interest or spontaneous pleasure in social interaction, exploration or eating. Their behaviour is described as listless and autistic-type behaviours appear. Rhythmic rocking and head-banging within the familiar world of the cot or small bedroom are common. Most give up crying because nobody responds. Malnourishment is often associated with this condition.

Other infants and young children, many of them raised in residential institutions, show *disinhibited, indiscriminately social behaviour*. They are very attention-seeking, clingy and over-friendly. They exhibit promiscuous affection with strangers. Peer relationships tend to be poor, with a good deal of rejection by age-mates. According to Lieberman and Pawl (1988: 331), development shows major impairment in three areas: interpersonal relationships, impulse control and the regulation of aggression. There is a long-term incapacity to establish emotionally meaningful relationships. Notions of reciprocity and mutuality are lacking. As they progress through childhood, rates of criminal behaviour, anger, interpersonal conflict, poor concentration and problems with school increase. Throughout life, many of these children continue to cope best in environments that are socially and physically structured rather than those which are permissive and relaxed. They find relationships that are too close and loving too demanding, fearful and anxiety-provoking. This creates a major problem for new carers, including foster and adoptive parents.

In terms of mentally representing relationships, the individual with a history of non-attachment cognitively models the self as being without social value or interest or concern. A 'careless' style of self-management follows. There has been little or no experience of caring or meaningful engagement with other people, so relationships are experienced as of little value, import or significance unless they are a means to an end. Relationships with others are based merely on attempts to satisfy some immediate need. Once the need has been met, the relationship has served its purpose. Children show little upset when one carer leaves and another one arrives. People are interchangeable as long as the basic needs of food, attention, money and sex are met. In adulthood, relationships are casual and conflictual. Although some institutionalised children do show good developmental recovery when they are placed with new families, many substitute parents of more developmentally disturbed children do feel disappointment. They enjoy few emotional rewards. For these children, self- and social understanding are very low. For example, Rachel's mother felt she needed to 'manage' her adopted daughter.

Rachel (taken from Howe 1998: 193–6)

Rachel was first removed from home when she was 4 months old, having been diagnosed as 'failing to thrive'. She was malnourished and weighed less than her birthweight. From hospital, she went to a foster home. Three weeks into the placement, the foster mother said that she was worried that Rachel needed more expert care than she could offer. The baby was returned to hospital, where she stayed for 10 days before being discharged to a children's home. At the age of 9 months, Rachel was returned to her mother, who had made a few, half-hearted visits to the children's home. By this stage, Rachel was proving to be a very difficult baby. Six weeks later, she was admitted to hospital with a subdural haematoma, caused, it was suspected, by a non-accidental injury. Rachel remained in hospital for another 5 weeks before she was discharged to a short-term reception centre. She lived at the centre for 4 months, where the decision was taken to transfer her to a long-stay children's home. Two unsuccessful attempts were made to place Rachel with long-term foster parents during her third year. She was finally placed, aged 5 years, with adoptive parents.

Her adopters described her as a 'hyperactive' child who ran everywhere in a 'harum-scarum' fashion. 'She seemed totally unfazed when she came. She arrived in the house and treated it immediately as home, jumping on the settee, running up and down the stairs and wanting to know what everything was and where things were. You know, very friendly, but in that way you know has little depth to it.' Her adoptive mother said that Rachel was never cuddlesome. 'If she hurt herself, she'd never cry and go running to someone.'

Not long after her arrival, Rachel began school. The teachers found her 'a bit wild, leaping and crashing about more than most of the other children.' She swore a great deal, which did not bother her parents too much but did upset her class teacher. After a couple of years, she moved on to a local, private day school. 'She seemed to have no sense of the teachers being in some kind of authority and needing respect. She'd scribble on the other girls' books. She would get up and wander around the classroom whenever she felt like it. She'd chat away to the headmistress, inappropriately showing none of the distance that the other girls showed. But she did learn quite a bit, to everyone's surprise.' Teachers found her extremely difficult to manage. Rachel had no close friends. If she did invite anyone home, she would end up fighting them. Shirley, her adoptive mother, could never leave Rachel on her own with a friend for fear of what would happen.

Running about suited Rachel much more than sitting still. Shirley recognised that Rachel needed structure. 'I had to develop a rigid timetable with her for each day. Otherwise she just careered off out of control.'

When she was 12 years old, Rachel attended the local comprehensive school. She found the constant change of teacher for each subject difficult. The school was permissive about discipline, which did not suit Rachel. She became even more disruptive and was eventually suspended after two terms for 'bad behaviour'. Her parents then sent her to a boarding school. After one term, they said that they couldn't cope with her. The only thing that they discovered kept her still was when she was allowed to look after the school's animals – a rabbit, chickens and a dog.

For the next year, Rachel had a home tutor. Shirley and her husband were finding her more and more difficult to control. Aged 14 years, she was once returned by the police for 'disturbing the peace'. She stole small amounts of money from her mother's purse and her father's wallet. Whenever she felt frustrated or was denied something, she would erupt into a violent temper, breaking things and hitting people.

Psychological tests recommended that Rachel should be sent to a special boarding school for children with emotional and behavioural problems.

Throughout childhood, Rachel's adoptive parents remarked how emotionally uninvolved she was in family life. 'I managed her rather than mothered her. I realised that all I could do was support Rachel, but that she really had no strong feelings for me more than she had for anyone else.'

Rachel left school when she 16 years old and began a youth training scheme. This involved going to the local college and working in local factories. However, Rachel was unable to get along with the other students. She was not able to share, take advice or mix socially. If anything went wrong, she would get in a temper and cause a scene. The trainers and the factory owners asked her to leave the course. Rachel always complained that she was being treated unfairly. It was at this time that she began to smoke heavily. She was keen to have money, but it slipped through her fingers as soon as she had any. Whatever casual jobs she managed to find 'fizzled out after a few days or so'. After a year of drifting in and out of casual work, Rachel took a job as a kennel maid looking after cats and dogs. 'And that's where she's been for the last two and a half years', said her adoptive mother.

Adolescence and adulthood

Relationships continue to be both difficult and hazardous for those who show disorganised, disorientated and controlling responses in situations where there are attachment-related issues. Within the internal working model, the self and other people are viewed negatively. The self is seen as unloved or bad by those who are particularly disturbed. Other people remain essentially unavailable, threatening, frightened or frightening. Bartholomew and Horowitz (1991) describe this attachment style as *fearful*. Close relationships are typically conducted in a volatile, even violent fashion. When stressed, attachment behaviour swings erratically, unpredictably and in a strongly disorganised manner between approach and avoidance behaviours of a high intensity. Using self-report techniques, individuals classified as fearful are said to identify with the following description:

I am somewhat uncomfortable getting close to others. I want emotionally close relationships but I find it difficult to trust others completely, or to depend on them. I sometimes worry that I will be hurt if I allow myself to become too close to others.

Using the AAI, adults who appear to be still affected, disturbed and disorientated by their memories of trauma and loss, are categorised as disorganised and *unresolved* (U) with respect to the trauma or loss. The unresolved experiences of trauma usually involve the loss of an attachment figure or the suffering of physical or sexual abuse during childhood. Interviews generally reveal an apparent failure to mourn the loss of the attachment figure or resolve the traumatic childhood abusive experience. Main (1996) writes that the unresolved attachment status is indicated by interviews where signs of continuing disorganisation appear when the attachment figure or trauma is discussed. The disorganisation includes 'lapses in the monitoring of reason or discourse'. Interviews become less coherent as the individual tries to talk about the loss or childhood distress. There are indications of unfounded fears and guilt. Internal working models of adults classified as 'unresolved' remain confused, dysregulated and disorganised.

Lapses of the monitoring of reason or discourse during the attempted discussion of traumatic events need only be of short duration, often no more than a few sentences here and there throughout the interview. The intrusion of such lapses and episodes of disorganisation and disorientation represent not so much an overall pattern of interaction but more a collapse of patterning when traumatic experiences are discussed, particularly the loss of a significant person (Main 1995). The narrative might also include irrational beliefs, the inability to stay with the topic, prolonged silences and periods when the individual becomes lost with and absorbed by tales of loss or abuse.

It also has to be emphasised that, according to Main and Solomon (1986), the unresolved classification, as with the disorganised infant classification, is superimposed on a core, *best-fitting* organised attachment pattern (secure–autonomous, F; avoidant–dismissing, Ds; ambivalent–entangled, E). Adults can have either a secure or insecure attachment organisation, but remain unresolved with respect to major loss and trauma. The disorganisation is only discernible in situations where distress, attachment-related anxieties and traumatic childhood memories intrude into the present. The overall character of the rest of the interview indicates that either an F, Ds or E adult attachment classification is appropriate.

Many of the characteristics identified in the childhood controlling patterns also appear in adult form. There are adult equivalents of:

- coercive, punitive, fearful patterns in which issues of power and domination appear to be linked to aggression and violence
- compulsive caregiving in which deep insecurities draw people into co-dependent relationships with partners who have major attachment needs that they attempt to meet while denying their own emotional needs as a way of keeping the other available
- patterns of compulsive compliance in which individuals try to keep on the right side of partners who are potentially demanding, aggressive and bullying, again by denying their own attachment needs.

Psychiatric and clinical populations

People with childhoods of severe abuse and loss seem more vulnerable to psychiatric problems, including depression (see, for example, Bemporad and Romana 1992). People who remain 'unresolved' or disorganised in terms of past traumas are those most likely to have relationship and mental health difficulties.

In an interesting study of inpatient psychiatric patients and a control group of general hospital outpatients, Fonagy *et al.* (1996) found that 76 per cent of the psychiatric group's interviews produced *unresolved–disorganised–disorientated* transcripts compared with only 7 per cent of the control group. Sixty-five per cent of the psychiatric sample (compared with only 8 per cent of the control sample) reported childhood sexual abuse or severe physical abuse. Patients with anxiety disorders and borderline personality disorders (intense, demanding interpersonal relationships, emotional instability, impulsiveness, a lack of control over anger, a fear of real or imagined abandonment, and chronic feelings of emptiness) were significantly more likely to have suffered severe physical or sexual abuse than were other psychiatric classifications:

> The present study demonstrated that psychiatric patients' narratives of their childhoods could be readily distinguished from those of normal control participants... The study provided overwhelming support for the association of psychiatric disorder with unresolved difficult early relationships, in line with attachment theory. The vast majority of the personal histories in the AAIs of the psychiatric group are so compelling and beyond the ordinary range of experi-

ence that a model based on the social causation of mental disorder becomes intuitively hard to reject... The significant association between a diagnosis of anxiety and the unresolved classification supports the clinical validity of the unresolved category. Anxiety indicates the extent to which past traumatic experiences are felt to be in the present. (Fonagy *et al.* 1996: 28)

Criminal behaviour

Farrington (1995) has shown that boys at age 8 years with severe antisocial problem behaviours, poor parenting (including harsh and authoritarian discipline and poor supervision), the experience of parental conflict and family stress, and significant separation episodes from the parents are at the highest risk of developing delinquent and criminal behaviour in young adulthood. These observations receive confirmation from many other studies that take a retrospective look at the childhoods of adult criminals, particularly violent offenders. The majority appear to have had childhoods characterised by severe physical and sexual abuse. There appears to be a major inability shown by many extremely antisocial and criminal adults to resolve the powerfully negative feelings associated with childhood experiences of trauma and abuse (Garbarino and Plantz 1986; Dodge *et al.* 1990; Allen *et al.* 1996; Boswell 1996). Poor reflective function and mentalising ability, themselves products of childhood maltreatment, reduce the ability to develop a reflective capacity and thus empathise with others. These weaknesses remove essential inhibitions on criminal behaviour (Fonagy *et al.* 1997).

Looked at in terms of attachment histories, rates of conduct disorder and criminal behaviour are highest for those young adults classified as disorganised–fearful and disorganised–avoidant. Young adult criminal behaviour has generally been associated with men who 'derogate attachment issues' (Ds pattern) *and* remain unable to resolve the traumas and losses suffered in their childhoods (U pattern) (Allen *et al.* 1996). Not only is their behaviour criminal, but much of it is also likely to be violent.

Parenthood

Maltreating parents tend to cope less well with stressful life events. Many are also likely to misuse drugs and alcohol (O'Connor *et al.*

1987; Rodning *et al.* 1991), and have unsupportive, insecure partners. When levels of stress and depression are high, there is a tendency to resign from the parenting role. Mothers with the most severe depression experience the most stress. They convey a general feeling of helplessness and hopelessness. 'In general, maltreating parents have been found to be depressed, socially isolated and lacking social supports, and lacking in impulse control, especially when aroused and stressed' (Cicchetti and Lynch 1993: 102). Carers may abuse, neglect or both abuse and neglect.

Abusing carers

Abusing carers are more likely to have internal working models based on power, conflict, control and rejection. 'Interpersonal relations are guided by the expectation that others are out to dominate and subjugate them coercively, and that the self will be rejected if fulfilment of one's own needs is sought... Coercion and victimization are prominent interpersonal strategies, with anger being the predominant affect' (Crittenden 1996). Children's attachment needs trigger many of these feelings in their caregiver, producing parental behaviours that are controlling, punitive, hostile, anxious and lacking in warmth. In contrast, neglecting mothers have internal representational models organised around helplessness.

Crittenden (1988, 1996) observes that abusing mothers are often classified as 'best-fitting' dismissing (Ds) in their attachment status. They typically believe that the harsh, punitive parenting that they received in their own childhood is appropriate for their own children. They have high expectations of their children which, if not met (which frequently is the case), warrants strong, hostile discipline. These are heavily 'defended' parents who fail to recognise the relationship between the attachment-related issues of distress felt in their own childhoods and the difficulties they experience in parenting their own children.

Their children are more likely to witness domestic violence, suffer violence themselves and experience periods of foster and residential care. Abusing parents provide low levels of support, interact less and behave more negatively with their children. Their disciplinary style tends to use 'power-assertive control strategies' (anger, shouting, smacking, hitting, sarcasm and criticism), which often leads to poor impulse control and less compliance on the part of their children.

Strategies that employ reciprocity (give and take), reasoning, negotiation and suggestion appear to be much more successful in helping
children to achieve impulse control, compliance and self-reliance.
These strategies are largely absent from the repertoire of parents who
maltreat. 'Consistently harsh parental *punishment*, *rejection* of the
child, and *inconsistent discipline* tend to predispose to antisocial,
aggressive, and delinquent behaviour on the part of the child' (Wachs
1992: 37, original emphasis).

Abusing parents also seem less satisfied with their children's
behaviour, abilities and achievements. They express little pleasure in
the parenting role, finding it difficult and stressful. This makes them
both hostile, highly critical and low in warmth. The combination of
expecting their children to show precocious levels of independence
and capability, and feeling agitated by displays of their children's
attachment needs, generates a difficult, tense relationship environment for children.

Neglecting carers

Carers who neglect their children are more likely to have internal
working models organised around helplessness (Crittenden 1988,
1996). No-one seems able to provide love, support and competent
action. Feelings of emptiness, despair and depression are usual.
Parents have high levels of dependency coupled with an inability to
cope. They have few expectations of either themselves or their children. An air of resignation, unresponsiveness and withdrawal pervades
family life. The passivity of the carers means that children are under-
stimulated. This pattern of parenting is typical of carers whose 'best-
fit' attachment style is strongly passive and ambivalent (also see
Chapter 6 on parents classified as preoccupied and uncertain).

Abusing and neglecting parents

In their 'caregiving' interviews (Solomon and George 1996), many
unresolved–disorganised mothers reveal representational models of
disorganised caregiving. They feel *helpless*, ineffective and out of
control in their parenting. As with abusing carers, their internal
working model is based on notions of domination and conflict,
control and rejection. If the 'disorganised' individual seeks to fulfil

personal needs, there is the fear that the self will be rejected. In the presence of more powerful people, the unresolved–dismissing personality can be compliantly submissive, seeking acceptance rather than rejection. With weaker people, behaviours tend to be more dismissing, coercive, hostile and rejecting.

As a result, parents' caregiving can appear extremely unresponsive, insensitive, harsh, punitive and highly agitated. An air of depression descends on mothers and fathers as they attempt to describe their parenting. Parents feel helpless and not in control of either themselves or their children. In the case of parenting which is hostile, intrusive and abusive, children, even from a very young age, are felt to be *out of control*, wild and beyond help. Children throw things around the room, shout and yell noisily. They lock doors so that parents cannot enter. In the eyes of their parents, the children seem monsters, powerful, precocious and supernaturally bad (George 1996: 419). In the face of family life that grows increasingly turbulent and disorganised, parents lash out more and more in ways that are both frightening and unpredictable. As a result, children find it difficult to make sense of and predict parental behaviour. Children therefore feel helpless, bad, full of rage, dangerous, chronically anxious and uncertain (the controlling punitive–fearful classification).

Parents' feelings of helplessness can quickly erupt into rage or fear. Overall, carers feel unable to offer their children adequate care or protection; they abdicate responsibility. At these times, a mother, for example, 'may psychologically and behaviourally abandon the infant or child, threaten him or her, or appeal to the child to reassure and protect her' (Solomon and George 1996: 193). These caregivers have no defensive strategy to exclude negative information from consciousness. 'Helpless' mothers therefore feel that they are without behavioural strategies for protecting and offering safe care for their children.

Although many mothers classified as unresolved–disorganised in their AAIs have infants classified as disorganised in their attachment behaviour, not all disorganised infants have 'disorganised–unresolved' mothers. The key behavioural characteristic in terms of disorganised children's experience of being cared for is mothers who are periodically (or in extreme cases continuously) psychologically unavailable and absent. For the period of absence, parents are unable to respond to whatever attachment strategy is attempted by their children. During moments of their day-to-day care, some mothers may become absorbed with their own past painful, traumatic memories of loss or abuse. Past fears may suddenly intrude and alarm parents who themselves have been the victims of violence. Others may be severely depressed or psychiatrically ill. Some parents may be too drunk or high on drugs to be able to respond to their children's needs. Yet others might be the actual cause of the physical danger and source of the children's distress. These different forms of parental unavailability, including parents whose state of mind remains unresolved in relationship to past losses and traumas, point to the mechanism linking the type of caregiving and disorganised–disorientated behaviour on the part of young children. Infants have no way of organising their attachment behaviour to secure their carer's psychological availability.

Therefore, parents most likely to maltreat or disorientate their children are those whose own childhoods include major losses of or frequent separations from their attachment figures, a lack of care, emotional cruelty, rigid and unloving discipline, rejection, hostile intrusions into children's own psychological space, violence, physical abuse and sexual abuse (Crittenden 1988; Éthier *et al.* 1995). Maltreating carers also provide poor-quality parent–child interactions. Conversations lacks fluency, children are viewed and treated negatively, parental signals are often misleading and contradictory, and positive affect, including tenderness and affection, is typically thin. The family life of abusing and neglecting parents appears to be full of conflict, anger and chaos. In contrast, neglecting but non-abusing parents are more likely to have had childhood histories of insensitive and incompetent parenting rather than abuse and rejection. In the case of neglect, social isolation is more characteristic of family life (Crittenden 1985).

For example, handling her children and dealing with them emotionally activates Sharon's own unresolved feelings of distress and trauma. The origin of these fears is not clear to Sharon, but she experiences frightened feelings that she might do something terrible to her children. An unconscious way of ensuring their safety is constantly to involve health and welfare officials. This she does by believing that her children are unwell or even by promoting distress and illness in her children to legitimate their referral.

Sharon

Sharon is 26 years old. Her own mother's first baby was adopted. She then met Sharon's father and became pregnant again, but the baby died when only 2 weeks old. Sharon's parents separated when she was 4. She remained in the care of her father. There was no contact with her mother throughout the whole of her childhood. Sharon's father remarried to a woman who already had three boys, all older than Sharon. The couple then had a girl of their own. Sharon describes her father as distant and unloving. His idea of 'caring' was to go and punch her class teacher because she had said that Sharon couldn't wear long, dangling earrings to school. Sharon says her childhood relationship with her stepmother was violent. She describes her as selfish, two-faced and unlikable. 'She could never accept me. "I'll put you in a home; you're not mine; nobody loves you", she would say. I was treated like a punchbag. I could never relax. I had to bottle everything up and self-destruct.' Sharon learned to cope on her own. From the age of about 6 or 7, her two older step-brothers began sexually abusing her. 'I was raped and as I got older they would do quite violent and perverse things to me... I tried telling my stepmother, but she just laughed. I think she might have even encouraged them... I became very quiet and withdrawn; no friends.' She had an abortion when she was 13, her older stepbrother being the father.

After a difficult adolescence, Sharon met and married Pete, although she was pregnant by another man at the time. The couple then had a child of their own. Sharon is experiencing difficulties parenting the two children, a boy and a girl. She finds changing the children's nappies and bathing them uncomfortable. She feels anxious when she touches the children, particularly in the area of the genitals and bottom. 'I don't think I'd ever hurt them,' she says, 'but it feels like it sometimes. I kind of see my step-mother in my mind and it totally freaks me out.' Generally, she does not allow Pete to be on his own with the children, although on one occasion, Sharon left him for a week and did not take the children with her. Sharon is constantly referring the children to her doctor, the hospital, health visitors, dieticians, child psychologists and social workers for a whole variety of feared illnesses and worries. She says her daughter, Sonia, now aged 2, 'fits' several times a day, but when the little girl has been admitted to hospital, the medical staff can find nothing the matter. They witness no fits. Sharon describes a fit as Sonia 'going into trance with sweating and shaking before the fit'. Sonia screams a great deal, has poor sleep patterns and shows eating problems. The social worker describes the home as 'very sexually orientated... there's a lot of sexy underwear, aids and things that she sells at parties for other women.'

Conclusion

Children described as aggressive and 'controlling' are among the most difficult and taxing cases with which practitioners have to work. Many of the older children placed for adoption will show controlling behaviours and have histories of severe abuse, trauma, multiple moves and neglect. The caregiving and parenting skills of long-term foster carers, adopters and residential carers are often placed under great strain by children who feel distressed and angry when they experience love and intimacy. Similarly, the relationship backgrounds of many abusing, helpless, rejecting and confused parents will be ones burdened by unresolved losses and trauma. Sexual abuse, often coupled with physical abuse, commonly features in the histories of mothers, fathers and stepfathers who find the caregiving role difficult and distressing, feelings that easily erupt in confusion, anger and aggression.

Part II

APPLYING THE THEORY TO PRACTICE

Introduction

Theories help practitioners to make sense of what they know about people, their behaviour and their relationships. However, different theories suggest different ways of making sense of ostensibly the same situation. The influence of a particular theoretical outlook can be surprisingly subtle and wide ranging, affecting every stage of the practice process from observation to intervention, and assessment to evaluation.

Developmental attachment theory orientates practitioners to particular features of the psychosocial environment with a special emphasis on past and present behaviours, interactions, feelings and relationships. Thus, what *information* is gathered, and which aspects of the situation are looked at and *observed*, is guided by the practitioner's theoretical outlook. Moreover, the ways in which the information and observations are *described* are also heavily influenced by the theory's defining features. Attachment theory, like other theories, provides a conceptual vocabulary and framework within which observations and facts can be described, arranged and organised. The classification of what is known about people and their relationships is a necessary step if understandings and explanations are to be offered. Explanations suggest possible causal links between the behaviours observed, the feelings described and the relationships experienced, both past and present. It is only when the practitioner begins to make sense of what is happening that aims and interventions can be appropriately considered.

The social work process involves the following seven elements:

1. identification of the problem, concern or need
2. the gathering of facts and information by the observation, examination and investigation of behaviour, interactions, relationships, and feelings
3. the classification of the facts, information and observations
4. an assessment and analysis of the case
5. the formulation of aims, including help, intervention goals, the reduction of risks and the promotion of resilience and developmentally protective experiences

169

6. the choice of methods and sites of intervention, help, treatment and service provision
7. the evaluation of the intervention, help, treatment and service provision.

In practice, there is considerable overlap between these stages. For example, new information will continue to affect assessments, which therefore remain open to revision. However, the sequence is logical and encourages practitioners to be systematic. The success of each stage depends on the degree of rigour with which the previous stage was carried out. The next five chapters will expand on each stage of the process, concentrating in particular on: gathering information about children and their parents; classifying and assessing the information gathered; formulating aims; and designing interventions and packages of help.

It will now be apparent why it has been necessary to spell out in some detail the research and theorising associated with each of the four main attachment patterns. An understanding of these patterns and the concept of the internal working model is the engine that drives the action and content of each stage of the social work process.

Information-gathering

What information is gathered, and what behaviours and interactions are observed, will be influenced by the theoretical logic underpinning each of the attachment patterns. Information will need to be gathered about past and present behaviours, interactions and relationships, defence mechanisms, reactions to distress and the ways in which people try to regulate affect.

Classification, analysis and assessment

The information and knowledge gained can then be used to classify relationships and their associated behaviours as either secure or insecure, organised or disorganised. This aids in analysis and assessment. Each attachment pattern (internal working model) has a characteristic ensemble of relationship styles, defensive strategies, social behaviours and affective states that should allow social workers to make a hypothetical match between the information gathered and the attachment patterns likely to be present in the case.

Aims

Having analysed the case and made an assessment, the social worker is then in a strong position to formulate aims. Again, these will be couched in terms of a developmental attachment perspective and a relationship-based outlook. The guiding principles are to help children to develop organised rather than disorganised attachment strategies and establish secure rather than insecure internal working models of themselves and other people.

Help and intervention

The methods of intervention are designed according to the analysis of attachment and relationship-based issues, the attachment classification (internal working model) and the aims formulated. It is recognised that different interventions, treatment techniques and service provisions will suit some people more than others, depending on their attachment status and classification. The *choice of technique* or method of help will therefore depend on the socio-emotional characteristics of parents and their children (formulated in the assessment). Interventions are designed to increase other people's psychological availability, levels of felt security, self-esteem, self-efficacy, self-understanding and reflective capacities, self-control, social understanding and interpersonal confidence and competence. In short, by seeking to strengthen and promote more positive social environments for children, the intention is to disconfirm their insecure working models of both the self and others. If successful, this will increase children's resilience, thus enabling them to cope better with stress and adversity.

In practice, social workers need to identify which *intervention sites* need to be targeted if children are to experience more positive psychosocial environments. This is a strong reminder that children's social worlds range from the internal to the external, from family to school, from parents to siblings. Sites of intervention might include one or more of these 'worlds'. Social workers could therefore find themselves working with the child, a parent, a parent–child relationship, a parent–parent relationship, the family, a group of parents, groups of peers or the child's school.

A practice and assessment model

Each stage of the social work process is therefore influenced, guided and supported by an attachment and relationship perspective using the four patterns of attachment (see Figure A). The following chapters elaborate the basic character of the model.

Practice Process

Information gathering and observation		Analysis and assessment	Aims	Intervention		
Parents	**Children**			**Focus**	**Theoretical Domains**	**Techniques**
Mother (figure)	Child	Internal working model	Physical safety	Parent	Material	Attachment-based interventions:
Father (figure)	Siblings	Defences	Psychological well-being	Child	Emotional	prevention
Parents together	Peers	Attachment behaviour	Psychological competence	Parent-Child	Relational	support
Parent with child(ren)	Parents	Relationship style		Parents	Behavioural	treatments
Extended family	etc	Caregiving	Increase resiliences	Family	Rational	psychotherapies
Social worker		Resiliences	Decrease risks	School	Legal	training
Other professionals		Other's availability	Increase protective factors	Peers		
Files						
		Affect regulation	Increase 'felt security'	Community		
Past	Present					

Attachment Classification

	Secure/Autonomous	Avoidant/Dismissing	Ambivalent/Preoccupied-entangled	Disorganised/Unresolved
Infancy	Secure	Insecure-avoidant	Insecure-ambivalent/resistant	Insecure-disorganised/disorientated
Toddlerhood-Preschool-Schoolage	Secure-optimal	Defended-disengaged	Coercive-deprived	Controlling-confused
Adolescence-Adulthood	Autonomous-free to evaluate	Dismissing	Preoccupied-Entangled-Enmeshed Uncertain	Unresolved loss/trauma-disorganised Helpless
Parenting style	Secure-base	Rejecting		

Attachment patterns, internal working models, relationship styles and personality types throughout the lifespan: research evidence and theory development

Figure A   Developmental attachment theory: practice and assessment model

8

Gathering information for assessment

One of the major challenges in incorporating attachment theory into a model of practice has been to take what seems to be a highly relevant and useful developmental theory for understanding family relationships and translate it into the practice frameworks within which child and family social work currently operates. The theory has to be made to work within the context of investigations, assessments and interventions in family support and child protection, and be persuasive in team meetings, child protection conferences and courts. Each of these practice environments requires workers to have available to them good, reliable and, above all, useful information about the family situation with which they are dealing.

This chapter addresses the question in relation to parents and children of *what information is* going to be useful in the context of an attachment- or relationship-based approach and *which methods* are going to be most effective for obtaining it. It has to be borne in mind that not all referrals will need to be explored in the depth described here. What is important is to be sufficiently familiar with the model to be able to spot when the need for help with the electricity bill is simply that and when the signals being given by the referrer or the parents or the children are indicating that there are significant needs, risks or both.

What information?: sites of interest

We can list broadly what we need to know in order to make sense of the child and the family:

- the child's current and past development: physical, intellectual, emotional, social and behavioural
- the child's sibling relationships

- the parents' well-being and functioning, including the history of relationships in childhood within their family of origin and relationships with present and previous partners
- the parents' caregiving history in relation to this child and others
- the extended family: patterns of relationships, past and present
- peer group relationships, for both the parents (neighbours, friends and work) and the children (school and neighbourhood)
- the physical environment: housing and finance
- relationships between family members and agencies, including that with the social worker.

The target within these sites of interest is information that allows us to arrive at an understanding of the:

- internal working models of children and adults
- quality of the caregiving environment: physical, social and emotional
- risk and protective factors: factors in the child that might indicate the degree of damage or the degree of resilience, and factors in the parenting that will increase or decrease the likelihood that the child's needs for physical and emotional security will be met
- capacity to change: evidence of the parents' capacity to make the necessary changes within the timescale of the child.
- resources or interventions that are most likely either to bring that change in parenting about or to support the child in making better use of what is available in his or her social and emotional environment, or, where necessary, to meet the child's needs outside the family.

Methods

Here we will offer an outline of the methods most likely to elicit the information needed to apply a developmental attachment model to assessment and intervention with children and families. The focus is on:

- making enquiries of the files and the wider professional network
- observing
- interviewing parents and children.

Each of these three strands is explored in relation to gathering information that will assist in making sense of children and their parents in terms of the four basic attachment patterns.

Making Enquiries

Mastering the file records

Reading files is a central part of all childcare practice. Because, within this model, we are interested in patterns of behaviour and relationships, it is essential that files are used to identify indicators of relationship style, particularly in terms of parenting over time. When looking at relationships, it is necessary to examine the past and present histories of parents and children in as much detail as possible. In particular, there is a need to ensure that children's developmental histories are fully looked at. Attempts have to be made to find ways of appreciating how children experience different caregiving environments and relationships at each stage of their childhood.

Examinations of the file records need to identify the patterns of separation, loss and change experienced by children. Histories of abuse or neglect, or critical incidents such as injuries, illnesses and accidents, often show connections with other events. They might provide a barometer of family functioning. For parents who have had other children, details of the whereabouts and well-being of those children need to be known. Serious histories of abuse in the parents' own childhoods also need to be noted and connections made. These are not new ideas but they are often disregarded. For example, although much was known of Ruth Neave's history, the powerful links between extreme childhood deprivation and disturbance, and current relationships was not given the weight it needed in the assessments made (Cambridgeshire County Council 1997). One of the great difficulties for social workers is that it can seem as if all parents have difficult backgrounds, and it is problematic to know what kinds of experiences and relationship history to pay particular attention to.

Vera

Vera, a 25-year-old mother of three boys under the age of 3, had been sexually assaulted during her teenage years by her adoptive father. This was clearly so disturbing and seemed such an obvious key to her difficulties that little attention was paid to her early history. However,

> when files were obtained from earlier in her childhood, it became
> clear that as a very young girl she had been neglected, sexually abused
> and frightened. Her insensitive parenting behaviour actually made
> more sense in terms of this early experience of extreme rejection.

This mother's unresolved feelings from her early childhood needed
to be understood not only to appreciate the emotional risk posed for
her own children, but also to work with her in a more compas-
sionate fashion.

Information from other agencies

To grasp the full picture of what is happening in the life of a particular
child, social workers need to draw heavily on information provided
by other professionals. This information often appears as reports to
meetings and conferences by health professionals, teachers and
others. Useful though this can be, it relies on the other professionals
selecting information that they feel to be relevant. Social workers
using an attachment model need to explain to other professionals the
kind of detail needed, particularly information about early childhood
experiences. From this, it can be argued that face-to-face discussions
between the responsible social worker and other key agency workers,
such as health visitors and teachers, should occur at times when a
thorough assessment of a case is required, whether this is a new
referral, court proceedings or a long-term 'stuck' case.

The pattern of parents' involvement with other agencies is another
important source of information. There are very often patterns of use
of agencies and patterns of relationship with agency workers that are
themselves indicative of relationship style and the individual's
internal working model. One parent had made many phone calls to the
police, another parent had taken children to the doctor's on numerous
occasions, another issued frequent complaints – all of these behaviours may not be evidence of parenting in the usual sense, but they are
sites of evidence in relation to the parents' internal working model
and relationship style. Here, as elsewhere, it may be process rather
than content that is significant. It might not be so much the content of
the phone call or the nature of the complaint but the fact that it was

made, at that time, and that a particular meaning was given to it by the person involved. Parents act out emotionally in their relationships with agencies and their workers. The access of agencies to resources and the potential for being available or not available, responsive or rejecting, places agencies in a parent-like role which provokes powerful, unconscious reactions.

Observation of parents and children

One of the most powerful and most underused methods of gathering information is observation. Because the internal working model is played out in all aspects of behaviour, observation is essential for creating the necessary detailed picture. So much of the information we need to make sense of the quality of relationships and caregiving environment can only be gained by observation of the family's physical environment, the interactions between family members and the impact of those interactions on the individual, parent or child. Seeing how parents manage stress and anxiety will be particularly significant. Relationships reveal themselves in subtle behaviours, even when certain other parenting behaviours may be grabbing our attention. In practice, for example in cases of physical abuse, paying attention to the subtleties when there are more obvious behaviours causing concern is often difficult to achieve and defend, even when they may be the key to the persistence of problems.

Observational skills and the sites that need to be observed are considered under the following seven headings:

- observational skills
- the physical environment
- non-verbal behaviour
- verbal communication
- parental consistency
- parental sensitivity and availability
- the observation of children in other settings.

Observational skills

Observation is a practice skill in itself and one which is rarely given specific attention. It requires sensitivity to the detail of actions and interactions, to the nuances of facial expression and body language. To understand the nature of relationships, we need to take account not only of the behaviour of individuals, but also of the cycle of action and reaction between each participant in the 'dance' of a relationship encounter, over a mealtime, perhaps, or during the social worker's visit. The timing of approaches and responses, the tone of voice and the use of eye contact can indicate parental availability and sensitivity, rejection and hostility, or intrusiveness – all important indicators of attachment style and the quality of caregiving. The child's ability or inability to express needs appropriately and achieve parental availability and concern will also be apparent only by making close observations.

What is observed is actual *behaviour*. Behaviour indicates feelings that affect the quality of the relationship. Saying that a parent is 'hostile' or a child is 'sad' is based on an interpretation of the behaviours observed.

One mother presented as lively and engaging, and was often described as bubbly and fun-loving. She herself talked with great passion about her concern for her children and had caused difficulties in their schooling by moving them around because 'the teachers weren't good enough'. However, the pattern of observed behaviour during an extended visit over a lunchtime was of a woman who was preoccupied with her own emotional entanglements and had what was only a passing awareness of or interest in her children's well-being. Her children, aged 7 and 10, asked on numerous occasions for food and were ignored. She was emotionally unavailable and insensitive to their needs.

Observational skills do not rely simply on the ability to note specific behaviours. The fact that a parent *appears* to the observer to be unresponsive to a child could be due to a number of factors, including physical illness, depression and an insecure attachment style. It could even result from the observer's own expectations of an appropriate level of stimulation based on personal experience as a parent. Similarly, the child could be unresponsive or overdemanding because of a relationship problem or because of a specific stress on that occasion. Undeniably, much information will be open to interpretation. This demands both self-awareness and the capacity to look for evidence, using theory and research to explain it. The Tavistock model offers a good example of how to observe a child (Miller *et al.* 1989; Bridge and Miles 1996). The model emphasises learning to make sense of the world of the subject both through applying theory and through developing self-awareness.

Families at home are likely to find it difficult simply to be observed by the social worker. In practice, most observation is likely to take place during interviews with parents or the family. This makes it more of a challenge to note the reactions of the parents to the children or their reactions to each other. In some situations, it can be helpful or necessary to do joint visits in order to make assessments. This allows practitioners to pick up more of the detail. Whatever the circumstances, time needs to be taken to note down what has been observed in as much detail as possible. Links can then be made with the major dimensions of parenting such as the availability and sensitivity of the caregivers. It may not always be immediately apparent what is actually going on, and instant conclusions are to be resisted. The practice model should be that of formulating and testing hypotheses over time and against subsequent information.

The physical environment

Features of the physical environment as well as the behavioural indicators of the emotional and relationship environment will often be as significant for the assessment as is verbal communication. How it feels to be a parent or a child in this family will reflect and be reflected in the care of the house, mealtimes and whether there is bedding on the beds, as well as in whether parents feel in control of or are available to their children. The *physical environment* gives clues not just in terms of the care that is taken, but also in terms of the relationship environment and the more subtle messages given to children.

In one family, where there was a query about Münchausen's syndrome by proxy, there was observed to be a vegetable rack full of sweets that was in view of the two young children, aged 3 and 6, but kept out of reach. There were also stairgates at every door. The mother's apparent wish for control of the children was matched by an inclination, almost certainly unconscious, to provoke them. In this same household, the mother, who had been sexually abused herself, expressed fear of the children being sexually abused. Yet she was an agent for a catalogue of sexually provocative clothing and had parties in the home to sell the goods.

Non-verbal behaviour

Even the first step into the family home can provide useful information about the internal working model of the parent and the way in which this affects the quality of care given to the child and the child's emotional and behavioural strategies for dealing with it. A simple question to the social worker about what happens when she knocks on the door can produce a very revealing account of observed behaviour.

Maria, the mother, did not get up to answer the door but seemed to sit as if fixed to her chair in a room where curtains were often left drawn. Around her and even on her lap were children who were trying to get her attention in some way, to produce some kind of emotional response or indeed interest in them.

This image is powerful. It suggests something very important about the way in which Maria operates as a parent. In the subsequent research interview, it became clear that she was still closely involved with her own parents and spent most of her available energy preoccupied with the need to please them. Although the idea of being a mother was important to her, she was in practice unable to see her children as people with needs of their own. This included being unable to recognise the needs of her deaf child: she had not learned sign language because she had some erroneous idea that he might be able to hear one day. She rarely attempted to control her children, but when they were not with her, she was strong in expressions of love for them. For example, she was strongly disapproving of how the foster carers were caring for her teenage son, whom she had refused to have at home. Her mix of passivity and unpredictability as a parent and overinvolvement with her own parents is highly characteristic of an entangled or preoccupied attachment style.

The children's behaviour is also worth noting. Two-year-old Sally was intermittently passive and demanding, yet she was clearly highly preoccupied by her relationship with her mother. She was unable to play appropriately. Over time, as would be predicted in an ambivalent–resistant child, her behaviour became increasingly coercive, and it seemed likely that she would follow in the footsteps of her much older brothers and become aggressive and volatile. This observation needed to be seen in the context of other information but was in itself a helpful key to further exploration.

Verbal communication

Careful observations need to be made of the verbal exchanges between parents and children in terms of *content, choice of language* and *tone*. For example, speech to young children may be too adult in its language, or the tone may be aggressive and hostile. Such characteristics of parental communication effectively distance the child from the parent and are typical of a dismissing caretaking style in which the parent is uncomfortable with the demands made by the child. The parent may superficially be responding appropriately to the child's attachment behaviour, but the language and tone give the message 'I'm not available. Look after your own needs.' The child is likely then actively to reject subsequent offers of food or care and become increasingly self-reliant.

Where language from parent to child is apparently affectionate, perhaps sentimental in tone, but then shifts for no apparent reason into a complaining, rejecting, demanding or angry tone, the child becomes unable to trust the communication. Observation of the parents' overt expression of affection and the child's response to the initial approach by the parent may inform the observer about the quality of the relationship. The child may respond in the hope or expectation that the parent is genuinely expressing affection or may show a mistrust of this behaviour.

What is particularly harmful is inconsistency between the tone and the language, for example a caring tone and rejecting content, or vice versa. Alternatively, the messages can be so confusing that even older children find it difficult to respond or defend themselves. The following conversation was observed to take place between 15-year-old Jerry and his grandmother, with whom he was living following a row with his mother:

> Jerry's grandmother said, 'Would you like to come on holiday with us?' No reply from Jerry. 'You can't come on holiday with us because your behaviour would ruin the holiday for everyone. Well? Do you want to come or not? You can't say you haven't been given the chance.'

Jerry knew he had no real choice, and the confusing message at both a cognitive and emotional level was part of a family pattern that also characterised his relationship with his mother. Jerry's response was initially a startled, upset silence. He froze temporarily on this occasion, but the tension the conversation created for him and his sense of powerlessness to defend himself against such emotional assaults contributed to his sudden and violent outbursts.

When these confusing parental messages are linked with abuse, it is probable that the child will be unable to adopt any defensive strategy. The most obvious example of this would be the communication in sexual abuse cases that the child is the most loved child, yet the child is being traumatised by the abuse and threats to ensure silence. Although observation will not necessarily reveal the full nature of these damaging relationships, it is sometimes possible to observe that mix of 'special' affection with a sense of menace in the tone of voice and the pattern of parenting behaviour towards a particular child. Where children are receiving messages either verbally or non-verbally that are frightening and/or simply do not make sense, their own behaviours and verbal communications are distinctive. Such children may be extremely tentative or placatory. On the other hand, however, they may be extremely demanding and aggressive, as if provoking and defying the parent to act. They may also freeze, a characteristic response of many disorganised children.

Parental consistency

As with confusing or inconsistent verbal communication, inconsistent or uncertain parental behaviour can leave children confused and unsure of what or who to believe in their attempts to achieve proximity. If inconsistency is associated with levels of rejection that amount to emotional abuse, the consequences for the child are serious. The observation of such a pattern can give a very real insight into the quality of the emotional environment created by the parent.

Patrick

Patrick, aged 7, was observed at home with his mother and younger sister, aged 2. He repeatedly switched the cassette recorder on and off, playing a few notes of music each time. His mother, Janet, allowed this behaviour to continue for some time. She then told him that if he didn't stop, she would put him outside in the hallway. He carried on in a rather ritualistic manner, not apparently looking for attention. His mother appeared to laugh at his behaviour. After quite a long time switching the cassette recorder on and off, Patrick stopped of his own accord and walked over to the window where he stood quietly. After a while his mother turned to Patrick, suddenly shouting at him at the top of her voice that he was a very naughty boy and she was going to put him in the hall and tell his father what a bad boy he was and his dad would have to do something about him. In the face of his mother's anger, Patrick froze. He was no longer being naughty yet he was to be punished. His mother threatened to put him in the hallway but then did not do it. Patrick stood very still for a while and then, in a desultory way, picked up one of his sister's books. At that point, his mother flew at him and put him in the hallway, laughing and saying that that would teach him to touch his sister's things. Patrick could be heard crying outside the door.

From Patrick's point of view, here was a situation in which he simply could not predict what was going to happen. He could not prevent or protect himself from his mother's anger. The person who should have been the source of comfort was a source of fear, confusion and rejection. He showed symptoms of a disorganised attachment, freezing on the spot but also showing extreme outbursts of anxiety and rage. From his earliest weeks in school, small changes in his routine led to an attack on peers and teachers, to the extent that they required hospital treatment. This observation clarified the way in which frozen behaviour, stored up anger and confusion, can lead to violent outbursts.

Parental sensitivity and availability

Observation is likely to be a particularly powerful way of gauging whether parents are sensitive to their children's signals and physically and emotionally available to meet their children's attachment needs. When the parent is insensitive to signals and does not keep a space for the child in his or her mind (Winnicott, D. 1964), the child as a person is ignored and the child's signals are not listened to or taken into account.

Jane

Jane was observed during a visit to the paediatric ward to feed her 10-week-old baby, Liam, who was failing to gain weight. She was late arriving, and Liam was crying and in distress. Jane entered the ward and talked to some other mothers before approaching Liam. She was told that he was hungry and needed feeding urgently. She then very slowly started to change his nappy, glancing round the ward at other people as she did so but not at Liam. Liam continued to cry. Eventually, she picked Liam and the bottle up, then put him rather roughly across her shoulder when she realised that someone was putting up a new picture on the wall at the far end of the ward. Liam continued to cry. She wandered slowly down to talk to the person. By this time, about 15 minutes had passed. Eventually, a nurse suggested she really must feed Liam. Jane looked angry but wandered over to a chair and sat down to feed her baby.

It is only through this kind of observation that it is possible to capture the lack of emotional connection and the sense of desperation experienced by the baby. Throughout the whole episode, Jane failed to engage with Liam as a person. She did not attempt to soothe him or acknowledge his distress. She handled him very much like an object.

It was as if Jane was mentally somewhere else, not seeing in the baby what the observer was seeing. The point is perhaps best made by contrasting this interaction with the available parenting offered by the foster carer who subsequently looked after Liam.

Liam

Just after the observer arrived, Liam woke up in his bedroom and cried out. The foster carer immediately called out to him by name, and, as she walked towards the bedroom, she continued to talk to him to reassure him that she was coming . His crying diminished in intensity when he heard her voice. She changed him quickly before feeding him but talked to him throughout the nappy change, stroking him, putting her face and smile clearly in his vision and telling him that she was just going to feed him. After only 7 days in this placement, Liam was engaging in 'conversations', getting physically excited and showing interest in his environment. Emotionally, he was being clearly held in the interaction with the carer.

Both the change in Liam and the difference in the quality of the care-giving could only be fully described and understood by close observation. The foster carer was not just available to the child: she was also offering him an emotional and cognitive scaffolding to enable him to cope with the separation of waking up alone and the distress of waiting to be fed. His birth mother's behaviour, on the other hand, suggested that she was unable to see the world through his eyes – he barely existed in her consciousness. This was an intelligent, highly articulate mother with a traumatic early history of abuse and neglect.

Observation of children in other settings

Children's relationships with adults and peers outside the home can provide further evidence of their attachment style. For younger children in particular, observation in playgroups and nurseries is helpful in noting similarities to and differences from their behaviour in family settings.

Evidence of resilience may be apparent in the quality of children's play and their relationships with peers, particularly in terms of children's self-esteem and self-efficacy. Seeing children in different contexts allows for the observation of such things as their strategies for dealing with stress and distress, and the way in which children approach or fail to approach adults and other children for help. Other competencies that may not be evident at home, such as the ability to concentrate or negotiate, also help in the evaluation of children's developmental status.

Interviews

Interviewing parents

An attachment perspective requires social workers to be interested in parents in terms of not just their current parenting role, but also their sense of self and experiences of other past and present relationships. It is not sufficient simply to say, 'I am only interested in children.' The welfare of children is inextricably bound up with the welfare of the parents. We need to move away from fears that expressing an interest in the parents may mean losing the focus on the child. It is essential to understand parents' own sense of self and the quality of their relationships.

Content: self and relationships, past and present

Information about parents' own backgrounds and childhoods has been a traditional part of the social worker's assessment. Here, however, we are looking for information that illuminates the internal working model by showing patterns over the parents' lifespan. Just as the quality of other current relationships can illuminate the parent–child relationship, so stories and memories from the past can provide powerful keys to understanding present difficulties. These memories could be traumatic, such as of being sexually abused. Alternatively, they could be something less acute, such as a chronic history of perceived coldness and distance between parent and child that has caused the person who is now a mother to adopt a rejecting caregiving style. The content of parental histories needs to be looked at critically for evidence of both specific events and relationship patterns. Certain patterns are particularly relevant, such as those involving memories of the perceived availability of attachment figures and threats of separation. One mother gave this example during an interview:

> My mum was never there – out partying, drinking, socialising, sneaking off with her new boyfriend whatever… She'd think nothing of being in a queue of traffic with us and my dad in the car. She'd had enough of us kids. She'd get out of the car and walk away.

This mother's present view of self as a result of such relationship experiences is:

> I'm very scarred. Very insecure. Very lacking in knowing where I'm going and how to cope with it. Still needing to talk to somebody, anybody, just to help me.

In her present role as a parent, her reaction to stress includes threatening to or actually leaving her children. Her own awareness and even specific memory of the anxiety caused by separations has not prevented her from feeling despair and resorting to abandonment as a method of coping. These responses are not free, rational choices but are driven by the need to defend against anxiety in whatever way appears to have best aided survival in childhood.

The couple's relationship needs to be explored in interviews both because of what it reveals about the parents' separate attachment styles and because the combination will have an immediate impact on their parenting. If we think, for example, of couples where there is a dismissing father and an entangled mother, both will struggle with ways of responding to the normal emotional demands of children. The storms that break out between them as a couple may also put the child at risk. More specifically, however, the mother's parenting style leaves the child anxious and with attachment behaviour that is hyperactivated. Increasing attachment behaviour in such children is the very behaviour most likely to cause the father to feel highly anxious and to respond with rejection, departure from the family or, in some cases, violence.

What we can learn from the use of the AAI is to ask specific questions about self, others and relationships and then follow them up in ways that might seem rather more detailed and even persistent than the usual interview style. The effect, however, is to *surprise the unconscious*. The responses reveal characteristic ways of dealing with attachment-related concerns.

There are several levels of content to bear in mind. At one level, we have the purely factual: dates of birth of children, family of origin, names, ages, characteristics and so on. This includes events that have happened in the recent past to bring the family into contact with the agency. For an attachment-based model, we also need details about how people *feel* about other family members, past and present, their relationships and the events that led up to the referral. Finally, since the internal working model is essentially a cognitive structure, we need to explore what *ideas* parents have about other people and what is happening– *why* they believe events happened as they did or relationships turned out in a particular way. What did your mother do when you misbehaved? How did it make you feel? Why did she do this, do you think? Why did you feel the way you felt? Do these feelings or behaviours recur in your current parenting role? Because so much of the dynamic of relationships is driven by unconscious processes, the links between people, events, feelings and ideas may not be clear at an early stage, either to the parent or to the worker. It is often necessary to continue to talk and explore before new information and some kind of sense begins to emerge.

The idea of *evidence* is familiar to social workers preparing assessments. It is also relevant in the present model where we need to get past the superficial telling of a family story. Within any interview where there is an interest in relationships, it is essential to ask for specific examples of feelings and experiences that people have in particular relationships. Where parents offer general descriptions of relationships with 'loving' or 'hateful' parents or with 'wonderful' or 'impossible' children, there needs to be a further exploration. The apparently simple question to one father, 'Which five words would you use to describe your relationship with your father?, produced the answer: 'fear, revulsion, guilt, anger, misunderstanding'. He was able to give examples of incidents that supported these adjectives. In contrast, a mother described her relationship with her own mother as 'loving', but, when asked for detail, she talked of the fact that she could never please her mother and that her mother preferred her siblings. It is important to stress that such words alone do not give us the basis for an attachment categorisation, but they provide a starting point for a detailed examination and discussion of how that relationship was experienced.

Process

One of the important aspects of an interview apart from the content is the process, not just *what* is talked about but *how* it is talked about. In any interview, it is clear that the way in which the story is told, the pattern of story-telling and the use of language will be giving an additional source of information about the person who is telling the story. For example, is the account brief, lacking in detail and remembered feelings? Is it long and detailed but incoherent and inconsistent? Was the parent's own childhood objectively very difficult, yet the parent talks about it in a way that suggests that he or she has an appropriate recall of feelings and has been able to reflect on childhood matters and resolve any associated affect?

A mother talking of her relationship with her stepmother, said:

> I was terrified of her. I still am, as old as I am now I am still terrified of her. I still feel sick when I get anywhere near that house but I love her.

Her feelings of distress in childhood remain unresolved. Her fear is as real now as it was when she was a girl, yet she talks of loving her stepmother. When she mentions trying to meet her stepmother's standards, the interviewer asked for examples:

> Oh silly things – but they weren't silly things when you were a child. You couldn't go to the toilet in the morning before your bed was made... I used to sleep on the top bunk and you couldn't just make your bed, it had to be done in a certain way, hospital corners and the sheet had to be dead straight in the middle of the bed and meet in the middle underneath the mattress and everything was precision and if it wasn't then the mattress would be stripped off the bed and you would have to start again... And you'd get a good beating into the bargain.

Such examples and the way in which they are told give us an insight into the quality of the memory and the vividness of the feelings. They also demonstrate the difficulty for this mother of resolving the feelings of distress and trauma experienced in her childhood. They explain how, in adult life, she is preoccupied with relationships but finds herself unable to trust, alternately expressing devotion to and rejection of her children.

Interviews and face-to-face work with children

Time spent with children on their own, talking, listening and engaging them in structured activity, is a necessary part of gathering information. It offers workers the opportunity to explore children's reality, their view of their world and their place within it. As with interviews with parents, these sessions with children should be focused and purposeful. They should be acceptable and supportive to the child but designed to maximise the amount of information about the child that is revealed. Research interviews with children have taught us that structured sessions with skilled workers who use age-appropriate materials to explore the child's world can be very informative, even with very troubled children. As with the AAIs, it seems that research instruments, suitably adapted, might play a useful part in information gathering and assessment.

Content: self and others

The aim of the interview with the child is to learn how children mentally represent themselves and others. This is likely to emerge in response to simple questions, most usually related to some shared practical activity such as producing a visual picture of the child and his or her family relationships. Jane, aged 11, said, 'My Mum can't look after me. I don't blame her. I was really naughty.' Dawn, a 5-year-old girl also separated from her mother, said, 'My mother is the best mother in the world, she's lovely. She never lets us down. She says that when she wins the lottery she is going to buy us lots of things.' Dawn's mother was a drug user who had left her and her sister alone on a number of occasions. What Dawn is offering the worker is one part of her mental representation of the world. She is defending herself against the distress of acknowledging her mother's inability to care for her. She 'splits' off the negative views of her mother and allows only positive thoughts to enter her consciousness. At some level, she also blames her 'bad' foster carers for keeping her apart from her mother.

Children may be thought to be confused or not meaning what they say when there is such a disparity between reality and their expressed views. Yet a knowledge of children's perceptions, the meaning they attribute to events and people, will be as significant in an assessment as a knowledge of the objective reality. Dawn was not challenged on the reality of her account of her mother and, later in the same session, was able to tell the 'Wise Hedgehog' puppet about her greatest fear, that her mother would die. This unexpectedly revealing response in the context of an otherwise artificially jolly presentation shows how effective the use of different materials can be with children. As with the AAI, useful information from interviews with children can be gained by 'surprising the unconscious', but the means need to be developmentally appropriate.

Understanding children's view of the world will of course require workers to be familiar with normal patterns of cognitive development and how these affect the sense of self and self-esteem in childhood. Preschool children, for example, will not have a global sense of self-worth that can be articulated. Instead, their self-esteem is likely to be manifested in their behaviour and play (Harter 1983). The nature and character of what children say needs to be thought about in the context of their developmental history.

Materials

The materials used with children should also be adapted to their developmental stage. For preschool children, play materials that encourage discussion about feelings and family members will be important, although not all young children will be capable of naming feelings and this has to checked first, perhaps by using drawings of faces or dolls with happy and sad faces and linking these to appropriate situations. Four-year-olds and older can be given 'projective stories' or 'story stem completion tests' (see Chapter 3). Although these 'tests' are mainly used by researchers in developmental psychology, their use, suitably adapted, can aid social workers in gathering information highly valuable for assessment purposes.

More familiar strategies in practice and research with school-age children include the ecomap (Fahlberg 1994) and other visual ways of describing and discussing families, schools, friends, feelings and so on. Visual images of relationships, such as charts, are often less threatening than asking children to put thoughts and feelings into words.

Although, with adolescents, the balance will shift from practical materials to conversation, visual prompts or materials can still be helpful in getting conversation going. At this age, however, because of cognitive developments in adolescence, it is more likely that young people will be able to reflect, and reflect in more abstract terms, on themselves, their relationships and their memories of early childhood. They will also be starting to tackle ideas about themselves as future adults.

Rebecca

Seven-year-old Rebecca drew a star chart of significant people in her life. When she was asked if she had included all her family, she became anxious because she realised that she had not included her father. She took some time to place him and settled on putting him right on the edge, half on and half off the paper. Although she had not seen her father for over a year, the fear of him lingered just below the surface.

Process

As the example of Dawn above demonstrates, even within one session, there can be a process as the child uses the materials over time in the context of a relationship with the worker. Each session with children of all ages must first allow the child the chance to see that the worker is there to listen and learn. However, even activities that are planned to build rapport with the child can be designed not only to communicate that the worker is interested in everything that the child wishes to say, but also to elicit information relevant to the developmental assessment and understanding of the child's relationship style. One 10-year-old boy, when offering a physical description of himself for a shared drawing, said, 'I've got green eyes. I'm the only one in the family to have the same colour eyes as my dad.' The significance of this glimpse into his story about himself can be noted and explored later in the session in terms of what he thinks and feels about the link with his father and areas of difference from his siblings.

Even very disturbed children with histories of abuse and neglect, who show clear signs of disorganised attachments, can cooperate in a play- and drawing material-based interview. For some children, evidence of their anxieties or defensive strategies will appear in glimpses. In the middle of an otherwise ordinary account of which school subjects a child likes and dislikes might come an extreme account of violent conflict and fear of peers, siblings or parents. A view of a frightening internal world is momentarily revealed. For other children, it is probable that conclusions about their attachment style will emerge from the process of the interview as much as the content.

James and Brian

James, a 10-year-old foster child, had violently killed ten chickens during his last visit to his mother at his grandfather's farm. Throughout the interview, he was polite and co-operative, and managed to sustain a reasonable level of concentration. He was, however, quite unable to respond fully to questions about feelings, giving either very short answers or repeatedly saying, 'I don't know'.

Brian, an 8-year-old boy, stared out of the window when asked about family members and went into a dreamy, trance-like state, talking rather bizarrely about magical animals.

Scheurer-English (cited in Grossmann and Grossmann 1991) suggests that short or absent answers are more typical of insecure children, while strange, inappropriate answers are more typical of children with an early ambivalent relationship. However, what seems particularly helpful in thinking about the interview process is that, in the research, the child's behaviour was itself indicative:

> The social behaviour of the children towards the interviewer was significantly related to early attachment quality. Insecure children were more often either openly ignoring to the point of impoliteness or overly close, inappropriately intimate, even seeking close bodily contact to the visitor. (Grossmann and Grossmann 1991: 106)

Evidence of certain aspects of resilience may also be apparent in this kind of focused work with children on self and relationships. Fonagy *et al.* (1994) outline the importance of the child's capacity to reflect upon mental states. A child who can think about and make sense of his or her own thoughts *and* make sense of what other people think will also be able to make the best use of the individuals available to him or her, including friends. Closely linked to the capacity to reflect upon mental states is the capacity for pretence. This ability to entertain a belief while at the same time knowing it to be false can be seen in its primitive stages in toddlers playing 'pretend' with toy people and animals. Fonagy *et al.* (1991b: 892) explain that, in a developed form, the capacity for pretence can provide a buffer in life:

The capacity to suspend the demands of immediate physical reality and contemplate alternative perceptions yet retaining the distinction between what is fantasised and what is real must offer a tremendous advantage to the individual in dealing with life's adversities.

Conclusion

This outline of some of the issues involved in gathering information highlights the need for an integrated but multimethod approach. Information from files needs to be thought about alongside observational material and the content and process of interviews. After observations or interviews with parents or children, the worker is likely to be left with a range of feelings. These feelings of liking or anxiety, of irritation or concern, need to be explored as further evidence of how the parent or the child operates in relationships. Reflection within supervision is needed to make full sense of this kind of 'information'. For example, if the worker feels overwhelmed by a child's unmet needs, it is worth considering how that child is experiencing, defending against and surviving his or her personal situation.

Each small piece of information, whether it is a file note or an interview, provides a piece of the jigsaw. The jigsaw pieces will vary from factual information to perceptions of and attributions given to events. The puzzle will never be entirely complete, but the aim of the process is to have enough pieces in place in order to see something of the picture and the patterns – and then to move on to the analysis.

9

Analysing, assessing and classifying the information

During the course of their work, social workers accumulate a great deal of information about individual cases. They know a lot about family members' behaviours, concerns and relationships. Much of what is known is the result of direct observation – always a powerful source of information – in 'natural' settings such as the home, playgroup or school. The previous chapter outlined how such information can be gathered and collected systematically. However, information in itself does not help the social worker to explain or understand what is happening. Before facts can be used for explanatory effect, they need to be organised by theory. Developmental attachment theory offers clear guidelines on how to theorise facts. The theory suggests how information and observations might be arranged and ordered to help practitioners make sense of people and their relationships.

We have already seen how an attachment and relationship perspective helps social workers to *describe* what they see and know. Chapters 4–7 provided a fourfold framework of attachment patterns for *classifying* the information gathered. The task now facing us is *to classify the descriptions* of children's and parents' behaviours, emotional needs and relationship styles into one of the four attachment status groups. In other words, we need to organise what we know using attachment theory. We need to add theory to fact, conceptual order to what would otherwise be miscellaneous description. To the extent that this is successful, it should reveal deep regularities in the way in which parents and children behave, feel and relate.

The assessment process is based on marshalling and analysing the information known at the time. Assessments should be seen as ongoing as new facts become available, although there will be a need formally to present analyses at case planning meetings, case conferences and courts. The steps taken in the analysis of case material are guided by attachment-related issues and the mental representations that make up individuals' internal working models. At the end of the analysis, the practitioner hypothesises the possible internal working model and its associated pattern of attachment for each key individual. This aids practitioners in developing working understandings of family members so that their behaviours, feelings and relationships make some provisional sense.

In all cases, there will be a dynamic interaction between *past* and *present* experiences. Over time, social workers learn a great deal about people's past and present behaviours. The analysis will therefore need to explore and hypothesise possible connections between past relationship experiences and current psychosocial states. In practice, the essence of the assessment is captured by answering three questions (Mayseless 1996: 214):

- How does this person handle attachment-relevant issues?
- How is the self viewed and internalised?
- How are others viewed and internalised?

Expanded versions of these three questions give us the information upon which the analysis takes place. The information gathered about each individual's past and present behaviours, feelings and relationships is reviewed, analysed and assessed under the following eight headings:

1. statement of main concerns, problems, needs and, if suspected, type of maltreatment
2. description of the individual's appearance, health, material circumstances and environmental stressors
3. relationship and attachment history, including descriptions and memories of family and childhood relationships
4. mental representations of the self
5. mental representation of others
6. types of attachment behaviour
7. quality of caregiving
8. defence mechanisms.

Based on an analysis and assessment of the individual's history, behaviours, relationship styles and personality, a provisional hypothesis is made of his or her probable attachment pattern and internal working model (Table 9.1). Understanding the individual's attachment behaviour helps practitioners to make sense of what is happening in terms of behaviour, relationships and family life.

Further information and observations will confirm or disconfirm the working hypothesis.

Table 9.1 Assessment and attachment classification

Assessment categories	Secure–autonomous	Avoidant–dismissing	Ambivalent–precoccupied	Disorganised–unresolved
Statements of main concerns				
Appearance, health and environment				
Relationship and attachment history				
Mental representations of self				
Mental representations of others				
Attachment behaviours				
Caregiving style				
Defence mechanisms				

An understanding of attachment patterns and their personality correlates also helps practitioners identify the stressors, risk effects, protective effects, and resiliences present in the lives of both children and their parents. This is an important step and will help in the formulation of aims and objectives (see Chapter 11).

Statement of main concerns, problems, needs and type of maltreatment

Although statements can be a fairly descriptive account of the main needs and problem behaviours, the analysis is sensitive to both the type of concern expressed and who expresses that concern. A series of preliminary questions will help to orientate the practitioner towards making a case appraisal (see, for example, Cox 1994: 22; Rutter 1975):

1. What is the amount and nature of the personal distress or suffering?
2. What is the extent of social competences and social activities?
3. What is the restriction of social competences and social activities?
4. To what extent is normal development being interfered with and hindered?
5. What is the effect of the child's behaviour on others?
6. What elements and forces are maintaining the need or problem?
7. What elements and forces are facilitating the child's normal development?
8. What are the strengths and competences of the child and the family?
9. If there is no intervention, what is the likely course of events?

Understanding child welfare concerns depends on recognising the interactions between individual characteristics, past and current relationships, and the qualities of the social and material environments. An attachment classification cannot be based solely on material found in this section, but it might trigger first thoughts that can be tested and revised in the light of further information. For example, reports by health workers that an 18-month-old child of a parent with learning difficulties is very passive and has limited vocalisation and poor motor skills might alert the worker to the presence of some form of insecure attachment, possibly of the passive ambivalent (C2) kind reported by researchers. Such children are often observed in cases where there is severe physical neglect, typical of parents whose caring skills are very limited. Young children may lapse into a passive, listless, depressed dependence. In contrast, a parent who threatens to kill herself unless social services 'do something' about her 'out-of-control' aggressive 9-year-old appears to be operating on a non-trusting, attention-seeking, maximised attachment strategy that hints at an adult entangled–preoccupied attachment style.

However, such early thoughts must remain extremely speculative. They merely act as first steps in the assessment process, encouraging practitioners to wonder why a carer might be expressing her anxieties this way rather than that, or why a child of that age has developed a particular set of behaviours under those caregiving conditions. Parents with entangled–preoccupied attachment styles are more likely to self-refer than, for example, carers whose attachment behaviour is more typically dismissing and avoidant, who are more likely to be reported by others as 'a cause for concern'. These are very rough-and-ready thoughts that simply serve to raise the practitioner's curiosity, sharpen her observations and allow her to test out preliminary hypotheses that may well be overturned in the light of new information.

Description of the individual's appearance, health, material environment, living style and possible environmental stressors

We have heard that researchers have identified a number of broad correlations between attachment status and such things as symptomatology, domestic organisation and perceptions and distress in both self and others. In themselves, such observations are not conclusive, but, allied with information gathered elsewhere, they tend to consolidate the social worker's emerging picture of a client's attachment style. For example, preoccupied patterns are often associated with higher rates of declared symptomatology, more personal disorganisation and increased feelings of distress. In contrast, dismissing patterns downplay illness and personal need – life is more ordered, and there is a preference for environments that feel structured and under control.

The final assessment of the following two examples classified one parent as E (enmeshed–preoccupied–uncertain) and the other as Ds (dismissing–avoidant–rejecting) respectively. The following descriptions of typical home visits were made by social workers.

Lorraine, mother of three children: enmeshed–preoccupied behaviours

The doorbell wasn't working so I had to knock hard on the door. Lorraine shouted to let myself in. I tried, but there was a tricycle lying behind the door which I had to climb over. All this commotion set the two dogs barking and they were dashing in and out of the hall getting very excited. This finally roused Lorraine who got out of her chair, yelled at the dogs and dragged them into the kitchen and closed the door to keep them in. She sank back into her chair and lit a cigarette.

She always calls me either 'love' or by a shortened version of my first name, which I hate! Jen instead of Jennifer! Ugh! She says it's because she's got a sister called Jen and I'm a bit like her, so she says… Lorraine is thirty two, smallish, a bit plump, you know, likes wearing sweaters and track suit bottoms. I suppose the house is reasonably clean but it's definitely cluttered. You can't move for CDs on the floor, cups, kids' broken toys, that sort of thing, clothes drying. Anyway, she says she prefers to sit down and not get up for visitors because she's got some kind of back trouble. Generally she has health problems of one kind or another which she puts down to the estate where they live being too close to the river. Too damp, she says. Makes her feel wheezy, chesty. Says she wants to move house… She's generally quite welcoming – on her good days – when she wants something! Always gets one of the kids to make us a cup of coffee.

Alison, mother of 5-year-old Emily: dismissing–avoidant behaviours

Alison prefers to visit me at the office. If I do feel the need to make a home visit I either write or phone to make an appointment. Having said that, the house is fine. Rather discreet taste, I would say. Nice objects arranged nicely. Never any clutter. Everything in its place, if you know what I mean. She is always polite with me but her manner is cool, correct. She says what she has to say but absolutely no more, and I always feel that she can't wait to see the back of me. Emily is a quiet little girl. I don't think I've ever seen her smile. It's hard to understand why Alison feels that she can't cope with her. But there's no denying that Emily is not a very happy little girl. She doesn't have any friends at school and there have been incidents when she has jabbed things like pens and sharp sticks at other girls and injured them. Alison comes across as impatient, confused even. The only time she gets at all animated is when she talks about how she regrets being unable to pursue her career. She says she was determined to make a go of her life and become independent of her family as soon as possible. She was beginning to get promoted in her job as a beautician when she agreed with her partner to have a baby. She now regrets the decision, believing that she was too young and not cut out for being a mother… She's tall. Wears very smart clothes all the time… I know

> she's bulimic, but she wouldn't talk about it. Alison likes to see herself as a coper, you know, independent, that sort. Mind you she does get rattled when things don't run to plan. Then she does lose her cool. Like once, when her partner accidently unplugged the freezer and everything melted, she couldn't believe someone could be so stupid. OK it's annoying, but she couldn't let the subject drop. It really got to her.

Relationship and attachment history, including descriptions and memories of family and childhood relationships

The quality and character of relationships from infancy onwards provide powerful clues to the possible origins of current internal working models, behaviours and interpersonal conduct. Specific instances and concrete examples of parent–child interactions, family incidents and significant events help to support the analysis. Children's personality and attachment styles will be affected by the type of caregiving provided. Caregiving that is and has been neglectful, physically abusive, sexually abusive, rejecting, inconsistent or repeatedly interrupted (multiple serial carers) will greatly increase the risk of children developing an insecure attachment pattern, which in turn increases the risk of later developmental disturbance.

Adults' memories of attachment-related experiences in their own childhoods also provide evidence that aids in developing an understanding of present behaviours and relationships. Analysing adult attachment styles is not simply a matter of recognising whether or not the quality of care experienced in childhood was good. Instead, it is the way in which those memories are being processed in the present that tells us how adults are handling attachment-related issues. For example, people who have suffered abuse in childhood but who are able to access and accurately reflect on the full emotional character of those experiences may well develop a sense of security and autonomy in adult life.

Secure–autonomous patterns

Children and adults who are free to evaluate attachment-related experiences in a balanced, accurate manner are likely to show secure, autonomous attachment styles. Cognitive strengths can be brought to bear to make sense of and understand emotions. Bad as well as good times can be accessed and reflected upon in measured terms. This means that individuals have the ability to deal with the world realistically without too much distortion. This increases the chances of behaviour being appropriate and effective.

Ambivalent–preoccupied patterns

Caregiving that is or has been neglectful, unpredictable and unresponsive often leads individuals to maximise their attachment behaviour and develop a preoccupation with relationships and their availability. Adults who show *preoccupied* patterns become easily absorbed by issues of love and hate when recalling childhood memories. Anxieties over parental availability and love dominate both the past and present. There is an overinvolvement in family relationships and emotional conflict. Uncertainty and ambivalence about other people's interest and responsiveness lower self-esteem. People become preoccupied by and entangled in their close relationships. Accounts are coloured by strong emotions. There is little evidence of the ability to step back, think about and reflect on the nature and origin of feelings and how they might be affecting social interaction. Dependence on others remains high. People appear to be caught up in relationships and seem unable to move beyond them. Joy, a mother of two 'out-of-control' boys, is still preoccupied with doubts about her own parents' emotional availability and whether or not they love her.

Joy

We were always moving house as kids. My mother could never settle anywhere. She'd meet me outside the school gate and say 'Hop in the car. We're moving.' She had lots of boyfriends, too. Mum and Dad were always fighting. Dad was having affairs. Mum was having affairs. I always felt split between the two of them… My mum was never there – out partying, sneaking off with her new boyfriend. She was violent with me. I was always getting the blame, even though she knew I was ill with psoriasis. I used to hate her… I was told I was unplanned, not wanted. Even today she throws that back at me when we're arguing… When I married my first husband, I asked dad to come to the wedding, to heal the feud between him and my mum. My mum and her boyfriend took me to the registry office, but my dad was furious for letting this man, who wasn't my dad, take me to the wedding. My dad said to me 'As far as I'm concerned, you're dead. You are no longer a daughter of mine. I don't want anything to do with you.' And to this day, he's never spoke to me which is 13 years ago now. I've tried writing letters, phoning him, everything, but he won't see me. I still can't talk about him without crying. All I want to do is see my dad and give him a cuddle… I suppose my dad loves me. But my mum doesn't. No way. As long as she's getting what she wants, she's OK… I love my mum immensely, but I hate her so much. I'm very close to my mum. I love her in her own selfish way.

Avoidant–dismissing patterns

Anxiety that others might reject you if you make too heavy a demand on their care leads to an avoidant strategy in which attachment needs are played down and affect is suppressed. People tend to minimise the emotional effects that relationships, both past and present, have on them. In particular, there is an avoidance and dismissal of negative experiences and painful memories – a derogation of attachment-related issues. Vagueness, even idealisation, of parent–child relationships is not untypical. Descriptions of childhood relationship experiences are often terse, underdeveloped with little specific detail. This apparent detached attitude to relationships is described as disengaged or 'dismissing'. Individuals such as Jim described below see themselves as strong, independent, able to cope with adversity and untroubled by feelings of distress in either themselves or others.

Jim

Jim is 45 years old and married to Maggie, who is 10 years younger. He is a stepfather to her two very behaviourally difficult young adolescent boys. He would like to administer severe physical discipline, but it never seems to work and only makes matters worse. He describes his own childhood relationship with his mother as 'distant' but claims that this has not affected him. 'Being the eldest, I was just left to get on with things. My parents used to go off down the pub most nights leaving me to look after the little ones.' His father was very strict with him. There was much physical discipline. Even now, Jim says he feels scared of his father. He has never felt close to him. He finds it extremely difficult to talk about his father: his words seem to choke in his mouth. 'It's easier to put him completely out of my mind.' Jim left school and joined the Air Force as a technician. 'I liked it there. You knew exactly where you were and what was expected of you.'

Disorganised–unresolved patterns

Close relationships have been experienced as unsafe and frightening. Proximity to others has and may continue to arouse feelings of distress and confusion, sometimes leading to fear and anger, sometimes sinking people into helplessness and despair. Adults who appear to be easily disturbed by old memories may still be caught up in *unresolved* childhood traumas and losses. The unresolved experiences usually involve the physical or psychological loss of an attachment figure, or the infliction of severe physical or sexual abuse. Talk about past attachment relationships can be difficult and confused, incoherent and disorganised. Fears, phobias and guilt intrude into and easily disturb current functioning without any obvious triggers. Psychological disorganisation becomes most pronounced in situations of distress and relationship difficulty. The feelings of despair and helplessness when faced with situations that activate attachment needs, such a being a parent, are graphically illustrated by Tracey.

Tracey

Tracey experienced severe neglect as a child. Her father sexually abused her over a number of years. 'She has been unable to deal with this trauma, which still flashes into her mind', reports her social worker. Tracey is functioning very poorly in adult life. She is now 36 years old, overweight, has a history of drug misuse, suffers 'self-induced fits' and shows very poor personal hygiene. She loves animals and in her small flat keeps a zoo of guinea pigs, birds, hamsters and a dog. Her first two children were adopted as babies. Efforts were made to help her keep her third child, a boy named Frankie. She tried to strangle him at birth. When she did not feel well, Frankie would be left for days totally neglected. She regularly left him with unreliable friends while she disappeared for several days. Tracey also has a violent, unpredictable temper and found caring for Frankie very stressful and distressing. As a result, Frankie suffered physical and emotional abuse. Periods of short-term foster care were eventually followed by permanent placement with long-term foster carers when Frankie was 5 years old. In the early years, Frankie showed high levels of disturbed behaviour – aggression with peers, vandalism, nightmares, hearing voices telling him to do 'bad things', and drawing pictures full of violence, gore and death. He also suffers bad eczema.

Mental representations of the self

Internal working models are cognitive structures in which the individual mentally represents the self, others and relationships. These representations form in the context of close attachment relationships during early childhood.

The caregiver's responses convey how the self is regarded by others, particularly in times of need, distress and raised affect. Thus, the quality of relationship with the caregiver has a profound bearing on the child's understanding of self: Am I loved? Am I of interest? Is there concern about how I feel? Can I influence other people's availability and responsiveness? Am I cared for? How do I appear to affect other people? The result is that the self is represented either positively or negatively (Figure 9.1).

Positive +	Negative –
1. Lovable	1. Unlovable
2. Worthy	2. Unworthy, unvalued
3. Interesting	3. Uninteresting
4. Effective	4. Bad, evil
5. Autonomous	5. Ineffective
	6. Dependent

Figure 9.1   Internal working model: representations of self

Secure–autonomous patterns

Self-esteem is moderate to high. The self is viewed as lovable, likable and of interest to others. At times of need, care and attention are provided. Social understanding is sound and is associated with a broad feeling of being socially and practically effective (self-efficacy). There is confidence in the self. There is a sense of personal autonomy – a self that is not at the mercy of strong feelings or the whim of others. The combined effect of these positive characteristics is a robust, competent, constructive self that copes well with setbacks and moderate adversity.

Ambivalent–preoccupied patterns

The inconsistent, unpredictable love and interest of caregivers means that the self is experienced as inherently not very lovable, unworthy and of no great interest. Self-esteem is therefore low. The lack of synchrony and attunement with carers means that children find it difficult to get others to recognise, understand and respond to their needs. Attachment behaviour operates at maximum in an attempt to gain other people's attention. The self is experienced as socially ineffective. Self-reflexivity is poor. Dependence is high and autonomy low. Feelings are difficult to suppress; other people's reactions have a powerful affect on individuals' emotional states. For example, feelings of low self-esteem and a sense of unworthiness and ineffectuality are described by Sheila, the mother of two disruptive adolescent boys.

Sheila

I can stay angry with my mother and sister but not my children... I can't stand up for myself. I generally let people walk all over me. I think that it's because I'm frightened that if I say no, they will think she doesn't want to do this or that; she's no good... I can't say no to my mum and dad... even if it puts me ten miles out of my way. I worry that if I refuse they'll think I don't love them, but I do, very much. My mum is the hardest to please. I think I did please her once, when I had Jamie, when he was born. It was her first grandchild... My mum has always seemed to me more for my sister and my brother... She had that little bit more time for them than me. I felt very hurt. There were times when I felt that I didn't belong to this family. I must be adopted... I'm fairly easy with the children but they do wind me up. They laugh if I say anything to them and I just hate that. It makes me feel as if I'm inadequate, not doing my job right.

Avoidant–dismissing patterns

The self is seen as strong and independent, although esteem is fragile: self-worth and self-confidence can be surprisingly low. Experiences of rejection or care that feels distant, reluctant or reserved raise doubts about the value and likability of the self. Only when the self is under emotional control and performing well does the individual feel confident, accepted and valued. It is more comfortable to engage people factually, cerebrally, than emotionally. Autonomy feels easier than intimacy. Self-containment and emotional self-sufficiency are not only preferred, but are also regarded as strengths. The self is achievement orientated.

Eric

Eric sees himself as strong, independent, 'even bloody-minded'. 'I'm very stubborn and won't budge. It takes an awful lot for me to change my mind.' He says that he likes to keep his feelings to himself: 'I bottle things up inside; I can't open up.' After leaving school, he spent the following 23 years in the Air Force as a technician. He liked the routine. He says that he had no sexual relationships during this time, but drank very heavily: 'Drink was cheaper than sex.' He adds, 'Until I met Maggie, I felt that it was best to get on with things myself.' He likes things to be in order and is very uncomfortable with the wild, undisciplined behaviour shown by his two stepsons. He thinks that strong, hard discipline, such as he received in his childhood, is the answer, even though he has tried this course of action and it has manifestly not worked. 'When they wind me up, I just seem to end up blowing a fuse.'

Disorganised–controlling–unresolved patterns

Controlling children have a deep underlying insecurity in which the self is experienced as not only unlovable but possibly bad, powerful and dangerous. The sense of autonomy is low; individuals remain affectively vulnerable in the face of their own and other people's distress and fears. In the case of children and adults who feel unable to control what happens to them, there is a sense of profound helplessness and hopelessness. These feelings place people at high risk of depression. There is little self-understanding. Feelings arise and constantly threaten to overwhelm the individual. The one way in which to introduce some certainty into frightening situations is to try to develop heavy *controlling* behaviours and *avoid* intimacy and close relationships. In the past, proximity with caregivers and attachment behaviours have led to feelings of fear and distress. Only the self can be relied upon as a source of comfort and safety. Seeing the self as powerful and invulnerable is a way of trying to keep frightening experiences at bay and out of consciousness. Lee is an example of a boy who has to feel in complete control of what is happening to him. His deep fear is that, unless he is in control, he will be overwhelmed and annihilated.

Lee

Lee is aged 9 years. He suffered neglect and sexual abuse throughout his early years. Although never proven, there are strong suspicions that he was abused by men in a paedophile ring. Teachers and other children found him 'spooky', 'chilling' and 'very manipulative'. His play and his drawings are full of violence and sexuality. 'He draws people with their hands cut off with blood everywhere', said his therapist. 'His stories arouse him. He gets completely scary and he soon gets over-excited and totally out of hand. The only way he can resolve things is for him to suddenly become a magic person, a powerful wizard. This makes him in total control and he magics away all the difficulties. He also becomes a powerful wizard with his teachers and his foster parents. No-one knows the magic inside him and no-one can touch him in any way; no-one can ever stop him. Whenever he plays, he has to be the most powerful person. If you try to outwit him by trying to be more powerful, he just kills himself and comes back as an evil spirit to get you. Even in real life he does things that. I really do think he would carry through unless he was stopped. Like I had to stop him jumping through a second floor window because he wasn't prepared to do what I was asking of him, like something minor, like put his dirty clothes in the wash basket. He is self-harming more and more; digging his nails into his arms to draw blood, that sort of thing.'

Mental representations of other people

The responses that children receive from their carers indicate the extent to which other people can be trusted and relied upon to be emotionally responsive, to understand and to cooperate. Internal working models seek to represent other people's interest and psychological availability. Different defensive adaptations arise to deal with particular caregiving environments.

Other people's psychological availability can be represented either positively or negatively (Figure 9.2).

Positive +	Negative −
1. Available	1. Unavailable
2. Loving, caring	2. Neglectful
3. Interested	3. Hostile
4. Responsive	4. Rejecting
5. Sensitive	5. Unloving
6. Accessible	6. Uninterested
7. Cooperative	7. Unresponsive
8. Trustworthy	8. Inaccessible
	9. Ignoring
	10. Untrustworthy

Figure 9.2   Internal working model: representations of others

Different combinations of these positive and negative mental representations occur within each of the four basic attachment patterns. As Mayseless (1996: 218) notes, each pattern reveals whether an individual's attention is directed towards either other people (an increase of attachment needs) or objects (a minimisation of attachment needs).

Secure–autonomous patterns

At times of upset, distress or need, other people are approached positively. They are perceived to be caring and understanding, responsive and emotionally available, warm and protective. Parents and friends can be relied upon and trusted. Attachment behaviour operates in a balanced way. Relationships are conducted with emotional reciprocity, harmony and synchrony; people give as well as receive. Relationships are experienced as satisfying.

Ambivalent–preoccupied patterns

Other people's emotional interest and responsivity is represented as unreliable and cannot be trusted. There is the constant anxiety that the availability of the other might be lost at any time. There is an oversensitivity to other people's moods and responses. Emotional neglect and abandonment are feared. The result is that attachment behaviour remains high, with great emotional demands being made of others in an attempt to keep them engaged. There is social over-involvement. The approach to others is strong but negative, tinged with feelings of insecurity, anger and frustration. The combination of need/dependence and anxiety/low trust produces feelings of ambivalence towards others. There is thus a preoccupation with other people's sensitivity, interest and psychological responsiveness. Dependence on others is therefore high. People become overinvolved, demanding, anxious, intense, possessive and easily roused to jealousy. The need for attention and approval is strong. This highly demanding approach to relationships is wearing. There is a good deal of emotional taking but not so much emotional giving. If others threaten to give up on the relationship, conflict, despair and anger quickly flare up, with counter-threats of abandonment and the removal of love and availability, but letting go of intimacy and involvement is difficult. Boundaries between the self and the other become blurred and entangled.

Tina

As a little girl, I had all these feelings but nobody was ever interested. They wouldn't listen. It's always been like that for me. It always ends up in arguments. Even when I was sixteen and got pregnant, my boyfriend blamed me and disappeared... Sex. I think I started when I was about 13. Anything to get noticed. I've never thought I'd got anything to offer anybody. Whatever I try to do, no-one appreciates it, like when I tried to help my mum and the problems she was having with boyfriends, she told me to stop interfering. I still need someone to talk to, but all I get is arguments... Most of my relationships with men seem to be stormy... Mal [her present husband] is the most important person in my life. I don't care about anybody else. I'm terrified that he might leave. So I'm always pushing him to see how much he loves me. [Three months after this conversation, Mal does leave Tina after a fierce quarrel.]

Avoidant–dismissing patterns

Mental representations of other people as emotionally distant or even hostile and rejecting mean that individuals are not people orientated. Relationships are often approached instrumentally via an interest in objects, practical pursuits or ideas rather than feelings or emotions. Social comfort is greatest in task-orientated environments. Minimising attachment needs leads to an avoidance of intimacy. There can be a dismissing attitude towards too much closeness in relationships. There is social underinvolvement, and the need for others is downplayed, even denied. It feels more comfortable to remain slightly detached and self-contained, with claims of being self-sufficient. Emotional proximity reawakens feelings of anxiety and discomfort. However, this does not mean that people are necessarily uninterested in relationships: it is just that they find them difficult. They can be reserved, socially gauche or smoothly evasive. Some people behave as social 'loners'. Emotional independence is seen as a strength. Others experience dismissing individuals as emotionally unrewarding and socially hard-going.

Elaine

I was a manic flirter, you know. I had lots of men, but I had no intention of ever committing myself in any way. I didn't want a relationship, just for them to adore me. I didn't want responsibilities. I still don't like relying on people. I'd rather do things for myself and not depend on others even though I need them to like me, think me able, you know. I need to be in control, not let others know me so I fit in with the occasion.

Disorganised–unresolved patterns

This is a complex category in which children's attachment behaviour remains generally disorganised but may be modified in one of three possible ways:

- a continued failure to develop an adaptive strategy to the distress experienced in relationships

- the development of an overlay of an avoidant strategy
- the emergence of a controlling, role reversal strategy.

In all three types, relationships with other people continue to have the potential to induce feelings of anxiety and fear in children, but each handles it in one of the modified ways. Chapter 7 identifies and discusses three basic disorganised–avoidant–controlling patterns: coercive–punitive, compulsive caregiving and compulsive compliance. In all three cases, interpersonal life remains difficult and, with little provocation, capable of causing great distress, manifested as violent anger, anxious dependence or hopeless depression. Deep, unresolved losses and traumas, coupled with profound feelings of other people's emotional hostility and general dangerousness, mean that, whether conducted aggressively or passively, closeness and intimacy are a potential source of anxiety, distress and fear in which strong feelings threaten to overwhelm the individual. Josh displays a number of these anxious, aggressive controlling behaviours.

Josh

Aged 8 years, Josh has a history of severe physical and sexual abuse coupled with neglect. He cannot bear any adult to be in control. Even mild situations, such as asking him to put his coat on to go outside, trigger difficult, oppositional behaviour. He is now in foster care, but he will not allow his foster mother to care for him. According to his carers, each confrontation sounds incredibly petty, but Josh makes everyone who comes into contact with him feel extremely irritated and angry. 'He always has to be in charge. He always has to be the one who decides where his younger sisters sit, what time he goes to bed. Everything we ask him to do takes up so much emotional energy and so much time. It's totally exhausting. If he wasn't getting his own way, he would close his eyes and say that none of us were here; that we could do absolutely nothing to affect him; he was beyond our reach whatever we might do. Scary, really. I always felt that he daren't let others take charge in any way.'

Types of attachment behaviour

How do individuals react in situations in which there are relationships stresses and strains? What attachment behaviours do they display when they experience anxiety, need and distress? People tend to behave in highly characteristic ways that provide strong clues about their general attachment style.

Secure–autonomous patterns

Other people are approached positively with the expectation that they will be psychologically available and responsive. Positive and negative feelings in both the self and others are recognised and acknowledged. As well as emotional recognition, individuals employ cognitive processes to understand and handle attachment-related issues. Self-reflexivity and social understanding are high. Attachment behaviour remains balanced and flexible. Needs are accurately expressed and actions negotiated with others. There is emotional give and take: relationships are reciprocal and cooperative.

Ambivalent–preoccupied patterns

Other people's psychological availability can be neither taken for granted nor trusted. Not only might they fail to respond when needed, but they might also be the cause of the distress itself by threatening to abandon the relationship or remove their emotional interest. The preoccupation with other people's responsiveness means that anxiety remains high. In turn, this means that attachment behaviour operates at maximum – it is 'hyperactivated'. There is therefore an exaggeration of distress-signalling behaviour – attention-seeking, not letting go, distress, provocation, anger, demandingness and inconsolability. Coercive strategies predominate as a way of trying to ensure other people's continued involvement. Threatening behaviours play on other people's guilt. Babyish sentimentality and coy helplessness are used to placate and seduce others when they become angry, exasperated and threaten abandonment. In relationships, there is more 'take' than 'give'. For example, resentment and jealousy of other people who were dependent and having their needs met resulted in Susan increasing her attachment behaviours in reaction to her changing family life. She became attention-seeking, needy, helpless, demanding, petulant and angry.

Susan, mother of Maria (10 years) and Melissa (7 years)

Susan, aged 31, is married to Tom. Three years ago, her husband suffered a major stroke, leaving him physically disabled. No referrals had been received prior to his illness. Tom used to work, was responsible for running many aspects of family life and was the organiser behind the children's social life. After his stroke, Susan 'went to pieces' and said she was unable to deal with the girls' emotional distress. Matters got worse when, 3 months later, Tom, who needed high levels of care, was returned home. Susan resented this decision: 'No-one asked me if I wanted him home.' She said she could not cope with this arrangement. Maria and Melissa began bedwetting. The social services were called in. A week's respite foster care was provided for the girls, followed by a 'respite link family' to whom the girls might go in the day time if their mother felt in need of a break.

Over the following months, Tom's behaviour deteriorated. He could not speak and he began to lose his temper, becoming increasingly aggressive, all in marked contrast to his personality before he suffered the stroke. Susan's regular visits to the family doctor also resulted in the children being referred to a psychologist. A few months later, Tom was transferred to a nursing home. Susan wished that he would die and appeared to resent and feel angry about the sudden 'loss' of the husband whom she had originally married. Susan developed agoraphobia. Various community supports were brought in. The local vicar took her in his car to visit her husband, while his wife did the family shopping. The following year, Maria's attendance at school dropped. Susan encouraged her to stay at home. Maria's teacher, who felt sorry for the family, agreed to pick up the children in the morning and drive them home again in the afternoon.

More recently, Susan has said that Melissa has developed epileptic fits, although medical investigations have been unable to confirm their presence or cause. Social workers have also become involved. The house is rarely cleaned by Susan; it is untidy and dirty. She is also 'letting herself go'. Her hair remains unwashed, and she says that she thinks that she is going to have a breakdown. Susan is now suffering severe migraines. After taking her medication, she goes to bed for the rest of the day, leaving the children to fend for themselves. As a result, several episodes of short-term respite care have been provided for the children. Now, whenever Susan feels a migraine coming on, she telephones the vicar, who contacts the social worker who dashes round and arranges for the girls to stay with their respite carer until their mother recovers.

However, all Susan's support networks are beginning to feel worn out, impatient and increasingly irritated. The vicar says that he can no longer devote so much time to one person. The schoolteacher feels that she cannot continue indefinitely 'acting as a free taxi-service'. Much of the community's frustration is diverted on to the social worker, who is being told to 'do something about it', but the social services also feel that they are being 'manipulated' by Susan. 'It's all one way traffic with her; take, take, take.' Her migraines are becoming more frequent and intense. Susan now never ventures outside the house unless taken by car.

Avoidant–dismissing patterns

In the past, other people have withdrawn emotionally when needs and distress signals have been expressed. Relationships with others therefore appear to work best when they are conducted via practical or intellectual pursuits. Distress is handled by trying to ignore it, denying that one is upset or refusing to let it affect one (the stiff upper lip, seeing the self as strong and able to resist being affected by emotions). 'Going-it-alone', compulsive self-reliance, insisting on being independent and being able to manage on one's own even though being helped by others seem perfectly reasonable and appropriate, all suggesting an avoidant attachment style. Attachment behaviour, normally expected when levels of emotional need rise, is deactivated. There is also an impatience and irritation with other people's attachment needs. Partners or children who appear overly dependent, needy and emotionally demanding (for example at times of upset, illness or anxiety) cause irritation, even rejection. Such needs provoke discomfort and distress. This is handled by either trying to control the other person's state ('You don't have attachment needs; stop making demands on me', 'It's only a scratch, what's all the fuss about; you're not hurt'), or avoiding it by walking away. Poise and emotional equilibrium are maintained as long as individuals have things under their control and not too much is being asked of them. Whatever they do, they will do well, but only as long as no more is asked. When demands are felt to be high, and things are in danger of getting out of control, old feelings of failing to please and consequent rejection flood in. The result is raised anxiety or an outburst of anger.

Ainsley

Although Ainsley had a very strict childhood, he remembers it as happy. He feels that he did not really know his father ('Out at work all day and every day'). His mother was described as very loving and firm, 'but you knew where you were with her'. She was 'not a very physical person, if you know what I mean, no cuddles or anything like that'. His parents separated when he was in his teens, and he has not seen his father for the past 20 years.

When he left school, Ainsley went to sea on a merchant ship. 'The best days of my life. Lots of money. No commitments. I had control of my life… Then Lorraine burst into my life. I was quite reserved with women I suppose, but she was bubbly, exciting, fun to be with and I fell in love with her.' Lorraine already had two children and a long history of crises, problem behaviours and failed, violent relationships. Ainsley felt out of his depth. When the emotional heat felt too high, Ainsley simply walked out and left. He describes himself as a 'weak person' who cannot deal with major emotional problems. 'All I wanted was a normal family life, a good job, a holiday once a year and to go out in the car with the family on a Sunday. Lorraine started to have affairs and that left me at my wit's end, so I had to leave. I loved her but I felt depressed… I'm just not very good at relationships. They always seem to fall apart. I get paranoid that if I get too involved or I feel I get too pushy it won't work out. If someone's miserable, I always think it's my fault, it's got to be me. Every time I get a girlfriend I feel panicky now. I feel paralysed that whatever I do, it'll be the wrong thing and so everything will go wrong… I like control in my life. I'm happier when I'm in control. This is the reason why relationships are difficult. I find that when I do get into relationships, my standard of life deteriorates. And when it does fall apart, I just shut myself away. I don't speak to anyone. I stop eating. I shut everything down.'

Disorganised–unresolved patterns

In situations of distress and confusion, children and adults have no strategy that allows them to regulate their own affect or influence the other's availability. Infants may 'freeze' or show a confused mix of approach and avoidant (A–C) behaviours. When aroused and upset, older children may erupt in a helpless, aggressive rage. Adults faced with emotional demands (a baby's hungry cry, for example) may feel overwhelmed by powerful feelings of distress that leave them feeling helpless, angry, depressed or rejecting. Unresolved feelings of loss and trauma retain the power to resurface and disturb current functioning whenever experiences resonate with past hurts. Kylie, for example, becomes very distressed when well-meaning foster carers try to offer her comfort and closeness (S. Fearnley 1998, personal communication).

Kylie

After a childhood of physical abuse, neglect and five foster care placements that had all broken down, Kylie went into residential care when she was 9 years old. She had also been excluded from school for aggressive behaviour in which she regularly attacked other children. She continues to feel angry and hostile towards any woman who cares for her. 'It is as if she had learnt that you first have to experience some kind of physical hurt before you get a cuddle. She only got her mum after there had been some kind of violence. There is a lot of confusion between hurting and caring for Kylie.' She witnessed a lot of violent and bloody incidents between her mother and various stepfathers. Whenever she is in situations that she experiences as stressful, she literally pulls out clumps of her hair, so that she has many bald patches. She also runs around screaming very loudly. On one occasion, she ran out into the street, yelling, 'They're going to kill me; they're going to kill me.' At such times, she is completely out of control. 'Someone only has to knock on the door of her room or go to touch her and she goes mad, screaming and looking wild and distraught.' When she is not in a distressed state, Kylie is often found curled up in the corner of a room.

Quality of caregiving

Internal working models formed in childhood continue to guide interactions into adulthood unless 'disconfirmed'. Adults who become parents find that their mental representations of the self and others continue to guide their interactions, including those with their own children. As we have seen, the construction of the self as a caregiver is structured around the answers to two questions: will I be a good mother (= will I be able to protect this child?), and will I have a good child (= will I want to protect this child?) (Solomon and George 1996). The defences and strategies established over the years to cope with attachment-related issues operate when parents provide care for their children. Ainsworth *et al.* (1978) identified four dimensions of the caregiving system (sensitivity, availability, cooperation and acceptance). Each of the four attachment patterns and their transformation into caregiving behaviour is characterised by particular positionings along these four dimensions.

Secure caregiving styles

Parents who, on the whole and in a 'good-enough' fashion, tend towards the positive end of each of the four dimensions are able to acknowledge and handle the demands and delights of their infants in a balanced manner. The attachment needs of their children are fully recognised without overly distressing and disturbing the parents. Parents remains sensitive and responsive, accepting and cooperative, available and reliable.

Uncertain (preoccupied) caregiving styles

In uncertain styles of caregiving, parents are not sure about how they feel and how they should react to their children. There are extreme switches between feeling very loving and positive about children, and feeling very critical and 'put-upon'. The more demanding the children become, the more ambivalent and uncertain the parents feel. Parental preoccupation with their own needs and anxieties means that children experience their caregivers as unreliable and insensitive, poorly attuned and unresponsive. There is difficulty in acknowledging and dealing with both the positive and negative aspects of children, the parent–child relationship and their own feelings as parents. Doubts appear in the minds of parents about whether or not their children love and like them. Children's growing independence is interpreted as a threat to the relationship, a potential abandonment. Being a caregiver, a protector and a secure base triggers feelings of anxiety. As children grow older, the lack of confidence in knowing what to do increases. Carers do not always recognise dangers, remaining unsure of when it is appropriate to intervene and help. The caregiving style is both uncertain and neglectful. The growing demands made by Carol's children amplified her anxiety that needs can never be met. Uncertainty, despair that it was 'all getting too much' and the wish for other people to take over began to set in.

Carol

Carol's four children, aged 7 years and under, have all suffered severe physical and emotional neglect. In the space of 5 years, Carol and the children have moved house 10 times. She suffers from depression and has on three occasions taken overdoses of her medication, each time ending up in hospital while the children are temporarily looked after by foster carers, where they are said to 'thrive'. Her relationships with her various partners are described as 'stormy'. Carol and her current partner make accusations that the other has either physically or sexually abused the children, only for the accusation to be retracted the next day. Social workers, health visitors and teachers regularly report that the children are undernourished, suffer lice infestation, are poorly clothed, are rarely washed and receive poor supervision. The house is dirty. There is little furniture and no toys. Carol, who is overweight and suffers poor health, regularly stays in bed all day, with the result that the older children often fail to go to school. She says that she finds looking after them all 'too stressful'. Her requests that the children be temporarily looked after by foster carers are increasing in frequency. Carol says, with mounting alarm, bewilderment and exasperation, that she can no longer control the behaviour of the two oldest children: 'You'll have to take them. They're doing my head in. I can't cope.'

Rejecting (dismissing) caregiving styles

The basic caregiving style is one of *rejection* of children's attachment behaviour and emotional needs. In response to distress, parents deactivate their attachment/caregiving systems. Children's safety and protection are therefore compromised. Caregiving tends to be intrusive and controlling as parents either ignore children's distress or instruct them to deny attachment needs ('You're not ill; stop crying').

The basic wish is to suppress behaviours in others that might cause the carer to feel needed. The caregiver's experience is that the expression of needs leads to rejection, so attempts to express attachment behaviour are discouraged. Parents such as Sandra therefore feel uncomfortable with the caregiving role.

Sandra

Sandra has a 4-year-old boy, Tim, and a 2-year-old daughter. Sandra is requesting that he should be adopted. 'It sounds terrible to say it, I know, I can't stand him. I can't bear to look at him or have anything to do with him.' She says that she never took to him, even when he was a baby. Sandra dresses very smartly. She is trim, neat but quite tense. She always appears 'immaculate' according to the health visitor involved in the case. The home is beautifully decorated and furnished. Her husband runs his own heating engineering business, working long hours. Most evenings, he does not arrive home until the children are in bed. He cannot understand his wife's rejection of his son but feels there is nothing he can do about it. Tim is an attractive-looking boy who is also dressed very neatly, with new, very fashionable clothes. He walks around the house 'like a little robot, like an automaton', said his social worker. 'It's weird and very upsetting to watch him and his mother together.' She can no longer bear to be in the same room as him, and if he does enter, she talks about him as if he is not there. Sandra said that she cannot explain her feelings. Meanwhile, Tim's behaviour appears to become more and more desperate and defended.

Helpless (unresolved) caregiving styles

Faced with the emotional and physical needs of their children, caregivers with a history of unresolved losses and trauma feel that they could be easily overwhelmed. The inability to develop any behavioural strategies to help to regulate raised affect means that, for these carers, the demands of children engender feelings of confusion, disorientation or anger. Caregiving therefore remains disorganised. Parents feel potentially *helpless*, ineffective and out of control in their parenting. As a consequence, caregiving can be unresponsive, insensitive, aggressive, agitated, hostile and rejecting. Issues of power, control and subjugation are felt whenever attachment-related experiences occur. And as children trigger such feelings, they represent relationships in which such issues inevitably arise. Children experience their carers as highly unpredictable. One moment a mother might be very loving and protective, while at another, for no apparent reason, she might be hostile and aggressive, or depressed and totally unresponsive. Not surprisingly, because children find it very difficult to develop an effective attachment strategy in this context, their behaviour becomes increasingly unregulated and difficult to control. And in turn, parents' own feelings of helplessness can quickly erupt into rage or fear. Unable to offer their children adequate care or protection, many parents abdicate responsibility. They may withdraw emotionally or literally abandon their children by walking out on them. The caregiver's availability is always in doubt, and this causes children to feel great distress and rage. Young children can therefore develop no way of organising their attachment behaviour to secure their carer's psychological availability. Older children might attempt to meet their parent's needs (parenting the parent) while denying their own needs as a way of maintaining an attachment relationship. For example, a sense of simmering anger and resentment underpinned Vicky's attempts to control both her own unacknowledged feelings of distress and the desire of other people to help.

Vicky

Vicky is 23 years old. She describes her own mother as 'cold, cruel and untrustworthy' but is very vague and evasive about the details. However, there is no doubting the strength of her hostile feelings. Vicky's social worker describes her as 'hostile, terse, avoidant'. Vicky's husband is an alcoholic. Most nights he returns home drunk, wets the bed and contributes very little to the running of the home. Although she talks about him disdainfully, she is making no effort to leave the marriage. She gave birth to Nicholas 12 months ago. Immediately after he was born, Vicky made heavy use of the health visiting service for advice. She said that Nicholas was a very difficult baby who constantly cried. Nothing that she did soothed him. She said he seemed a very determined baby who assumed the world would revolve around him, 'but he'll have to learn that life isn't like that'. Vicky felt she had enough on her hands with a 'useless' husband without also having to care for a truculent son. When he was 3 months old, Nicholas suffered a subdural haematoma. He was in hospital for a month. When Nicholas was ready for discharge, Vicky argued with the paediatrician, saying that he was not yet ready to go home. The social worker arranged for Nicholas's maternal grandmother to look after him until his mother felt ready to resume his care. This plan upset Vicky, and she took Nicholas back a week later.

Social workers found it very difficult to supervise the baby and his mother. There was rarely any answer when workers knocked on the door. When she did let the social worker in, Vicky said that she was coping. She conceded that he was not an easy baby, but it was her first child, and, like all new mothers, she hadn't fully appreciated how much effort was needed to look after a baby, particularly a fractious one. She handled him very roughly when she was feeding him, although she was conscientious about hygiene and ensuring that Nicholas was well fed. Nicholas suffered severe scalding when he was 8 months old and was again admitted to hospital. Vicky explained the serious injury as an accident that had happened in the bath. Nicholas is currently being looked after by foster carers.

Defence mechanisms

The defences used to regulate affect and control attachment-related experience vary according to each of the four main attachment patterns. Defences represent attempts to keep feelings of attachment-related distress out of consciousness. However, the kinds of relationship experience and perception that trigger anxiety depend on the individual's attachment style. Therefore, particular defence mechanisms are typical of some attachment patterns but not others.

Secure–autonomous patterns

Individuals generally deal with anxiety and distress in an open, realistic fashion. They are able to acknowledge the origins of an upset and reflect on its possible causes. The effect of the self on others and others on the self is understood so that a fairly balanced view can be taken about what has led to misunderstandings and strong feelings, rejection and insensitivity. Although such situations cause hurt and upset, individuals can use their cognitive understanding to make sense of and handle their emotional distress. This leads to constructive behaviours including discussion, compromise and negotiation. Reason can be used both to appraise emotion and control it. This is not to say that defence mechanisms will not be employed. Instead, secure–free to evaluate individuals have the capacity to develop good levels of reflective function and examine what has taken place so that social as well as self-understanding is achieved. This allows people to increase their autonomy. They have a greater repertoire of responses at their disposal, thereby increasing their range of options in demanding situations.

Ambivalent–preoccupied patterns

The internal working model represents other people as unreliably available, insensitive and not to be trusted. They are therefore approached with an attitude that presumes that they will be denying and unresponsive. There is uncertainty about one's own likability and worth. In more extreme cases, the approach is demanding as well as complaining. In addition, as other people's perceived emotional withholding is the cause of the distress, other people are blamed for relationships going wrong. For example, anger may be defensively *projected* onto the other, who is accused of being angry and blamed for causing the argument.

The defences are employed to try and keep distressing attachment-related issues out of consciousness. For those classified as ambivalent–entangled, distress is particularly acute when other people threaten to withdraw their care and interest. It is the uncertainty that increases anxiety. One way of trying defensively to exclude such ambiguity is to respond to only one component of the other's reactions. By seeing the other person as all-denying and bad, the individual feels justified in reacting angrily with threats of abandoning the relationship. In contrast, by seeing others as all-giving and good, it is possible to sentimentalise the relationship. These perceptions of the other as loved or hated are often quite short lived. One day someone can be described as 'absolutely wonderful' while the next they are dismissed as 'total rubbish'. This defence of *splitting* occurs in an attempt to deal with and respond to ambivalent feelings about other people, who are both desired as potentially responsive and hated as potentially denying. Integrating contrasting feelings within the same strategy is difficult. The mixture of good and bad points in others is hard to handle.

Feelings are not contained or held back. They are not thought through; they are *acted out*. The emotional state of those classified as ambivalent tends to be transparent. Moods affect the whole of their body language. For ambivalent–preoccupied types, emotional agendas feel much more potent than cognitive ones; feelings drive behaviour more readily than does thought.

Avoidant–dismissing patterns

Feelings of anxiety arise in situations in which emotional proximity and dependence increase, and in which attachment-related issues are brought to the fore. The individual's internal working model suggests that one should expect rejection and withdrawal if one gets too close to and dependent on others. The basic defensive ploy is to keep attachment-charged information and experiences out of consciousness. Emotional involvement increases discomfort; it is better *avoided*. Independence and emotional *self-containment* are valued. The self is seen as strong and unaffected by feelings. Displays of strong affect in the self and others is *suppressed*, or its presence and impact are denied. Avoidant individuals dismiss the importance of attachment (derogation of attachment) or the influence it has on them. When interpersonal matters do become distressing, relationships and feelings are handled in a detached, rational, thought-based way – emotions and emotionality are *intellectualised*, they are analysed theoretically, often in a manner that appears to others to be cold, detached, smug and complacent. In more extreme cases, individuals might try to avoid feelings of worry and distress by developing compulsive behaviours and obsessions. These behaviours are an attempt to gain some personal control over events; they lock the individual into a closed loop of compulsive self-absorption in an attempt to shut out anxious thoughts and feelings.

Disorganised–unresolved patterns

By definition, those who cannot organise their attachment behaviour to gain proximity and experience protection have failed to develop any defensive strategies to cope with raised affect. In times of distress and difficulty, confusion and puzzlement, feelings quickly flood and overwhelm the conscious. All feelings of control and regulation are then lost. Rage and helplessness are mixed with fear and disorientation. Behavioural consequences vary from violence and aggression through apathy and despair to disengagement or trance-like states. When people feel either out of control or not in control, their response may be one of thrashing anger or passive, depressed fatalism. Feelings of guilt can surface. Irrational fears and phobias can easily disturb routine functioning as individuals encounter situations that seem to evoke old traumas.

For disorganised, abused children, the most prevalent secondary attachment style is avoidant–dismissing with its attendant defences. With experience, some abused and traumatised children will clearly learn that displays of distress and attachment behaviour fail to bring comfort; indeed, they compound the distress as carers not only fail to deliver comfort and protection, but are also the source of the fear and danger. A small number of individuals (although the number is much higher in at-risk populations) combine a disorganised attachment pattern with a secondary resistant, preoccupied, coercive pattern in which the use of projection, splitting and acting out are not only present as defensive behaviours, but also often exist in exaggerated levels. Nevertheless, it must be remembered that, in the more serious cases in which loss and trauma remain unresolved, disturbance and disorganisation continue to operate at high levels, with few signs of effective defensive behaviours.

Classification and analysis of attachment patterns and relationships, risks and protections

In order to develop a working classification of a child or parent's attachment history and style, it is not necessary to have confirmatory evidence from every one of the above eight psychosocial dimensions. It is not therefore required to explore and evidence every aspect of an individual's past and present relationships and behaviours. Based on an analysis of available information, a provisional hypothesis is made of the individual's probable attachment pattern, internal working model and mental representations of the self and others. New information, which will continue to accrue, will either confirm or disconfirm the working hypothesis.

In practice, it is not usually long before sufficient knowledge is obtained to classify with a high level of confidence. Confidence tends to be greatest between deciding whether or not an individual should be classified as secure or insecure. It is also easier to feel greater certainty in classifying adults rather than young children. Third, confidence is often higher in judging between children who show organised and disorganised patterns. For example, maltreated children from high-risk populations who show very disturbed behaviours are most likely to be classified as insecure–disorganised.

Pieces of information and scattered observations appear as discrete outcrops of evidence, the causes of which lie beneath the surface. It is the job of the practitioner as assessor to theorise what might connect the various behaviours and relationship patterns. Practitioners therefore move from *description* to *classification*. We have said that theories help to organise what we know. Theories also provide an economy of effort. They allow conceptual short-cuts to be taken. If the theory is a powerful one in terms of accounting for and explaining a wide range of phenomena, it might only take a few observations to locate a particular phenomenon as an example of a class of objects or behaviours. Practitioners generally need only a few major indicators of typical behaviours and relationship responses to hypothesise an individual's attachment classification. Hypotheses help to guide future observations, the results of which aid practitioners in further testing and refining their initial assessments and understandings.

Once in possession of a working classification and the theory that underpins it, the character and logic of people's behaviours and relationships begin to make more sense. The confusion and turbulence that can sometimes surround difficult cases begins to dispel. This not only increases their sense of understanding and sureness, but also increases their professional and psychological availability to those with whom they work.

An analysis of people's relationships and attachment behaviours also helps practitioners to identify and locate the stressors, risk effects, protective effects and resiliences present in the lives of both children and their parents. Stresses and insecure relationships pose risks to children's psychosocial development. By adversely affecting children's self-esteem, self-efficacy, self-reflexivity, sense of autonomy and social competence, insecure attachments lower children's resilience to cope with stress, frustration and setback. As caregivers are the main generators of children's close relationship environments, any factors that adversely affect parents' psychological availability need to be identified. Such factors might include material poverty and stress, an insecure caregiving style, an unsupportive partner or a rejecting social environment.

On the positive side, assessments also need to identify possible experiences and effects that might boost children's resiliences. These protective effects can also be understood within a developmental attachment framework. For example, exposure to steady, reliable, secure close relationships provides the capacity to improve children's self-esteem. Success in some practical or social task might increase feelings of self-efficacy. Assessments need to map these risk and protective effects if case aims are to remain developmentally informed.

10

Formulating the aims of intervention

In a sense, the aims in all cases will be the same: to ensure children's physical safety and well-being, and to promote sound psychosocial development, or, in Werner and Smith's words (cited in Fonagy *et al.* 1994: 231), to produce the child who 'works well, loves well and expects well notwithstanding profound life adversity'. The assessment and analysis tell the social worker what factors are hindering and helping the achievement of these developmental goals. Thus, in short, the basic objectives will always be:

- to remove or ameliorate those forces and factors which appear to be hindering or threatening development
- to introduce and promote those forces and factors which appear to be aiding development.

Attachment is a lifespan concept. With the prospect of new relationships at any stage in the lifespan, a reorganisation of existing internal working models is always possible. Relationships provide opportunities not only to acquire new strengths and understandings, but also to develop new vulnerabilities. Practice interventions aim to disconfirm insecure working models and promote the protective effects of secure attachments and positive relationships.

In practice, once thinking about purposes develops along these lines, social workers need to be very clear about a small number of important developmental concepts. Six in particular, all closely linked, inform and guide talk about practice aims and objectives; these are stress, risk, resilience, vulnerability, protection and coping.

Risk and resilience, vulnerability and protection

The effective prevention of social maladjustment and disorder 'should be based on a model of human development in which risk and protective factors, arising from both biologic and social influences, shape the paths by which individuals become vulnerable or resistant to psychiatric symptoms and disorders' (Beckwith and Sigman 1995: 684).

Risks

Risks indicate those features in children's make-up or experience which might adversely affect their psychosocial development in some direct or indirect way. Risks increase children's *vulnerability* to adversity and stress. For example, children who suffer physical abuse have an increased risk of developing aggressive behaviour and, in turn, of becoming parents who abuse their own children. Maltreated children appear to be more aroused by aggression. They also see aggression as a solution to interpersonal problems. Risks also include such diverse things as having a parent who is alcoholic, being cared for by a mother who suffers severe depression, living in a high crime community, experiencing marital discord, suffering repeated changes of carer, witnessing parental conflict and receiving a poor education. The more risk elements to which a child is exposed, the greater the likelihood of later social and psychological disturbance. However, exposure to any one risk does not mean that a child is fated to suffer a developmental impairment. Instead, it merely increases the chances of a child being psychosocially disturbed. Children who manage to resist being adversely affected are said to show *resilience* in the face of that particular risk.

Many risks, for example parental neglect or the misuse of drugs, decrease children's experience of good-quality social interaction. This loss interferes with children's ability to conduct themselves in a socially competent manner with peers, parents and others, further cutting them off from the potentially corrective experience of positive relationships. The inability to conduct relationships is regarded as not only a major personal problem, but also a defining quality of being a social problem.

In these examples, we see that individuals might be exposed to different amounts of risk and that, in some cases, these differences might be the result of the individual's own behaviour, which appears, in part, to shape their social environment. Children's inborn *temperamental* characteristics may influence how they respond to others as well as how others might respond to them. Children with 'difficult' temperaments are more likely to be scapegoated and treated critically and irritably by parents. Critical, hostile parenting constitutes a risk. Thus, in the case of a child with a 'difficult' temperament, we can see how a train of negative, adverse interactions might cascade out of interactions between the child and his or her parents. Equally possibly, positive chain events might be seen to develop in the case of children with easy temperaments who possess sociability, a good sense of humour and an optimistic outlook.

Aggressive children tend to elicit more aggressive responses in others, concentrate less well at school and thus enter the adult world with fewer skills and qualifications, enjoy less social support and so on. Children with a conduct disorder have an increased tendency to marry a spouse who has also exhibited antisocial behaviours (Quinton *et al.* 1993). Champion *et al.* (1995) found that children who showed emotional and behavioural problems aged 10 years were twice as likely as other children to suffer severely stressful events in their mid-twenties. Spirals of negative experiences – *negative chain events* – are often experienced by those children who are most vulnerable to stress.

Experiences are defined as a risk only if and when there is some statistical association between the experience and some specified impairment in development: 'The demonstration that *X* is a risk factor for *Y* simply means that, if *X* is present, *Y* is more likely to occur' (Hay and Angold 1994: 4). Therefore, it must be understood that the *risk variable* may not itself be the direct risk agent. Poverty, for example, is associated with an increased rate of certain diseases, illnesses and anti-social behaviours, but it is not material deprivation as such that causes these problems. Instead, poor diet, overcrowding or psychological stress may be more prevalent in poor households. It is these factors which constitute the risk agents. Poverty and social disadvantage make good parenting more difficult, and it is failures in parenting that are more directly involved in the actual psychological mechanisms that increase the risk of children becoming emotional disturbed and behaviourally difficult (Rutter 1995: 76). It is important:

> not to mistake risk indicators for risk mechanisms. On the whole, at any one time, poverty and social disadvantage *are* accompanied by an increase risk of psychopathology. The secular trend data, however, are persuasive in showing that it is most unlikely that the risk mechanism lies in either poverty or poor living conditions per se. Rather, the evidence suggests that the effect comes about because poverty is, in turn, associated with family disorganization and breakup, which are rather nearer to the relevant risk mechanisms. (Rutter 1997: 363)

Nevertheless, the demonstration that something is identified as a risk factor is often the first step in recognising that some other thing is more directly involved in the cause of the problem or dysfunction.

Rarely does a single risk event in itself leads to developmental impairment. A single stressor such as parental divorce usually acts as a marker for a whole complex of diverse adverse experiences, including family conflict, diminished parental availability and scape-goating of the child. Contextual models of risks and their affect on development appear more realistic (Gore and Eckenrode 1997). The total number of risks is a better predictor of developmental impairment than is exposure to any specific risk (Zeanah *et al.* 1997: 168).

Resilience

Simple exposure to a risk might not, however, lead to a dysfunction or developmental impairment. Children who appear to be able to surmount or resist the stresses posed by exposure to the risk are said to show *resilience*, at least in the face of that particular risk. Resilience is concerned with how individuals vary in their responses when exposed to a risk. Stress-resistant children are able to retain competence in environments of stress and adversity. No-one, as Rutter (1995) reminds us, has absolute resistance to stress. As the number of stressors increases, either at the same time or cumulatively over time, psychodevelopmental risks also increase. 'At-risk' children are those children who are likely to find themselves in social and physical environments that increase the likelihood of their development and adjustment being compromised.

Resilience is not just a matter of constitutional strength or the possession of a robust temperament: it is also a product of how people perceive, appraise, approach and tackle stresses and challenges. These latter abilities are more likely to arise out of family life and interpersonal experiences – factors that initially lie outside the individual.

Connell (1990) suggests that people have three basic psychological needs:

1. the need for *competence*
2. the need for *autonomy*
3. the need for *relatedness*, reflecting the need to feel securely connected to other people, the need to experience oneself as worthy and the need to love and be loved.

The fulfilment of each of the needs appears to increase resilience.

More widely speaking, factors that have been associated with resilience include (Fonagy *et al.* 1994: 232):

- higher socio-economic status
- the absence of neurobiological problems
- the possession of an easy temperament
- the absence of early loss and trauma
- secure, warm attachments
- positive social supports
- good educational experience
- a high IQ
- a good problem-solving ability
- task-related effectiveness
- high self-esteem
- autonomy and self-control
- social understanding, awareness and empathy
- the ability to plan
- a good sense of humour.

Secure attachments predict many of the characteristics of the resilient child. 'There is thus a prima facie case that *resilient children are securely attached children*; that is that secure attachment is part of the mediating process where resilience is observed' (Fonagy *et al.* 1994: 235).

Continuing their review of resilience within an attachment perspective, Fonagy *et al.* (1994) pose the idea that the individual's ability to represent both the self and others mentally without defensive distortion might be a major factor in understanding many aspects of resilience. Thus, maltreatment that disturbs children's ability to represent and understand their own and others' emotions and behaviours reduces their ability to make sense of and cope with distress, conflict and social failure. However, if a maltreated child can relate to a responsive figure outside the abusive interaction (for example, with the other parent, an aunt, a teacher or a psychotherapist), he or she might be able to develop the capacity to represent relationships mentally with increased accuracy and understanding, without distortion, self-blame or negative self-image.

Within secure internal working models, children and adults are able to reflect on the self, others and relationships in a relatively non-defended way. This allows people to *think about* their own and other people's actions, feelings, beliefs and behaviours. It is a cognitive capacity used to deal with emotional issues and attachment-related concerns. It is a recognition that human behaviour can only be understood as a set of interactions between feelings and thoughts, and that these have to be reflected upon if social interaction is to become intelligible and manageable. Fonagy *et al.* (1994) refer to this as a *reflective function*. It occurs not only when people recognise what they have felt, said or done, but also when they can reflect on the causes and motivations that lie behind such feelings, words or actions, for example 'I know I was an awful teenager, but I used to get upset with my mother and frightened because she drank such a lot which I know she did because my father was such a bastard.'

The possession of a high 'reflective-self' function appears to confer resilience; it allows people to step back and review what is happening in complex social interactions. This helps people to contemplate responses; it gives them options; it increases autonomy. It also helps them to *think through* situations, plan effectively and learn from past experiences.

In Fonagy *et al.*'s studies (1991b, 1994), high self-reflectivity also produced more secure caregivers who were much more likely to have securely attached children. Mothers, for example, are better able mentally to contain their babies' needs and distress. As they reflect on the mental state of others, they can understand their children's internal states and react sensitively and appropriately. Thus, the promotion of secure attachments is a highly worthwhile goal of intervention. Early relationships that help us to make sense of ourselves and others therefore offer high levels of protection when individuals are exposed to the potential risks of social misunderstanding, confusion and conflict. In contrast, insecure attachments frustrate children's ability to develop self-reflectivity. Instead, children become anxiously absorbed with their own distress and other people's availability. Parents' internal working models fail to represent their children's needs as they actually exist. As caregivers, they represent and project their children's needs in terms of their own attachment anxieties.

Main (1991) considers similar matters using the concept of 'metacognition'. Although people may be able to represent their experiences in the form of a statement such as 'I have low self-esteem', the ability to reflect on that representation (a metarepresentation) further increases one's cognitive fluency – 'I am someone who thinks that she has low self-esteem which is why I feel anxious in new social situations.' *Thinking about thoughts* (rather than just *thinking*) allows people to reflect on their experiences in terms of origins, motivations and effects. The ability to step back and consider one's own cognitive processes (that is, to think about thoughts or use *metacognition*) appears in some children as early as 3 years of age but nearly always in secure attachment relationships. Main (1991: 134) quotes Brown and colleagues, who describe metacognitive knowledge as 'relatively stable, statable, often fallible, and late-developing information that human thinkers have about their own cognitive processes and those of others'. Such self-reflective abilities clearly advantage children and adults in social situations. The ability to use cognitive and metacognitive processes to access, understand and handle their own and other people's feelings, behaviours and actions appears strongest in children who have enjoyed secure attachments. The ability to develop metacognition and self-reflective capacities is often weaker in children classified as insecure, and it is particularly weak in those classified as insecure–disorganised with histories of maltreatment.

Vulnerability

Children who are adversely affected by a risk event are said to be *vulnerable* in the face of that risk. What makes some children resilient and others vulnerable when exposed to a particular risk can, however, often be the end product of a complex interaction between a number of psychosocial events ranging over time. The loss of a close love relationship – for example, the death of a spouse – can directly precipitate depression. However, as Rutter (1990: 186) points out, the continued lack of a close relationship (rather than its sudden loss) constitutes a *vulnerability factor* (rather than a direct risk factor) if other life stressors are met. The lack in itself may not be a risk. It only renders individuals vulnerable to psychological dysfunction if they subsequently experience stressful or adverse events, such as parental divorce or being bullied at school.

Brown *et al.*'s (1986) studies of depression in women explored similar ideas. The loss of a parent in childhood makes adult women vulnerable to depression, but it is not the direct cause of their depression. It is exposure to the subsequent risk of not receiving warm, affectionate parental care that makes such women vulnerable. Such losses create feelings of helplessness (an inability to control key emotional experiences) and low self-esteem. It is the emotional vulnerability created by these feelings, coupled with the risk of later affectionless care, that appears to lead to the depression. Parental loss in itself is not associated with depression if children subsequently receive good-quality emotional care, that is, they do not experience the risk variable of poor-quality care.

Protective influences

In contrast, other characteristics and aptitudes serve to *protect* individuals against the potentially disturbing consequences of being exposed to a risk. 'Protective factors are those characteristics or conditions that increase resistance to later psychological disturbances' (Beckwith and Sigman 1995: 685). Protective factors may exist within:

- the infant (temperament, intelligence or skill in self-regulation)
- the relationship with the parent (secure)
- the supportive relationships enjoyed by the parent with other adults.

Again, it is necessary to note the difference between protective indicators and protective mechanisms. Protective influences (such as a secure attachment) are often those events which children experience that statistically increase their ability to resist being developmentally impaired when exposed to a stress or an adversity. The actual mechanism by which this is achieved may be more subtle and might depend, for example, on developing a strong sense of self-efficacy or social empathy within a secure attachment relationship.

Protective mechanisms operate in a variety of ways, including avoidance of the risk, immunity to the provoking agent and positive cognitive processing of the negative experience. It is helpful to remember that protective processes only become apparent as they interact with a risk variable. Many of the most effective protective mechanisms promote self-reflectivity, self-esteem and feelings of self-efficacy in the individual. For example, although children who have a parent who is mentally ill are at increased risk, some protection is achieved for those able to recognise that their parent is ill and who enjoy positive emotional relationships outside the family. Stable caregiving relationships in which children avoid many and frequent moves between carers ('interruptors') allow them to develop secure attachments, which in turn facilitates the growth of self-esteem and social empathy.

> The inability to develop a set of protective resources early in life not only produces early dysfunction, but additionally provides the basis for both enhanced lifetime exposure to stress and vulnerability to dysfunction. (Gore and Eckenrode 1997: 56)

Some factors in themselves do not protect individuals directly against risk, but they might increase people's positive self-evaluation of themselves or their effectiveness so that, when they experience a setback or a hostile experience, their view of self is not too deeply disturbed. Characteristics that help individuals to cope adaptively with stress are identified as *resiliences*.

> the loss of a love relationship (through rebuff, bereavement, or separation) is important not so much because a loss is painful in itself but because it causes people to question their own ability to maintain relationships. The concept of 'neutralization' suggests that if the threatening life event is accompanied or followed by some other event that counteracts this damage to self-esteem or self-efficacy, the risk should be reduced. (Rutter 1990: 204)

Rutter (1990) is keen to point out that protection is not just a matter of avoiding adversity or enjoying positive relationships. The deeper search is for processes that protect us against risk mechanisms: 'Protection... resides not in evasion of the risk but in successful engagement with it' (Rutter 1990: 186). Children who have coped well with spending a night away from home without their parents might be better protected against the risk of separation entailed in going into hospital. Protection therefore develops from the ability to cope with or adapt to stressful and challenging events. This has major implications for interventions, help and treatment.

A range of variables, found in either the *person* or the *environment*, operate as protective factors that predict increased resilience (Garmezy 1997: 14). These include:

- personality features such as good health, easy temperament, autonomy, self-esteem and a positive social orientation
- problem-solving abilities
- a sense of self-efficacy
- attractiveness to peers and adults
- family cohesion, warmth and absence of discord
- the availability of external support systems that encourage and reinforce children's coping efforts.

Many protective factors, however, stem from the same process. For example, social support and high self-esteem buffer stressful experiences. A positive sense of self forms in the context of good social support, and social support is likely to be enhanced if the individual responds to others non-defensively and with warmth. 'Over time,' continue Gore and Eckenrode (1997:40), 'this process is certainly reciprocal, with persons possessing relatively high levels of self-esteem being more capable of maintaining existing relationships, forming new relationships, and eliciting the positive responses (social support) of others.' Processes can, of course, work in the opposite direction, those with low self-esteem avoiding or failing to respond to social relationships in a competent manner. It is generally the case that many of the parents and children seen by social workers experience the highest levels of stress, are rarely on the receiving end of experiences that protect them against risks, and possess or develop few resiliences. They therefore remain vulnerable and low on coping resources.

These are extremely important observations. People's own behaviours play a large part in creating the social environment with which they have to deal. Boys who are found to be antisocial suffer much higher rates of unemployment, disrupted friendship and broken marriage in adolescence and early adulthood (Robins 1966). Turned around, however, this also means that people can increase their resilience by attempting to re-think and reflect on what they do and how other others react. Quinton and Rutter (1988) have shown the strong protective effects that stem from young people learning how actively to plan the ways in which they might deal with difficult and demanding life events. In their study, it was the ex-institutional girls who felt at the mercy of fate and failed to take active steps to deal with personal challenges who fared worst. Feeling in personal control of one's life and shaping what happens significantly increases resilience.

Furthermore, this same research also showed the important protective influence of entering a harmonious relationship with a non-deviant partner. It was those girls from disadvantaged backgrounds who developed the capacity to plan who were most likely to find supportive partners. Further back still, the successful 'planning' group appeared to have benefitted from positive experiences at school – an interested teacher, a talent in music or sport that was recognised – that gave these particular girls increased resilience based on raised self-esteem and self-efficacy. The result of these pleasurable successes raised confidence to take active steps to deal with life's daily demands. Such results are a powerful reminder of the importance that school life can play – for good or ill – in children's psychosocial development.

Rutter (1995: 85) summarises matters of risk, resilience and recovery in six points. Individual variation, he says, derives:

- from personal characteristics, including temperament
- in part from previous experience

- in part from the ways in which the individual copes with negative experiences
- in part through indirect chain effects stemming from the experience and how it is dealt with
- in part by subsequent experiences
- in part from the way in which people cognitively process or think about and see themselves as individuals.

Formulating aims

The basic purpose of the assessment is not just to understand what is happening, but also to use that understanding as a guide to future action. In practice, it is possible to disassemble the somewhat global nature of the overall developmental goals and recognise that there is a hierarchy of aims and sub-aims that cascade downwards to the level of risks and protections particular to the individual child in his or her psychosocial context. Each level of the aim hierarchy supports those above. This means that, when thinking about overall objectives, it is necessary to build up case aims from the lowest level upwards, beginning with reducing risks and increasing protective forces. A developmental attachment perspective helps to define each level. This ensures that good practice is built up systematically from children's immediate concrete experiences to more global developmental goals. Figure 10.1 describes the hierarchy of aims implied in practices that apply developmental attachment theory.

I	(i)	To ensure the child's physical safety
	(ii)	To promote the child's psychological well-being and psychosocial development
II		To increase resiliences
III		To increase 'felt security' and disconfirm insecure internal working models
IV	(i)	To decrease risk effects and stressors
	(ii)	To increase protective influences, buffers and supports

Figure 10.1   Hierarchy of aims

An understanding of the concepts of risk and resilience tells us something about how people respond to stress. Developmental perspectives also guide practitioners towards identifying and fostering experiences that have the potential to offer children protection in situations of adversity. The planning sequence runs through the hierarchy of aims, building up from aims that seek to reduce risks and improve protective experiences so that children's ability to resist stress and adversity increases.

Level IV aims

To decrease risk effects ands stressors

Life stressors place vulnerable children at increased developmental risk. Stress may be experienced within relationships or the physical environment. The assessment identifies the psychosocial risks that appear to have disturbed and continue to disturb children's emotional development and social behaviour. These include one or more of the following:

- *child effects*, for example, difficult temperament or possible neurobiological problems
- *parental adjustment*, for example antisocial behaviour, psychopathology, neglect, depression, drug/alcohol misuse, parental conflict and violence, perceived parenting hassles or marital dissatisfaction
- *parental discipline*: harsh, coercive, inconsistent, unpredictable, aggressive, violent, non-negotiable or ineffective
- *demographic risk factors*: low socio-economic status, poor housing, overcrowding, low family income or a high-risk social environment
- *insecure caregiving*, particularly *disorganised, uncertain, rejecting, controlling, helpless, neglectful* or *abusive* caregiving, leading to insecure, possibly disorganised attachments.

Although it will not be possible to remove or ameliorate some of these risks (for example, neurobiological problems), the assessment should indicate which risks (a) appear to be having a particular adverse affect on the child's current behaviour and development, and/or (b) are most amenable to reduction. There are likely to be close links between some of these risks such that to tackle one is to do something about another. For example, insecure caregiving by a mother could be made worse by the presence of an unsupportive, even violent, partner. Both of these pose a risk for children's psychological development. Aiming to reduce these risk effects might therefore see a dual focus on improving parental relationships (counselling, separation or improved finances) and increasing caregiver responsivity and availability. Throughout childhood, a major risk is for a child to experience many and frequent switches of caregiver. Practitioners should as much as possible avoid children being moved repeatedly between birth parents and other carers, including foster parents, adopters and others.

To increase protective influences, buffers and supports

A wide range of experiences and accomplishments are capable of encouraging children to develop personal strengths and psychosocial skills in order to help them cope with life's difficulties. These protective processes act in complex ways. The more robust individuals are in terms of self-worth and interpersonal competence, the less disturbed they will feel in the face of setbacks, the fewer setbacks they will encounter and the more skilfully they will deal with them. Resilience is increased. A parallel set of aims runs alongside those intent on reducing risks and stressors. These are designed to increase the number of protective processes, partly to increase children's resilience and partly to avoid risks. A stable, long-term relationship with warm, loving and consistent caregivers is perhaps the most potent protective experience.

Level III aims

To increase 'felt security' (disconfirm insecure working models/ negative mental representations of the self and/or others)

Research repeatedly suggests that children's experience of secure early relationships promotes feelings of high self-esteem, self-efficacy and self-reflexivity. 'To that extent,' says Rutter (1990: 206), 'secure, harmonious parent–child relationships provide a degree of protection against later risk environments.' Children's 'felt security' is likely to increase if their carers (and possibly other adults important to them) become more emotionally available and sensitive. To the extent that children feel that the world is more predictable, reliable and responsive, they will feel more secure. They will generate a more positive view of the self, other people and the emotionally supportive and constructive value of relationships. In other words, if carers and others repeatedly behave in ways that 'disconfirm' children's mental representations of other people as unavailable and the self as unloved, unlovable and ineffective, there will be modest shifts of the internal working model from insecure to secure.

New or old relationships that provide more positive interactions always have the potential to bolster people's concept of self. Indeed, the ability to intervene and positively impact on parent–child or child–other relationships should be a major component of good practice. The concept of 'turning points', whereby an individual's life course can be shifted to a more positive, adaptive trajectory, lies behind many intervention plans.

Such shifts in the way children mentally represent themselves and others can come about through (a) changes in the behaviour and understandings of carers and other important adults, and/or (b) changes in the behaviour and understandings of the children themselves. In essence, many of the attempts to reduce risk and increase protection will result in improvements in parent–child interactions such that views of the self, others and relationships become more positive in outlook. Increased feelings of security have a number of linked benefits:

- Children experience less anxiety about attachment-related issues: there is increased confidence in other people's availability and interest.
- To the extent that elements of children's insecure working models are disconfirmed by the more responsive behaviour of others, children actually experience *fewer* attachment-related issues and anxieties.
- Within more secure relationships, children are able to develop a more resilient self so that stress and adversity are less likely to lead to disturbance and emotional turbulence. The self can withstand more 'knocks'.

Increased 'felt security' therefore implies that children feel more positive about both themselves and other people. They are better able to regulate their own emotions. This gives them the opportunity to reflect more freely, flexibly and accurately about their own and other people's feelings and thoughts, and how these might relate to behaviour. The cognitive processing and undistorted mental representation of negative life experiences acts as a protective mechanism. The self-reflective function identified by Fonagy *et al.* (1994) is something that might be taught to parents of insecure children to improve self and social understanding, and thus help them to focus better on their children's mental states. In the case of children, rather than seeing their poor relationship with their carer as the result of their own fail-ings, those 'free to evaluate' might recognise the difficulties stem-ming from their parent's depression or violent marriage.

Level II aims

To increase resiliences

Experiences that help children to develop psychological integrity, reasonable emotional composure and the ability to resist stress increase their resilience. Resilience, as we have seen, arises in a number of fields, including characteristics naturally present in the self and characteristics acquired via interaction with the social environ-ment, one of the most important being children's positive relationship with their carers. As little can be done by welfare practitioners about children's innate biological qualities, they are looking to increase resilience by bringing about changes in the interpersonal environ-ment. These might include changing people's responses to the child and/or the child's responses to other people and activities. In extreme cases, it might be necessary to remove children from relationships that seem irremediably damaging to their psychosocial development.

By a careful analysis of children's behaviour, needs and relation-ship history, social workers can plan to reduce risks and stressors, and increase protective and supportive factors, including 'felt security', so that, within the context of more positively experienced relationships, children can increase those resiliences based on a robust sense of self. These resiliences include:

- self-esteem
- self-efficacy
- social understanding and relatedness
- self-reflexivity
- autonomy.

In formulating aims in terms of changing the balance of risks and protections, social workers need to anticipate their effect on one or more of these five psychosocially based resiliences. Seeking to increase self-esteem helps children to feel good about themselves, valued and socially worthwhile. Improved self-efficacy encourages children to respond more constructively to the demands of interpersonal life. Self-efficacy includes the possession of skills to bring about desired social and environmental changes as well as the belief in oneself as an effective operator. According to Rutter (1995: 84), a positive self-concept comes about through three different routes:

- the experience of secure, supportive and warm reciprocal relationships in childhood with one's parents and friends, and in adulthood within love relationships
- the successful taking on of responsibilities and accomplishment of tasks
- successfully coping with stresses and challenges.

Increases in 'felt security' established within good-quality close relationships provide children with experiences that allow them to improve their understanding of their own and other people's feelings, actions and behaviours. The more that one's own and other people's behaviour appears to make sense, the more measured, thoughtful and flexible become one's own behavioural and emotional options. The ability to be self-reflective is a powerful skill that positively influences people's ability to understand and regulate their own emotions. In turn, this provides them with a wider range of responses so that interpersonal life is handled more fluently and constructively. The result is a more autonomous self, less bound by raised, unregulated affect, and more free to respond cooperatively.

Level I aims

The end result of thinking about aims hierarchically is the promotion of children's physical, emotional and social well-being based on a sound assessment of their past and present relationship history.

Conclusion

The last two chapters have classified and conceptualised the personal and interpersonal behaviours of parents and their children that practitioners meet in their day-to-day work. We will now outline a range of methods of help and intervention strategies than can be used to achieve the aims of a particular case.

11

Introducing protective mechanisms and processes

Within a relationship-based model of children's psychosocial development, interventions are premised on the belief that the quality of children's close relationships, particularly in the early years, profoundly affects their behaviour and development, and that, by changing the quality of close relationships, children can be helped to achieve their developmental potential. Practices that are culturally sensitive and family orientated, and foster support, can prevent problems and be cost-effective. Broadly speaking, interventions seek to modify the quality of interaction between children and their social environment (which includes parents, family, peers and other adults).

As Sroufe (1988) points out, it is not so much that the relationship between young children and their carers inevitably determines later development, but rather that children's initial relationship experiences with their carers probabilistically predict later social development because they affect 'expectations about others and relationships, feelings about self, and social skills used in other social contexts' (Belsky and Nezworski 1988: 5). Thus, according to attachment theory, modifications to (a) the quality of care provided, (b) the child's internal working model, or (c) a carer's internal working model of self and relationships, should result in shifts of children's developmental trajectory.

Attempts to improve or recover children's psychosocial well-being will therefore be concerned with trying to bring about changes in the quality of interaction between children and the people with whom they have a close relationship. In this sense, any technique or resource that promotes such an end is appropriate.

A number of common features run through all interventions based on a developmental attachment perspective. These include:

- practitioners acting as a 'secure base' and developing a 'therapeutic alliance' with clients

- efforts to increase the sensitivity, availability and responsiveness of carers
- an emphasis, particularly with younger children, on increasing the trust, attunement and understanding between parents and children
- increasing resiliences, particularly those based on self-esteem, social empathy, self-reflexivity, social relatedness and self-efficacy
- consideration of the internal working models and mental representations that parents use to guide their interactions with their children and partners, and how the attachment experiences of carers may be contributing to the relationship difficulties that they have with their children.

Internal working models of the self, others and relationships drive so many of people's perceptions and behaviours that they are an obvious target for intervention. McMillen and Rideout (1996: 386) suggest that insecure working models can be shifted towards more secure ones through three types of experience:

1. repeated interaction with people who disconfirm models acquired earlier
2. changes in relationships with early caregivers
3. powerful positive relationships.

The providers of such positive experiences might include parents with good reflective function, stable partners, interested teachers, supportive social workers, substitute carers or long-term reliable friends.

Developmental attachment theory acts as a guide to a range of practices so that the interventions chosen and decisions made have the aim of increasing children's resilience, 'felt security' and social competence. Social competence is based on social understanding, which is achieved in reasonably harmonious, warm and trusting relationships. In such relationships, children learn to make sense of both themselves and others. In the process, they achieve autonomy, self-reflexivity, behavioural flexibility, emotional regulation, social understanding and interpersonal skill. This and the following two chapters therefore act as a *guide* to social work interventions organised around a number of psychosocial and developmental concepts. A small number out of a growing volume of intervention studies are used to illustrate some of the methods available for those using a developmental perspective.

The choice and targets of interventions are not arbitrary. They are determined by the character of the assessment, which includes an understanding of the client's internal working model, the way in which the self and others are being mentally represented and the attachment classification based on these understandings. In particular, a clear understanding of the risks that have contributed and continue adversely to affect children's psychosocial development underscores both the choice of interventions and the sites where they are to be carried out. An attachment perspective systematically guides the practitioner through a number of conceptual stages of the intervention process until he or she arrives at particular responses, services, decisions and treatments. There are three conceptual stages that help practitioners to clarify and determine their choice of intervention:

- the introduction and/or growth of protective mechanisms and processes
- the site and focus of intervention
- the psychosocial domains to be influenced or changed, leading to the identification and implementation of specific responses, services and treatments.

So, for example, based on her assessment, a social worker might decide:

- to increase a young child's *self-esteem* (a protective factor)
- by improving a *parent's* caregiving skills (focus of intervention)
- in terms of the parent being more *emotionally attuned* and sensitive to her child's psychological needs (psychosocial domain)
- through the use of *parent video-training* in which mothers and fathers observe and analyse their own caregiving competences (treatment technique).

Each of the three stages will now be discussed in more detail in the remainder of this and the next two chapters.

Introduction of protective mechanisms and processes

By definition, the children dealt with by social workers are those about whom there are concerns. In the language of developmental psychology, these concerns translate as developmental risks. However handled, social workers respond to these concerns in terms of trying to decrease the psychosocial risks to which children are exposed, mitigate against the consequences that have accrued as a result of previous exposure to risks, and increase the number of protective influences that are known to help children to adjust emotionally and socially. Rutter (1990, 1995) helpfully reviews research and thinking in this field and suggests that basically five groups of *protective mechanism* can be identified that help children to develop increased *resilience* when faced with the risks posed by a range of life stressors and adversities:

1. those which involve a reduction in the personal impact of the risk experiences
2. those which reduce negative chain reactions stemming from the risk encounter
3. those which promote self-esteem, self-efficacy and social empathy through the availability of secure, supportive relationships or success in task accomplishment
4. those which open up positive opportunities
5. the positive cognitive processing of negative experiences, including the promotion of self-reflexivity and social under-standing.

Reduction of risk impact

There are two basic ways of reducing a child's exposure to a risk or hazard. The first involves *removal of the child from the risk* (for example, removal from abusive parents, a severely depressed mother or a delinquent peer group) to an alternative type of care or location.

The second requires *removal of the risk from the child* (for example, a legal injunction on a sexually abusive father not to visit the home, reduction in family poverty or a lessening of parental conflict). Milder versions of risk reduction by removal, for example, might include: parents implementing tighter forms of supervision to stop an 8-year-old boy roaming a criminally active neighbourhood with delinquent friends after dark; a less intense involvement with a mentally ill parent (compensated by an increased involvement with the mentally well parent); and providing contraception to prevent a sexually active 14-year-old girl becoming pregnant. Parental conflict and violence is particularly disruptive to children's development as it increases feelings of insecurity and emotional distress. Efforts to improve the quality of marriages or partnerships not only remove risks for children, but might also introduce more positive, protective relationships into family life. Intimacy between parents (supportive, sharing, confiding relationships) has been found to have a positive impact on children's development and the emergence of secure attachments (Cox *et al.* 1989). The provision of family support services has repeatedly been found to be effective in reducing *long-term* problem behaviours in children.

Family support for depressed mothers

A study by Lyons-Ruth *et al.* (1990) examined the effect of a home support visiting service provided to the mothers of at-risk infants. The mothers were depressed, lived in poverty and showed poor caregiving skills, including maltreatment. The mothers with family histories of conflict, severe punishment and lack of warmth were most likely to parent their children in a hostile, intrusive way. Interventions provided a trusting and accepting relationship, helped with meeting basic material needs, modelled more positive interactions with children and decreased maternal isolation. The most effective intervention appeared to be improvements in parent–child interactions. Subsequent follow-up studies found that the children were more securely attached than children in similar conditions who had not received the services. Children of matched families who did not receive the intervention showed higher rates of the angry, rejecting behaviours characteristic of children classified as disorganised.

Another way of reducing the impact of a potential risk is to change its meaning, thereby decreasing its ability to disturb a child's social development. Children who successfully deal with a mild exposure to a risk become 'steeled' to subsequent, possibly more severe risk encounters. A child who has regularly stayed with a grandparent overnight might cope better with her mother's hospitalisation. Bridging placements between foster care and adoptive placements allow children to maintain concurrent contact between centres of 'attachment'. Such placements mean that children do not suffer some arbitrary, abrupt change of carer for which they might feel in some way to blame (Fahlberg 1994; Morris 1996). Protection in these cases lies in helping children to understand and experience the potentially upsetting event more positively.

Bridging attachments

'Bridging' attachments are used to aid children in moving from foster care into adoption. Bridging placements help to minimise the trauma of further moves. It is now understood that foster parents can encourage the formation of an attachment bridge that enables children to cross over to their adoptive family with less trauma and more security. Fahlberg (1994: 167–223) points out that abrupt moves that break caring relationships with attachment figures are psychologically injurious. The trauma of losses and separations can be lessened if children are carefully prepared for transitions. Honesty, openness and sensitivity are recommended. Emotions have to be supported, and explanations need to be given to children about all that is happening and is planned to happen to them.

The use of pre-placement visits is strongly recommended. They help to diminish fear and can be used to transfer attachments, allowing the grieving process to take place at a psychologically healthy pace. Considerable contact between foster carers and adopters, particularly in the case of transferring preverbal children, is required. 'Unresolved separations may interfere with the development of new attachments. New attachments are not meant to replace old ones. They are meant to stand side-by-side with existing relationships' (Fahlberg 1994: 160). Post-placement contacts with previous carers are therefore advised. This helps to prevent denial and avoidance, develops a sense of continuity and trust in others, decreases loyalty issues and facilitates the transfer of attachment relationships from old carers to new ones. An attachment perspective demands that adults give much thought to what is likely to decrease children's feelings of anxiety and distress on the one hand and increase their feelings of security and being understood on the other, particularly during periods of major transition.

The 'neutralisation' of a risk occurs when a setback or loss is quickly followed by a success or recovery. For example, children who lose their mother through death, abandonment or rejection may feel that they are less lovable, less effective and less able to maintain close relationships. However, children are known to adjust better to such losses if they receive heightened levels of good care from the remaining parent or a relative who becomes more involved with the child. Such positive experiences counteract damage to self-esteem and social effectiveness (Brown and Harris 1978). In contrast, children who lose a parent and then fail to receive warm, supportive care find themselves at increased risk of feeling unlovable, helpless and depressed during adolescence and adulthood.

Support also helps to dilute the impact of potential stressors – 'a trouble shared is a troubled halved'. Demanding tasks can be distributed, talked about and approached differently. In adulthood, supportive partners in whom one can confide have been found to be particularly effective providers of psychological protection.

Practitioners therefore need to (a) identify the risks to which children are currently being exposed, and (b) work out how to reduce the presence and impact of those risks.

Reduction of negative chain reactions

Exposure to a risk can very easily set in train a series of further risk encounters, creating a vicious circle of negative experiences, each one of which further denies the child opportunities to develop adaptive behaviours. For example, a baby with an innately difficult, irascible temperament may undermine a carer's confidence in her parenting skills. This increases the carer's anxiety and reduces her availability, both of which raise the baby's distress to even higher levels. There is nothing that can be done about the infant's temperament, but interventions might concentrate on helping the carer to understand, stay with and soothe her baby, thus bringing to a halt the negative chain reaction. Teaching parents more sensitive ways of engaging with their children allows children to feel less distressed and more understood. Videotaping parent–child interactions is proving to be a popular and effective method of encouraging parents to develop more sensitive and attuned caregiving.

Video-parenting: promoting positive early parent–child relationships through interaction guidance

Interaction (relational) guidance approaches aim to help parents to gain enjoyment from their children. They also aid parents in developing an understanding of their child's behaviour. It is a coaching base method used during parent–child play. 'Treatment involves a videotaped play session in which mother and/or father (or parenting partner) play with the child as the therapist supports the caregiver's positive interactions with the infant. Following the play session, selected portions of the videotape are viewed with the parents. The therapist uses these taped sequences to highlight for the parents their interactions with their infant and to provide feedback about the caregiver's own behavior. The therapist seeks to empower families by focusing on identified positive caregiving behaviors during the videotape replay and by attending to problems and insights that the family initiates' (McDonough 1995: 662). To assist parents in developing an understanding of their children's growth and behaviour, they become actively involved in making observations and reflecting on the videotaped material, including their own style of interaction and play with the child. The videotape allows immediate feedback on the *parents' behaviour* and its *effect on the child.*

'Through viewing samples of parent–child interaction, family members become more aware of important interactive behaviors that are positive and need to be reinforced, elaborated, and extended, and those interactions that were less enjoyable or inappropriate and require redirection, alteration, or elimination. The use of the videotape also provides parents with the opportunity to listen more carefully to what they say to their child and the manner in which they say it' (McDonough 1995: 664). The technique is consistent with attachment theory as it aims to enhance maternal sensitivity and responsiveness towards young children. It is also involves a joint, dyadic, interactional focus on both mother and child.

Many maltreated children find it difficult to understand or cope with their own and other people's distress. They react with agitation and aggression. As a result, their peers either reject them or respond with hostility, reactions that increase the maltreated child's rage and confusion. Interventions that try to break these vicious circles might concentrate on helping abused children to manage their anger; teaching them in small, closely supervised groups with a good deal of rewarding, self-enhancing attention; or providing them with psychotherapy.

Interventions that improve the social, emotional and problem-solving skills of either parents or children can act as powerful breaks of negative chain reactions. In terms of improving children's socio-emotional development, therefore, protection lies in controlling the response of either the children or their social environment. For example, in relationship play therapy, mothers not only experience positive interactions with their children, but also enjoy considerable emotional support from each other.

Relationship play therapy

Direct work on the mother–child relationship has been developed by Binney *et al.* (1994). The children with whom they work generally show extremes of problem behaviour. Their ages range between 4 and 7 years old. Problems of parental control are associated with high levels of maternal distress. Mothers' attitudes to their children range from rejection to intense overinvolvement and guilt. Many of the mothers suffer depression and poor marital relationships, and have histories of poor-quality caregiving themselves. Many have had backgrounds of abuse, trauma and loss. Relationship play therapy is designed to break down habitually insecure patterns of relating between mothers and their children. The play is complemented by a mothers' 'talk group'. The general atmosphere created by the therapy team is one of security so that both children and mothers feel safe to explore.

Familiar games are played between children and parents with an emphasis on fun, relaxation, warm affect and reciprocity. They are designed to entice children into new ways of relating. Over the 12 weekly sessions, the games become increasingly intimate, beginning with light group games and ending with paired face painting and storytelling, with the child sitting very close to his or her mother. In other words, there is a kind of regression from playground-type games to more infantile levels of play involving bodily contact.

The mothers' 'talk group' that runs in conjunction with the play typically evolves through four stages:

1. complaints about the children's behaviour
2. distress and anger towards partners for lack of support or abandonment
3. feelings about their own mother, in terms of past and present support
4. feelings about power and powerlessness in relationships.

Mothers begin to make connections between the child's behaviour, their own distress and relationships between them, their partners and their own experiences of being parented as a child.

Relationship play therapy appears effective:

- in building warm, therapeutic relationships between mothers and therapists, and mothers and other mothers
- 'in making some impact on well established defensive styles of relating between mother and child' (Binney *et al.* 1994: 58).

Promotion of self-esteem and self-efficacy

There is strong research evidence that to view the self as worthy, competent and understandable is highly protective. These resiliences mean that social challenges and stresses less easily undermine the self, which continues to be perceived as likable and effective. Individuals approach difficulties with the confidence that they might be able to resolve problems and control what happens. We might also add to these resiliences the ability of children to understand their own and other people's affective states. This facilitates the fulfilment of the need for *relatedness* – the need to feel securely connected to other people, the need to experience oneself as worthy, and the need to love and be loved. Throughout life, but particularly during toddlerhood, people search for a balance between relatedness and autonomy – the inner mental correlates of attachment and exploratory behaviours (Lieberman 1992: 563).

Sroufe (1989a) provides the good example of two preschool children dancing to music. As new children joined the group, a little boy, classified as avoidantly attached, asked another child to dance. The child refused and the boy sulkily withdrew, feeling hurt. A young securely attached girl similarly asked newcomers to dance with her. At first, she too suffered a rejection, but she skipped over to another child who did accept her request to dance. Whereas the boy cut himself off from the opportunity of enjoying a more confirming experience, the girl went on to experience herself not only as acceptable, but also as someone who was socially effective. Her sense of self was sufficiently robust to see her through the setback and propel her along a chain reaction of positive experiences.

As Gilligan (1997: 15) makes clear, it is those aspects of resilience that develop within social relationships that are of particular interest to social workers. They are the ones that can be influenced or sponsored. *High self-esteem* develops most strongly within the context of *warm, supportive secure relationships*. Feelings of *self-efficacy* arise as a result of *successful task accomplishment*, often facilitated and encouraged within secure relationships with interested attachment figures. Many intervention strategies are therefore designed to raise children's level of felt security. Secure, reciprocal parent–child relationships offer protection against risks and adversity. This generally means, particularly in the case of younger children, that social workers will be working heavily with parents with a view to improving and supporting their emotional availability, responsivity and interest.

Although feelings of self-worth and esteem form within early relationships, they need not remain fixed. It is within negative caregiving relationships that low self-esteem becomes established, but later experiences of more positive relationships – at any age in the lifespan – can help to improve poor self-concepts. People who take an interest, who listen, care and love us, make us feel better. They improve our self-image and bolster our self-esteem. Children who are not loved at home may nevertheless develop feelings of self-worth if a relative takes an interest, a teacher appears concerned and caring, or a residential worker responds with kindness and consistency.

In adulthood, one of the most powerful positive, protective experiences is to be found in intimate relationships with a stable, responsive partner. Quinton and Rutter's (1988) study of girls raised in institutional care found that those who enjoyed long-lasting relationships with secure partners showed much higher levels of psychosocial adjustment than girls who entered a series of volatile, unstable relationships with poorly adjusted men. Similarly, Egeland *et al.* (1988) found that abused mothers who (a) were able to form an emotionally supportive relationship with a non-abusive adult during childhood, (b) participated in therapy during any period of their lives, or (c) had a non-abusive, stable and emotionally supportive and satisfying relationship with a partner were able to break the cycle of maltreatment. The positive relationships provided a degree of developmental protection.

However, although it is always possible that children with low self-esteem may recover a more positive concept of self by experiencing a future relationship that is warm and supportive, it still remains the case that good-quality caregiving is the most potent form of self-enhancement for children. To be loved and valued by one's parents is a source of great comfort, security and pleasure. Social workers should thus always consider ways in which parents might be helped to engage more positively with their children, either by attempting to meet the parent's own emotional needs or by trying to improve their caregiving skills. Good-quality caregiving confers high levels of protection against the vagaries of life.

Children's ability to affect and influence the world around them, to believe that they can make a difference, to feel that they have some control over what happens, increases their sense of *self-efficacy*, a known resilience factor. Children who learn to concentrate, persist with seeking solutions to problems or successfully complete tasks enjoy raised levels of both self-efficacy ('I can affect and influence what happens to me') and self-esteem ('I feel good about myself as a person who accomplishes things and performs well'). Social workers should be aware of the places and people who provide, or could potentially provide, children with such positive experiences. Success at school in sports, music and practical skills as well as academic matters is likely to increase self-efficacy. Children who are given or who assume responsibility for important and valued activities at home and school have been shown to achieve better outcomes (Elder 1979 cited in Rutter 1990). Such accomplishments are not only satisfying in themselves, but also bring social recognition and esteem from peers, teachers and parents. Positive chain reactions in which other people are prepared to relate with increased interest and regard further raise children's positive feelings about the self. Will is a case in point.

Will

Will, aged 11 years, is one of four children. He has an older sister, Karen, and three younger sisters. His mother is pregnant again. Although Will and Karen have the same father, his younger sisters each have a different father. The mother, aged 31, with an early history of prostitution, has a boyfriend, but he does not live with the family. Whenever the social worker visits, a wide variety of other people seem to pop in and out of the house. There is a general feeling of confusion. The home is also physically cluttered. Karen appears to be carrying out a good deal of the parenting of her younger siblings. All the children, including Karen, are bed-wetters. Will's mother says that she cannot control him. Several times over recent years, she has requested his removal to foster care. From the age of 2 years, he has had temper tantrums. His mother says that he is argumentative and violent, impatient and easily upset. He quarrels with his younger sisters and behaves competitively. However, on the rare occasions when he is alone with his mother, he is said to behave well and with affection. Will is not a problem at school; indeed one of his teachers has said that he was 'a nice boy who liked to please', He also gets on well with his father and paternal grandparents, whom he visits once every 2 or 3 weeks. Whatever help has been given or offered either has not been followed through or has been said by the mother to be 'not working'. Social workers see her as demanding but find her frustrating and uncooperative.

The assessment suggested an enmeshed family. A working hypothesis classified mother's parenting as 'uncertain'. Will's demands make her feel anxious and rejecting. Will in turn increases his coercive attachment behaviour in relationship with his mother. However, he operates reasonably well in other relationships that were judged to be protective. Intervention plans were based on supporting and increasing two key positive relationships/activities. The first involved attempts to consolidate contact with Will's father and his paternal grandparents. The second was based on a recognition that Will was good at football. This brought him into relationship with a group of equally sports-orientated, non-deviant boys who formed the nucleus of the school football team. Liaison work with Will's schoolteachers helped them to understand his needs and how they could be met within the school context.

A sense of achievement at any age is rewarding and boosting. Successful task accomplishments can also generalise so that people feel more confident about tackling other challenges. Many problem-solving, task-centred, solution-focused techniques have the effect of not only resolving the particular issue, but also increasing feelings of self-efficacy. Capturing many of these themes, Gilligan (1997: 17–18) offers a number of key messages for practice including:

- encourage purposeful contact with family members and other key adults from the child's past
- encourage positive school experiences
- encourage friendships with peers
- actively foster interest, involvement and talents in sport, music, hobbies or cultural pursuits

● help the child to rehearse, observe and discuss problem-solving and coping skills and strategies.

Many maltreated children find it difficult to recognise, differentiate and access not only different emotional states, but also physical feelings derived from the senses. The identification and differentiation of basic feelings normally takes place in infancy and early childhood. Difficulties in this area mean that children find it difficult to understand and regulate themselves and others in emotionally charged situations. Social competence and social relatedness therefore tend to be poor.

Cognitive restructuring of the self and others within the context of holding therapy provides an example of how children can be helped to connect with their senses and feelings (see, for example, Cline 1992; Howe and Fearnley 1999). The physical proximity provided by 'holding' therapy allows both child and therapist to access feelings that are not always verbally expressed. More generally, the treatment not only helps children to release and demonstrate feelings, but also aims to help children to recognise, label and understand them. Not until children can distinguish between despair, anger, guilt, happiness, shame, rage and fear ('sad, mad, glad and scared') can they begin to regulate their own affect and understand the nature and origin of other people's feelings and behaviour. Indeed, many children find it difficult to differentiate even feelings associated with their basic senses, including touch, smell, taste, sound and sight. Bodily signals, such as pain, hunger or the need to urinate, are easily misread and lead to inappropriate behaviours (putting a winter coat on for a hot summer's day, or wanting to eat when they are already full). The experience, recognition and labelling of feelings comprise the first important step to help children to get in touch with themselves; to help them access and deal with their early experiences of loss and abuse, anger and rage; to recognise their true origins and make sense of how they continue to affect current feelings and behaviour in close relationships. Some forms of play therapy allow children to explore, experience and identify many of these basic physical and emotional states.

Positive opportunities and turning points

That not all insecure or maltreated children become socially maladjusted, and that there are many examples in which there are breaks in the intergenerational transmission of abuse and neglect, reminds us that many children otherwise destined to repeat the behavioural problems of their parents achieve social success. Throughout the lifespan, there are always opportunities to respond to new experiences. Children who are able to take advantage of these opportunities may experience a developmental 'turning point' that projects them along a more positive trajectory. School life, with its rich environment of new relationships and tasks, presents children with occasions to identify, develop and establish fresh, more robust and socially valued aspects of the self. A child's talents may be recognised. New skills may be acquired. Supportive friendships may form. A non-deviant peer group may be joined. These experiences are potentially protective. 'Success in coping with these challenges', writes Rutter (1990: 208), 'may be protective in children from seriously disadvantaged homes, just as failure may create psychiatric vulnerability or risks.'

Children who avoid, resist or scupper such opportunities not only miss out on protective experiences, but also increase their exposure to risks including social isolation, skill incompetence and academic failure. Insecure children, particularly children who have suffered neglect and maltreatment, are those most likely to avoid, resist or feel anxious about new opportunities. Interventions may need to help these highly vulnerable children to recognise and respond to such opportunities. Practitioners might alert and train those who are in appropriate positions (a youth worker, a school teacher, a volunteer) to encourage children to respond to social opportunities when they might normally refuse.

The world of work and adult relationships continues to throw opportunities and hazards in people's way. Successes and failures in task accomplishments and relationships provide further potential turning points along an individual's developmental pathway in directions that might adaptively be either positive or negative. Downes reports the positive impact that skilled foster carers can have on adolescents.

Foster care for adolescents

Downes (1992) describes the potential developmental opportunities available to troubled adolescents placed in foster care. She classifies fostered adolescents in terms of the main attachment styles, with children developing either avoidant, coercive or anxiously passive behaviours in the care context. The simple provision of foster carers holds no guarantee in itself of a positive impact. Carers and children have to be helped and supported if psychosocial benefits are to be achieved.

Downes sees the foster carers as ideally offering adolescents a 'secure base' for negotiating the transition to adult life. The secure base, if established, allows children to explore difficult issues, past, present and future. Part of the social worker's task is to ensure that the total caregiving system is supported so that the secure base effect is realised. Foster carers need to be helped to support adolescents' efforts to reappraise (reflect on) their relationships with their own parents. The ultimate aim is to help children to develop their capacities for relationships and mature independence in adult life.

Positive cognitive processing of negative experiences, and the promotion of self-reflectivity and social understanding

The ability to step back and think about not only what one thinks or feels, but also *why* one might be having those thoughts or feelings increases autonomy and social understanding. The cognitive processing of potentially negative experiences lessens their impact. Self-reflection, positive cognitive processing, metacognition and the ability to accept the reality of negative experiences act as protective mechanisms. The ability mentally to represent difficult interpersonal experiences is more likely to arise within secure attachments, in those predisposed to have a positive outlook, in those with strong cognitive capacities and in the presence of other variables associated with increased resilience.

One of the most striking examples of the protective power of accurate and positive cognitive processing of negative experiences is the ability of some adults to develop secure–autonomous attachment styles even though they have suffered loss, abuse and trauma in childhood. These reflective abilities are nicely picked up in Main and Goldwyn's (1985–1994) AAI, in which adults abused and neglected as children and classified as 'secure–autonomous' talk about their childhood hardships in a way that is coherent, evaluative and able to access attachment issues without defensive distortion. Thus, rather than see emotional problems and hurts as personal failings, secure adults are better able to see such reactions as a consequence of, for example, their mother being depressed or their father being violent. It is not what happened in childhood that matters but how it is thought about and processed in adult life. In practice terms, this highlights the value of self-reflection and cognitive awareness, capacities that might arise in counselling, psycho-therapy or everyday conversation (with a loving, stable partner; with a social worker; or with other women in a support group).

Parental reflections on their own childhood experiences

A study by Beckwith (described in Beckwith and Sigman 1995: 691) looked at the effects of a bi-weekly home visiting service with a special emphasis on issues surrounding children's development. The parents of the intervention group showed an increased ability to shift the quality of their reflections on the quality of relationships with their own parents compared with parents who had not received the intervention. Moreover, those parents able to engage in such reflections and make shifts in their perceptions of their own childhood adversity were more likely to have children who showed an increase in the security of their attachment.

Prevention, treatment and protection

It is also possible to combine ideas about increasing protective processes with different types of prevention and treatment. Epidemiologists distinguish three modes of intervention: primary, secondary and tertiary. These can be used to guide thinking and practice in work with children and their families.

Primary prevention involves practices designed to prevent children being exposed to the risk in the first place or, if the risk cannot be avoided, to help children build up some resistance (resilience) to that risk. So, for example, early interventions by health workers teaching the mothers of 'at-risk' babies how to increase their emotional availability and responsivity represents an attempt to increase parent–child confidence and security. Health visitors who visit and support vulnerable mothers have been shown to be very effective in protecting children developmentally. For example, the Prenatal/Early Infancy Project in Elmira, New York, involved nurses targeting their visits on mothers who were either teenagers, unmarried or poor (Olds *et al.* 1986; also see the STEEP program, Erickson *et al.* 1992). Visits continued for the first 2 years of the infant's life. The positive effects of the programme included longer gestation, higher birthweights, less reported child abuse and neglect, and mothers postponing their next pregnancy.

The introduction of community supports (family centres and mother and toddler groups) provides parents with emotional, social and practical resources to help them to meet their own needs (Whittaker 1993).

Family and community support

Gibbons *et al.* (1990) studied the impact of family support provisions in two geographical areas. Family support services were successful in attracting parents and families with the highest level of need. Parents receiving the support reported gains, and there was evidence that they were coping better as a result of the support. 'The research provided some reasons to think that parents under stress more easily overcome family problems when there are many sources of family support available in local communities. The most useful form of provision may be good quality day care' (Gibbons 1992).

The Yale Child Welfare Project (Provence and Naylor 1983) provided an intensive family support programme for the first two and half years of children's lives. The programme included supportive home visits, day care provisions and health care for the children. Comparisons were made with a control group who did not receive the interventions. When the children were 12 years old, the intervention group showed better school attendance and higher social adjustment than the control group. Mothers in the intervention group had had fewer children and had obtained more education. A similar programme with low-income families run by Syracuse University also demonstrated good long-term results (Lally *et al.* 1988). Project children at the age of 10 years showed lower rates of delinquency.

Family centres

There is considerable research evidence that family centres provide much valued support to families living in high-risk and stressful environments. For example, Smith (1992) reports that parents felt that attendance at the centres helped their children to 'mix' better with other children, provided adults with a chance to socialise and gain emotional support, and helped to relieve some of the pressures felt living in a stressful environment. One mother said, 'It's calmed me down a bit, I think. It's made me look at things a bit more in perspective instead of getting so wound up' (Smith 1992: 19).

Family and Schools Together Program (FAST Track)

The Conduct Problems Prevention Research Group (CPPRG 1992) has developed the FAST Track Program to develop, implement and evaluate interventions to prevent severe and chronic conduct problems in a sample of children selected as high risk when they first enter school. 'The intervention is guided by a developmental theory positing the interaction of multiple influences on antisocial behavioral development' (CPPRG 1992: 510). The programme recognises that the early signs of conduct disorder are seen in the preschool years, children showing irritability and discipline problems, and being inattentive and impulsive. These signs are typically found in families characterised by patterns of high stress and instability, parental psychopathology, marital discord, insecure attachments and harsh, punitive and inconsistent discipline. Given the complexity and pervasiveness of these many factors, prevention programmes need to be comprehensive, multidisciplined, long term and multistaged. 'We not only attempt to build appropriate skills, attitudes, and expectancies in each system (family, school, peer), but also focus on building positive relations among these systems' (CPPRG 1992: 524). The intervention takes place at the point of entry to school – a time of transition and increased stress for the family. The intervention seeks to:

- promote reductions in the display of disruptive behaviours in the home setting, with corresponding improvements in parent–child relationships through skills training, particularly in the area of discipline
- bring about reductions in the child's disruptiveness at school
- increase social-cognitive skills to help them to control strong feelings and improve social problem-solving
- improve peer relationships
- promote academic skills, particularly reading
- improve the quality of the parent–school relationship.

Secondary prevention describes those interventions that aim to treat or change problems while they are still in their early stages. Pre-school children who are beginning to show oppositional defiant disorders (often a precursor of later, more serious conduct disorders) in response to anxious parenting might be helped in a variety of ways. A lone parent might lack support and feel under stress financially. A mother may try to cope with her distress by becoming less involved and yet more punitive with her increasingly demanding toddler. Responses in these situations might include giving benefits advice, providing frequent but low-intensity supportive home visits or carrying out behaviour therapy to encourage a parent to reshape his or her child's behaviour along more desirable lines using techniques based on instrumental conditioning. Potentially more serious problems are nipped in the bud through combinations of increasing people's skill and efficacy, improving self-esteem, breaking negative chain reactions in their early stages and helping people to develop less distorted processes of cognition and reflection.

Tertiary prevention refers to interventions that aim to reduce the degree of psychosocial dysfunction and impairment suffered by those who have already proved to be vulnerable when exposed to risks. Attempts to rehabilitate vulnerable children with their families fall into this category. Helping children to control their anger, concentrate longer at school and play more constructively with their friends can also be seen as treatments designed to help children to improve their social functioning.

In social work, primary interventions are conventionally referred to as 'preventive' work, whereas secondary and tertiary level interventions are known as treatments. Prevention is, of course, always better than cure, but in practice, many children's psychosocial development has been severely impaired by prolonged exposure to multiple risks. Tertiary interventions, ideally curative, but more commonly containing and controlling, will therefore continue to be a major strand in social work practice.

12

The sites and focus of intervention

Interventions can take place in one or more of three prime sites:

- the family home
- 'clinics' or specialist centres
- key community locations (school, family centre and youth centre).

Practice in 'natural' home settings, although difficult to control, is often more apt and effective.

Interventions can also be classified in terms of their *focus*. The basic division is between those interventions which focus on changing aspects of the parents' experience and behaviour, and those which focus on changing aspects of the children's experience and behaviour. Many interventions focus jointly on both parents and children (Figure 12.1).

		Focus on child	
		Low	*High*
Focus on Parent	High	Parent focused: *parent* *parent ↔ partner* *parent → child* *parent → others*	Jointly focused: *parent(s) ↔ child* *family*
	Low	Family/ community support and monitoring services	Child focused: *child* *child → parent* *child → peers* *child ↔ peers* *child ↔ school*

Figure 12.1   Focus of interventions (adapted from Meisels *et al.* 1993)

A rough rule of thumb is that, with increasing age of the child, interventions gradually shift from a focus on the parents to a focus on the child. It is also broadly the case that, with increasing age of the child, there is a move from primary prevention, through secondary intervention to tertiary intervention. Adding these two rough and ready rules together suggests that preventive work with the parents of young children is designed to reduce children's exposure to risks, while therapeutic work with older children aims to treat and modify problem social behaviours that have already developed in response to prolonged exposure to high-risk environments and relationships. The most effective and economic interventions measured over time are preventive practices with young children and their parents.

Parent-focused interventions

For young children, the most significant social environment in terms of their psychosocial development is the caregiving relationship provided by their parents. The quality and character of that relationship is influenced by parents':

- own attachment needs
- own relationship history and experiences of care as a child
- response to attachment-related issues (especially those triggered by the needs of the child)
- internal working model and mental representation of the self and others (particularly the child)
- defensive strategies.

The more insecure, anxious, distressed, defended and emotionally needy is the parent, the less psychologically available and responsive will he or she be to the child. Insecure caregiving poses a major developmental risk to the growing child. Thus, a highly important focus of intervention in many cases will be the parent or parents. Cicchetti *et al.* (1995: 56) state that:

> Unless the level of caregiving dysfunction is so great that the child will be removed from the home, we believe that attention must be directed toward the representations that the parent has carried forward into the caregiving context. In many cases, efforts to establish a therapeutic relationship with the parent may reflect the first opportunity that the parent has had to feel accepted... it is only through empathy with the parent that a possible bridge can be established

between parent and child. Depending on the magnitude of parental distrust and insecurity, early work may need to focus exclusively on the caregiver.

Social workers may work *indirectly* on children's psychosocial development by offering parents:

- emotional support
- material support
- community support and self-help groups
- improved reflective functioning via *ad hoc* conversational opportunities, counselling, psychotherapy and self-help groups
- couple counselling
- advocacy and advice
- problem-solving and planning skills using task-centred, solution-focused approaches and family group conferences.

Parents become more available and sensitive to their children when their levels of stress are reduced and they experience an increase in their own felt security, confidence, self-esteem, self-efficacy and social understanding. Warm, secure caregiving offers children a protective experience by both decreasing the relationship risks posed by hostile or rejecting parenting, and increasing resilience as result of improved self-esteem, understanding and social competence.

It is generally recognised that a powerful source of protection for children derives from parents enjoying close, supportive relationships with other adults. Effective relationships include the presence of emotional, material, practical and social support. Such relationships act as a buffer against life stressors. Research evidence also indicates that mothers who enjoy satisfactory, stable relationships, particularly with their partners, display more competent caregiving. They feel more competent as parents and less stressed by their responsibilities, with the result that children feel more secure (Cochran and Brassard 1979; Crockenberg 1981). Therapy, counselling and support offered to couples therefore have the potential indirectly to improve the quality of care given to children.

Work that impinges *directly* on the quality of parent–child interaction includes techniques such as parent skills training, parent education programmes, behaviour modification programmes and changing parental perceptions of children's attributions. For example, abusing parents might be helped to focus on their patterns of miscommunication, particularly in the area of emotions.

> ## Conflict resolution between parents' and children's increased security of attachment
>
> Studies reported by Heinicke and colleagues (cited in Beckwith and Sigman 1995: 692) found that couples in conflict who had been helped by having their interactions videotaped and then discussed were more likely to have infants who showed an increased security of attachment. Young children of parents who are better able to regulate their conflict and negativity appear to develop more secure attachments and show increased autonomy. In more satisfying parental partnerships, mothers show more positive affect towards their children. 'Marital functioning therefore provides an important focus for preventive interventions' (Beckwith and Sigman 1995: 692).

Child-focused interventions

Direct work with children aims to improve their social, emotional and behavioural competence. Such interventions might work at a number of levels. Children might be removed from high-risk environments and placed with foster carers or adoptive parents. Play therapy, psychotherapy, music therapy, drama therapy and group work can help children to improve their emotional understanding of themselves and others by giving them opportunities to recognise and name feelings, think about motivations and actions, and reflect on past and present relationships and the way in which they impact on feelings and behaviour. Cognitive behavioural techniques may teach children how to respond more constructively to difficult, distressing or problematic situations. Group work with older children can help in terms of offering peer support, shared understanding and group solutions. The range of interventions is legion, but underpinning all of them are attempts to improve children's self-esteem, interpersonal competence, confidence, behavioural flexibility and emotional understanding of the self and others through improved cognitive representations and processing.

Recognising and naming feelings

In her work with children being 'looked after' in foster care, Morris (1996) describes helping those with a history of abuse and neglect to get in touch with their senses. Using a variety of techniques that re-create early attachment experiences, the children are re-alerted to the sensations of touch, taste, smell, sight and sound. She helps them to get in tune with their bodies so that feelings of hunger, pain, tiredness, hot and cold can be recognised and their meanings understood. The basic emotions of happy, sad, angry and afraid are talked about, labelled and discussed. These are children whose emotions are often mixed and confused, so that feelings of fear, sadness and anger might trigger inappropriate behaviours that make matters worse. The children's growing awareness of their senses and feelings reawakens memories and their associated feelings. Gradual improvements in the identification, differentiation and accessing of present feelings and past memories allows children to make sense of and handle difficult relationship experiences. These improvements also mean that they begin to handle current attachment-related issues in a more balanced, constructive fashion. Morris underpins her work using an attachment perspective.

Play therapy

Securely attached and socially well-adjusted children play well and with imagination. Many abused and neglected children must be taught how to play. Children who show less imaginative play tend to be more aggressive and less flexible in their dealings with others. Children with behaviour problems and insecure attachments use fewer positive and negative themes in their play, with the exception of diffuse hostility (Russ 1995: 375).

Play encourages children to express feelings, regulate affect and develop coping skills. Most play therapy is in fact a mixture of play and talk. Play is both a form of communication with the therapist and a way of expressing feelings, thoughts and wishes. A number of mechanisms in play that appear therapeutic have been identified (Russ 1995): catharsis, labelling feelings, developing a more varied and accurate vocabulary of emotions and feelings, providing a corrective emotional experience, insight, working through difficult feelings, and learning alternative problem-solving techniques and coping strategies. Therapists often combine other techniques with play such as cognitive-behavioural approaches, teaching behavioural alternatives, and making connections and offering interpretations.

Cognitive-behavioural therapy

Many children with histories of insecure attachment, particularly those who have experienced some form of hostile abuse, go on to develop conduct disorders. These children typically have problems behaving flexibly in difficult social situations. They are quick to attribute hostile intentions to other people. Cognitive-behavioural therapies aim to improve children's cognitive and problem skills in order to reduce problem behaviours and negative chain reactions. For example, Kazdin *et al.* (1987) teach adolescent children to follow a set of step-by-step procedures to solve problems. Modelling, role-playing and reinforcement are also built into the treatments. Anger control training can also prove effective with children who are already experiencing major difficulties in interpersonal relationships (Kendall 1993). Anger arousal is believed to be mediated by the children's expectation of hostile reactions from others. Adolescent children learn to identify the triggers and social cues that make them angry. They are then asked to consider alternative behaviours that might be more suitable and less conflictual. Relaxation techniques, to be used at times of high arousal, are also taught.

Psychotherapy and adolescent children

Reviews of the research literature recognise that effective interventions with young people showing conduct disorders remain very limited, whatever the treatment technique employed (Kazdin 1987). Early, preventive intervention with young children showing aggressive, impulive, restless behaviour should be the social response of choice. However, this is still largely not the case. Richards and Sullivan (1996) describe psychotherapeutic work with 'delinquents', based on attachment theory. They follow the model developed by Holmes (1993) in which attention is paid to establishing a 'secure base' relationship. Nearly all the young people had histories of abuse, rejection, violence and loss. Talking about (exploring) and trying to make sense of these difficult experiences allowed the adolescents to build a 'coherent autobiographical narrative'. This can become integrated 'into a resonant story of loss and pain as opposed to dismissal or enmeshment' (Holmes 1993). Self-reflection allows people to reconnect with unresolved feelings, hurts and angers. They learn to understand the relationship between difficult feelings and behaviour, and this frees them up from the tyranny of unregulated emotional arousal. Non-verbal therapies are also used alongside reflective talk. Actions are generally easier for teenagers. Music, art, drama and sport not only allow expression of feelings, but also help people to gain recognition, esteem and a feeling of competence.

Group work and group therapy

As children grow older, the influence of their peers increases. Group work and group therapy with adolescents can be used both preventively and therapeutically. Group tasks can be either based on skills or social influence. A wide variety of techniques may be used, including cognitive-behavioural therapies, skills training, problem-solving, behavioural rehearsal (how to cope with difficult situations) and group support.

Jointly focused interventions

Many of the most effective interventions involve both children and parents, who are required jointly to think about, reflect upon and try out behaviours and emotions that are more positive, constructive and supportive. Many of the techniques used with parents and children separately can be used to good effect with both parties present. The examination and modification of parent–child interactions and communications is often most powerful in jointly focused interventions. Lieberman (1992), for example, describes effective work using an attachment approach helping mothers who are experiencing problems with their toddlers.

Family-based methods, including family therapy, can offer very clear guidance in handling interactions between parents and their children. For example, Byng-Hall (1991, 1995) applies an attachment perspective to treatment in family therapy. The treatment method itself triggers attachment behaviours in all family members. Such behaviours, within the safety and 'secure base' generated by the care of the therapist, then become available for examination and reflection for the therapist, parents and children. A 'secure family base', in which there is a network of reliable attachment relationships, is promoted to allow the 'exploration' of difficult experiences. The *availability of the therapist before, during and after treatment* is regarded as important. Links are made between the parents' own attachment histories and their current patterns of interaction; that is, families are helped to become self-reflective and create a 'coherent story'. 'Family therapists have an opportunity to work on the communications about attachment needs as they occur in the room' (Byng-Hall 1991: 213). Family treatment using an attachment perspective is reported to have promoted more secure attachment relationships between family members (Byng-Hall and Stevenson-Hinde 1991).

Lojkasek *et al.* (1994) identify four models of intervention that aim to change the quality of the relationship between mothers and young children:

1. Indirect effects on the relationship:

   - the provision of emotional and material support
   - psychotherapy.

2. Direct effects on the relationship:

   - developmental guidance with a focus on increasing mothers' knowledge of their children's abilities, needs, milestones and responses
   - relational (interactional) guidance, the emphasis being on helping mothers to increase their knowledge of and experience with their children in the context of spontaneous interactions.

The following two practice examples illustrate these indirect and direct effects on the quality of the parent–child relationship.

Three generations psychotherapy

Watanabe (1994) describes a case in which help was given to a Japanese mother whose toddler son was becoming increasingly detached and unresponsive. Paediatricians initially considered a number of possible explanations, including brain damage and autism. However, clinical work with the young mother established that her caregiving was anxious, rejecting and dismissing. She was tense and harsh with her child. Over the months since his birth, the boy, named Bo, had become increasingly avoidant and disengaged, behaviour that his mother thought was wilful. Over the period of treatment, it was learned that the mother had been placed in residential care of a not particularly satisfactory kind after her own father died. The family was plunged into poverty, and the young girl went into the 'home', where she lived from the age of 8 months to 8 years. It was at a session in which the maternal grandmother attended that the therapist helped the mother to make a connection between her own childhood experiences of 'rejection', her unresolved feelings about her own mother, and the rejection of her son's attachment needs and attempts to be close and dependent. The resulting conversation between mother and grandmother was described as 'cathartic'. With further reflections and encouragement, the mother became increasingly able to accept Bo and enjoy his behaviour. The boy responded with an increased willingness to interact, show his feelings and display both affection and distress. The amount of relaxed physical contact also increased between parent and child.

Towards the end of therapy, Watanabe congratulated the mother on how well she had done to bring about so many changes in Bo. She replied in a sad, tender voice: 'When I look at Bo, I feel as if I am comforting myself when I was a baby.' The 'orphanage' where she lived was not a good one. 'I was a loner. I had no friends' (Watanabe 1994: 42).

Infant-led psychotherapy

This intervention is an example of 'interactional guidance' and requires mothers to get down on the floor with their babies. They are required to observe and follow their child's leads and respond to the child's initiations. The intervention recognises that babies are prosocial and potentially significant partners in all interactions. The mother must not initiate activity on her own; she must learn to be less intrusive and more responsive. 'By learning to relax with the infant,' write Lojkasek *et al.* (1994: 212), 'and realizing that she does not always have to intervene, the mother begins to observe and appreciate her infant's individuality. As a result, she comes to read her infant's signals more objectively and becomes more sensitive and responsive to the infant's needs. In the process, within the context of a safe and accepting environment, the infant is allowed to express his/her inner life as well as strengths and weaknesses and to develop a sense of self through play, exploration, and interaction with the mother.' Mothers are then asked to discuss their observations and experiences of the session. This provides mothers with an opportunity to reflect on their own internal working models of the relationship with their child and modify their representations in the light of the infant-led play experience. This part of the treatment also allows mothers to think about intergenerational issues on parenting behaviour as well as their own attachment histories. Mothers are encouraged to become 'experts' on their own children.

Psychosocial domains to be influenced or changed

Attachment security, the psychological availability of other people and increased resilience protect children and adults against the potential risks of stress and adversity. However, the assessment of an individual's relationship history and current attachment style indicates the ways in which that child or adult is psychologically denying or cognitively distorting affect-laden information. We have learned that different attachment patterns are supported by contrasting internal working models in which the self and others are represented more or less positively. Each pattern is characterised by a distinctive cluster of defence mechanisms and the relationship styles that are consequent upon them. The attachment classification hypothesised for a parent or child, along with the nature of the developmental risks posited, suggests the psychosocial domains in which it might be most appropriate to work.

For example, a parent who relates and behaves in ways that are strongly suggestive of an ambivalent–preoccupied attachment pattern would be unlikely to respond appropriately to techniques requiring systematic thought, conceptual logic and rational enquiry. Such parents learned not to trust thought and reason. People lie; they let you down; they are insensitive. Their availability is best obtained by increasing attachment behaviour, which in turn depends on maintaining a high level of emotional anxiety and distress. There is an internal working model in which the self is seen as unworthy of care and protection, and other people are perceived as denying and depriving, neglectful and not to be trusted. Interventions that are stronger on emotional support, acceptance and consistent availability are much more likely to be effective in such cases. Methods that rely on the logic of problem-solving, the rational identification of tasks, agreements and reasoned arguments might well be interpreted as cold and rejecting. The result might be that workers who employ rationally based techniques with enmeshed, coercive families merely increase their attachment anxieties, leading to an increase in the number of family crises and a rise in attention-seeking behaviour.

Alternatively, all interventions might simply be experienced as opportunities to gain attention, in which case a specious form of co-operation might occur. However, involvement rests on the continued availability of the therapeutic relationship rather than a serious commitment to the task. Social workers might feel let down and angry when they discover that agreed behaviours have not been carried out or that conflictual relationships between partners are back to where they were before the programme of intervention began.

Figure 12.2 is a reminder of the main attachment and behavioural styles across the three organised patterns: avoidant, secure and ambivalent. Individuals classified as insecurely attached (avoidant or ambivalent) feel more comfortable and familiar in some psychosocial 'domains' than others. This reflects the defensive and adaptive patterns that they have had to develop to ensure other people's availability and the best view of themselves as effective in social relationships.

For example, individuals with more pronounced organised avoidant–dismissing leanings will feel more comfortable with structured, ordered, concrete, task-orientated and relatively direct but impersonal approaches to problem-solving (Dozier 1990). The avoidant person, says Holmes (1997: 241) is detached but not autonomous: 'He longs for intimacy but fears he will be rejected; he

A–Ds *Avoidant–Dismissing*	B–F *Secure–Free-to-Evaluate*	C–E *Ambivalent–Preoccupied*
Avoid –	Approach and seek comfort –	Approach, seek and resist
Attachment behaviour is deactivated	←Balanced→	Attachment behaviour is hyperactivated
Cognition Thinking Disengagement Independence	←Balanced→ ←Balanced→ ←Balanced→ ←Balanced→	Emotion Feeling Enmeshment Dependence
Low separation distress	←Balanced→	Intense separation distress
Task and exploration	←Balanced→	Attachment and people's availability

Figure 12.2 Attachment patterns and behaviours

hovers on the shores of intimacy, ever fearful of taking the plunge.' Focused interventions are likely to be viewed with more enthusiasm than approaches that appear too diffuse or emotionally laden. Interventions that arouse too much affect and too many attachment-related feelings will result in disengagement from the service or treatment being offered. Approaches that allow people to think about, even 'intellectualise', difficult feelings may seem safer than those which attempt to tackle them directly. Typically, parents classified as dismissing may, for example, become expert in child care law, their legal rights or the textbook psychology of their alleged behaviour. Procedures and routines that help them to know who and where they are in relationships allow difficult feelings to be kept under control. It is easier to relate to others via a task or some knowledge-based issue. This helps individuals to form relationships without the intrusion of too much potentially distressing emotional intimacy, at least in the early stages.

In contrast, the ambivalent individual constantly seeks attachment experiences but finds it difficult to trust intimacy. There is a longing for autonomy and to be more strong and assertive. However, individuals fear that, if they do try to be more autonomous, they will lose the close involvement with others that they crave and without which they feel even more anxious. Their therapeutic need is for acceptance and empathy.

With similar ideas in mind, Crittenden (1992b) suggests that *practitioners should manage and plan their interventions and treatments in some broad developmental order*, each operating within a particular psychosocial domain. She also advises that parents, children and families should not be the subjects of too many therapeutic experiences at once. Individuals, generally need to be moved through some or all of the following developmental sequence:

- Begin with the *emotionally* and *materially supportive* techniques (to maintain availability, develop trust, be caring, be accepting, be empathic, contain anxiety, reduce stressors, increase security and improve self-worth). The resiliences being promoted here are *self-worth* and *self-esteem*.
- Second-stage techniques are essentially *semantic, cognitive* and *interpretive* in character (to define, recognise, name, understand and differentiate senses, feelings and behaviour with a view to managing them better, to improve reflective function and to develop positive cognitive processes). The resiliences being promoted here are *self-understanding*, *self-reflexivity* and *social understanding*.
- Third-stage interventions include those based on *behavioural* principles (to change behaviours, to do things differently, better or more skilfully). The resiliences being promoted here are *self-efficacy* and *interpersonal competence*.
- Final, late-stage interventions for individuals whose basic developmental and relationship needs are beginning to be met allow people to engage their capacities for *rational* thought and action (being freely able to choose behaviours and courses of action without defensive distortion). The resilience being promoted here is *autonomy*, including the ability to plan and cope.

The most basic domains, developmentally speaking, and those which have to be considered first in case management and intervention plans, are material and emotional support. Problems in personal and interpersonal functioning that bring parents and children to the attention of the statutory agencies bring a *legal* option to all interventions. Legal sanctions not only permit many social agents to become involved in the first place but, in their most potent form, they also give social workers and courts the power to remove children from major risk environments. Each of the above four psychosocial and developmentally sequenced domains will now be described in more detail.

Stage 1: Emotional and material support

Supportive interventions are based on workers acting as a 'secure base.' Emotional, material and practical support helps to reduce parental stress and thus free up carers to be more sensitive, responsive and available to their children. The initial phases of practice typically require social workers or others to form strong, supportive relationships with a parent or child (a helping or therapeutic alliance) in which warmth, availability, acceptance, understanding, empathy and interest are present in good measure. Such interventions raise self-esteem. They help people to feel loved and liked, valued and of interest.

In many cases, social workers may not be able to go much further than this first stage. The emotional needs of many uncertain, distressed, disorganised and maltreating parents are often so great that social agencies can only expect to contain and maintain children in their families at marginal levels of psychological well-being. Such cases are likely to be very long term, requiring regular, low-intensity support. Person-centred approaches, low-intensity/high-frequency support services, family centres and relationship-based social work offer examples of interventions that are appropriate in these situations. Material support not only has a symbolic caring quality, but also helps to reduce stress and anxiety.

New York State Preventive Services Demonstration Project (Jones 1985)

A high-frequency, low-intensity supportive service was provided to families living in a poor, disadvantaged part of New York State. Committed, but unqualified social workers recruited from the local community regularly visited families whose children were at risk of entering public care. They provided practical and emotional support on a long-term basis. The support workers were easily accessible, and emphasis was placed on their 'being there' when needed. Compared with a similar group of families who received shorter-term, task-orientated interventions from more highly trained workers, significantly fewer children from the experimental group of families receiving long-term, 'low-tech' support were placed in public or foster care.

Penn State Family Intervention Project
(Nezworski *et al.* 1988)

Therapists should strive to establish secure, safe and caring relation-ships with the parents of insecurely attached children. Within such interpersonal settings, therapists help to create contexts in which parents can explore past and emerging representations of self and others. By reacting consistently and responsively, therapists attempt to disconfirm the insecure internal models used by parents. 'Our therapy model represented an initial attempt to provide mothers of insecurely attached infants with "corrective emotional experiences" that could facilitate change in self-esteem, relationship functioning, and parenting effectiveness' (Nezworski *et al.* 1988: 361). The thera-pist's responses were designed to contradict mothers' negative core beliefs about themselves. The intervention programme was described to parents as an opportunity to talk about their day-to-day concerns with their children, motherhood and friendships. The therapists provided emotional support. Once the relationship was established, there was an increased discussion of parents' feelings, including those concerned with the quality of their caregiving. The more dissatisfied mothers who lived in very chaotic households experienced domestic conflict and considerable problems with their children:

'This style of household (dis)organization exacted its toll not only in breeding tension and frustration within parents, but also in its sapping their nurturing energy. The child was responded to only when its cries were intense and salient in relation to the other pressing needs. These parents could not characteristically enjoy playing with their child; they were too busy coping with the latest crisis' (Nezworski *et al.* 1988: 368).

As a result, many mothers found their children's growing frustration, anger and distress very threatening. They regarded their children exasperating behaviour as wilful and manipulative. The aim of the therapists was to try to explain and aid mothers in understanding the children and their developmental needs. Evaluations of the project indicated that mothers felt increased relief from stress, openness towards both the therapist and children, and overall satisfaction with the service.

Family centre work with adolescent girls in crisis

Schofield and Brown (1999) describe work with a small group of deeply insecure young women (average age 14 years) who had experienced a range of adversities, including sexual, physical and emotional abuse. They were drifting outside the systems of family, education and public care. At the time of referral, their behaviours included alcohol and drug abuse, self-injuring, non-attendance at school, numerous sexual relationships and aggression. A family centre social worker aimed to provide the young women with a 'secure base' from which they could begin to develop trust, more positive self-esteem and stronger self-reflective capacities. The most important inputs from the social worker were:

- simply 'being there' and available, emotionally and physically, particularly at times of crisis
- containing the girls' anxiety, particularly when they felt helpless, hopeless, worthless and overwhelmed by strong feelings
- finding safer places for the girls to live, including foster care.

Two years later, the majority of young women remained in contact with the worker, often travelling long distances to keep in touch. They said that they had valued the social worker's availability and consistency, their ability to trust her, the support of the other girls and the opportunities to talk matters through with an accepting adult.

Families in which there is severe neglect find it more difficult to respond to interventions that require systematic, behavioural and cognitively logical approaches. Community agencies generally have to take responsibility for many family needs, including intellectual stimulation and school attendance. Crittenden (1996: 164) advises that 'the limited social competences of neglectful parents suggests that only a very few individuals should deliver services, and their relationship to the family should be long and intensive.'

Stage 2: Semantic, reflective and interpretive practices

Techniques that invite people to think about the nature and origin of mental states aim to increase people's ability to understand, recognise, access and appraise strong emotions and distressing thoughts in themselves and others. The inability to understand the origins of distress in the self and others means that emotions remain difficult to handle. This leads to heightened arousal, anger, aggression and conflict. Self-reflectivity helps individuals to make sense of the meaning of their own experience. Social empathy is extremely important if children and adults are to behave in a flexible, adaptive and competent social manner.

Work in this area includes helping maltreated children to develop 'emotional scaffolding' by providing them with the words – sad, happy, frightened, angry and so on – to describe feelings. Play therapy, many forms of child psychotherapy, holding therapy and parent skills training can provide opportunities for children to experience, recognise, name and think about their feelings. Cognitive control and affect regulation depend on recognising the nature and origins of strong feelings. Many abused and neglected children remain confused between feelings of distress and anger, sadness and aggression, thus behaving inappropriately and often with considerable loss of control in situations that they find confusing or arousing (Cline 1992; Keck and Kupecky 1995; Howe and Fearnley 1999).

Crittenden (1992) stresses the value of providing anxiously attached preschoolers with accurate semantic and episodic representations of their experience, particularly traumatic experiences. Caregivers must accept and encourage children to express, name and articulate their feelings in an accurate manner. Children can be helped to explore mixed and confused feelings, 'discrepancies between felt and expressed emotions, and the occurrence of different attitudes towards the same situation' (Cicchetti *et al.* 1995: 53). The aim is to help children to understand, cope with and handle discordant and disparate feelings, other people's perspectives and the relationship between feelings and behaviour.

Cognitive-behavioural techniques recognise that the way in which people feel and act is often based on the meanings that they ascribe to situations and behaviours. Such techniques offer another form of semantic enhancement that leads to better understanding and self-control. Individuals make sense of their world through cognitive structures or 'schema'. However they are developed, such structures, once formed, influence the way in which things are perceived, processed and understood. Therapy is basically intent on helping people to reconceptualise problems so that they are seen not as problems but as situations requiring *coping*. Coping schema help people to reappraise and handle formerly distressing situations. The negative attributions previously assigned to situations are changed so that representations and expectations are spun more positively. The individual is encouraged to see the self as effective and capable of coping. Positive self-statements stimulate confidence that problems can be solved with thought, effort and behavioural flexibility. Such methods are known as verbal self-instruction training. Parents and children can be helped to recognise those experiences which are rewarding and which are aversive (and thus to be avoided).

Fonagy and his colleagues have explored the connections between clients' experiences of psychotherapy and improvements in their reflective capacities (Fonagy *et al.* 1991a, 1994). Individuals' ability to understand the nature and origin of their own and other people's mental states allows them to stand back and reflect on feelings, actions and behaviours. Successful exponents of this 'reflective function' can also be seen as those who are psychologically secure and autonomous in attachment terms: people 'free to evaluate' their own and other people's mental states without becoming overly distressed and defensive.

> In therapy over a prolonged time period, diverse remarks concerning children's perceptions of others, particularly the therapeutic relationship forces them to attempt to create internal working models of themselves and others as thinking and feeling. This can then form the core of a sense of themselves with a capacity to represent ideas and meanings rather than stripping the world to its concrete physical aspects. Psychotherapeutic endeavour in general... may bring about a general facilitation of mental functioning. Perhaps this is why *all* attempts, regardless of theoretical framework, at focusing on the working of the mental life of an individual have clear therapeutic effects. There is something unique about the therapeutic process that takes place between two individuals, where one person takes an interest in the mental life of another. The patient's thinking is facilitated and he or she can conceive of his or her world in new, more resilient and sometimes sadder and perhaps happier ways. (Fonagy *et al.* 1994: 251, original emphasis)

In their conversations with parents and children, social workers, too, repeatedly 'concentrate on the mental life' of those with whom they work. The cumulative impact of these reflective encounters should not be underestimated. It is within relationships that parents and children initially develop insecure attachments and defended patterns of relating, so it is within new relationships that they might hope to increase feelings of security, social understanding, resilience and interpersonal competence. The capacity for reflective functioning offers considerable protection against psychological vulnerability in the face of psychosocial stress and adversity. Interventions along these lines represent attempts to break the intergenerational transmission of insecure attachments (see Juffer *et al.* 1997, and van IJzendoorn 1995, for reviews of these interventions).

To the extent that social workers remain available, interested and engaged in trying to make mental sense of parents and children, they will be helping those who feel insecure to 'disconfirm' their internal working models (for intervention examples, see Egeland and Erickson 1990, and Fish 1996). With the consistent acceptance and interest of their social worker, individuals will be helped to reflect on the nature of their own and other people's psychological states. They will experience themselves and others more positively. Negative representations of the self and others, which increase anxiety and defensive behaviours, can change so that a more robust, resilient concept of self emerges. Interventions that seek to change the caregiver's internal working model are most powerful inasmuch as the caregiver's attachment style influences that of the child. Helping to improve the psychological security of the caregiver also helps to increase the felt security of the child, particularly the young child (for example, see the STEEP programme, Erickson *et al.* 1992).

Interventions with mothers and their anxiously attached children

Lieberman *et al.* (1991) ran an intervention study that allocated 12-month-old, anxiously attached children of poor, immigrant mothers to either an intervention or a control group (which did not receive the treatment). The intervention lasted 1 year. It involved weekly home-based psychotherapy sessions with the mother and her baby. The broad aim was to reduce parent–child conflict and promote more positive emotional relationships between children and their carers. The specially trained social workers and psychologists who acted as therapists sought to alleviate the mothers' psychological conflicts about their children and increase maternal empathy. They provided information about children's development, including the value of responding sensitively to infants' signals, encouraging exploration and the negotiation of infant–mother conflicts to promote goal-corrected partnerships. Benign, positive perceptions of children's behaviour and motives were woven into the treatment. The mothers' own attachment needs and feelings of anger and ambivalence were acknowledged and responded to. Where possible, the workers also provided practical help in the form of goods and services. The findings suggest that the intervention group showed enhanced maternal empathy and interaction with their children. The mothers' capacity for improved reflective functioning increased. The toddlers displayed less avoidance, resistance and anger. There was an increase in goal-corrected partnerships and the children's security of attachment. The improvement in the quality of caregiving was most marked in cases where mothers were able to use the sessions to explore and work through feelings of anger, sadness and ambivalence toward the important people in their lives, including their child.

Psychotherapy

In their work with Mrs Wales, a mother in her early thirties, and Sophie, her 18-month-old daughter, Murray and Cooper (1994) broadly followed Bowlby's five principles in the application of attachment theory to individual psychotherapy with adult patients. Bowlby (1988) maintained that it is necessary:

- to provide a secure base that permits the exploration of painful experiences
- to encourage the consideration of current personal relationships
- to encourage the consideration of the relationship to the therapist
- to explore how current perceptions, feelings and actions relate to people's past and present relationships with their parents
- to enable people to recognise that current models of self and others may or may not be appropriate, and to help people to imagine alternatives.

Sophie was classified as avoidantly attached – she resisted cuddles and comfort, and had settled into a pattern of independent withdrawal. Sophie's avoidance was a cause of considerable distress to her mother. After Sophie's birth, her mother said that it took some time for her to feel any real affection for her daughter. For much of the first year, Mrs Wales suffered from depression. In turn, Mrs Wales was also classified as avoidant–dismissing. Mrs Wales's recounted feelings of rejection and anger towards her parents, particularly her mother. She remembered her father as someone difficult to please. 'I have visions of me growing up being anxious to do what he wanted, and trying to sort out what he wanted, and then just not feeling that you're liked for your own sake, but because you can do the things that he wants, and that was quite painful for me' (Murray and Cooper 1994: 20).

During treatment, Mrs Wales began to resolve her feelings about her parents. She recognised similarities between their treatment of her and her own dealings with Sophie. As a result, she made a determined effort to become more open and emotionally available to Sophie. The little girl became less watchful. She felt more confident in showing her distress and was increasingly prepared to go to her mother for comfort. This, in turn, helped Mrs Wales to feel more confident. Six months after treatment, Sophie was classified in the Strange Situation as securely attached.

Stage 3: Behavioural and procedural practices

The ability of individuals to regulate their own feelings and actions in order to bring about a preferred state of affairs (within a relationship or social situation, or in practical tasks) allows them to feel in control of their lives. People need to feel that their environment is predictable and under their control. There is a need to feel purposeful rather than helpless. Whether the situation is social or physical, it is important for people to believe that they can make a difference (Gilligan 1997: 17).

Behaviourally orientated interventions are based on the way in which the environment, particularly the social environment, helps to shape behaviour. Such environments are a mix of rewarding and aversive stimuli in which some behaviours are reinforced and others 'punished'. For children, parental responses act as powerful behavioural modifiers. We have seen how some aspects of attachment behaviour are shaped by parental availability. Children classified as avoidant suffer rejection if they increase their attachment behaviour; they respond by 'deactivating' their attachment needs. However, parental availability and responsivity appear to increase when children behave in a non-distressed or task-competent manner. These behaviours are reinforced and as a result increase.

In contrast, children classified as ambivalently attached persist with their attachment behaviour, amplifying signals of distress and dependency until eventually they gain a response from their parent. The response may be an angry shout, a bag of crisps or a cuddle. All such responses reward the child's continued attempts to gain attention. In behavioural terms, attachment behaviour has been increased according to an intermittent reinforcement schedule. Although not every instance of attachment behaviour has been rewarded, the child sooner or later provokes a worthwhile response. Behaviours learned as a result of operating a schedule that intermittently and randomly rewards attention-seeking behaviour are extremely difficult to extinguish. The child has learned that although not every behaviour brings a response, it is nevertheless worth persisting with attachment behaviours running at high intensity as it will only be a matter of time before some form of parental reaction is secured. Some kind of attention is always better than no attention.

Helping and advising parents about how to change the way in which they respond to their children's behaviour in turn helps children to modify their attachment behaviour. 'Dismissing' parents who are rejecting and intrusive can be helped cognitively to read their children's signals more sensitively. Once they have raised their level of attunement, they can begin to respond more appropriately to their children's attachment needs and with increased reciprocity. Their children will begin to feel that expressions of attachment behaviour and the desire for intimacy are less hazardous. Felt security is increased, and, along with it, the self and others are experienced more positively.

In contrast, 'preoccupied' parents whose caregiving is uncertain have the effect of raising levels of attachment behaviour in their ambivalently classified children. Although parental availability is unpredictable and erratic, it is not perceived by children as rejecting or intrusive. In behavioural terms, parents need to be helped to be more predictable, consistent and reliable, responding only to desired, acceptable behaviours and not to those which are excessive, aggressive and clamouring.

Parent management training

Parents of children with conduct disorders showing serious social behavioural problems have been effectively helped by various types of parent management training intervention (see, for example, Patterson 1982). Parents are taught how to identify problem behaviours, code them and intervene effectively. Many of the techniques are based on behavioural principles, including the reinforcement of desired behaviours, ignoring undesired behaviours and improving negotiation skills.

Phobic behaviours are not uncommon in children classified as disorganised. Loss and maltreatment in the first few years of life pre-date language acquisition. Such traumatic experiences involve very high levels of distress, which overwhelm the infant. Organised attachment behaviours breakdown, particularly if the source of the distress is a frightening parent. Such traumatic memories are stored, but as raw emotions rather than semantic constructs. This means that such memories are difficult to access consciously and self-reflectively. They therefore often remain unresolved. However, their power to affect current experience is strong. Relationships that trigger memories of early traumas can suddenly precipitate feelings of great distress, fear, rage and helplessness that appear to arrive out of the blue. Individuals do not understand the origin of their strong feelings but nevertheless feel overwhelmed and helpless as these flood into consciousness. Some phobias have their origins in early traumas. Classical behavioural conditioning and desensitisation programmes have some success in many cases. However, there is growing evidence that the unresolved nature of the original distress and the primitive emotions that accompanied it still have the power to cause 'irrational' feelings of fear and anxiety to erupt into consciousness when old, pre-linguistic memories of fear or rage are triggered (LeDoux 1998). Even successful behavioural interventions with phobias begin to wear off over time.

Stage 4: Rational thinking, planning and learning to cope

The ability to handle difficulties in a considered, rational and logical manner is a hallmark of psychological maturity and emotional adjustment. It means that the individual is able to appraise and reflect on the characteristics of the situation and the way in which the self and others are reacting to it emotionally, behaviourally and cognitively. Based on the appraisal, plans can then be made. This is a definition of coping behaviour. Children's *coping responses* arise out of their ability to understand, evaluate and act upon experiences of stress and difficulty. Good coping skills offset the potentially harmful effects of stress. Conversely, increasing levels of stress can erode a person's coping resources. Tasks that help people to cope also help to preserve self-esteem, a sense of personal effectiveness and the continued willingness of others to offer support. Indeed, a major successful coping task, conducted either consciously or unconsciously, is the preservation of close relationships and continued emotional support. Much that is effective in child and family social work aims to preserve and enhance good-quality social relationships.

However, the ability to cope in a considered and rational manner requires people to be able to *access* and *think about* the origin of their own feelings, reactions and thought processes as well as think about those of others. Cognition is used to understand emotion, but emotions often drive people's behaviour and responses.

Secure, free to evaluate individuals can use their ability to reflect cognitively on difficult situations to plan the most constructive, least conflictual course of action. This increases their autonomy in the sense that they are not overly disturbed, confused and disorganised by the emotional demands made by relationships.

Insecure individuals suffer an imbalance in their ability to use and access their cognitive and emotional capacities. Those classified as avoidantly attached rely heavily on trying to think their way through situations but tend to deny the relevance or presence of their own strong feelings, which therefore remain active but unprocessed.

Ambivalent styles are characteristic of people who have learned to control interactions using a repertoire of exaggerated emotional moods (volatile feelings to provoke attention, simperings of helplessness and dependency to evoke sympathy). However, the nature, origin and deployment of these roller-coaster feelings remain largely outside cognition. There is an unwillingness, even inability, to reflect on them. The individual's agenda and response pattern remains largely emotional and immune to rational processes.

Those classified as disorganised–unresolved remain susceptible to eruptions of fear, distress and anger in situations that suddenly feel threatening or dangerous, including experiences of caring and being cared for. Thus, although rational courses of action can be agreed and followed for a while, they can abruptly come to a halt as angry, disruptive forces destroy even the best laid plans. Appealing to reason in emotionally highly charged worlds tends only to make matters worse.

It has often been remarked by evaluative researchers that treatments that appeal to people's rational capacities work best with those who need them least. In other words, such treatments have their greatest successes with people who show secure attachment behaviour and have a high level of reflective function. People with such capacities do, of course, run into difficulties and may come the way of social workers. Foster carers looking after disturbed and demanding children may seek guidance and help. Maltreated or neglected children who have increased their 'felt security' as a result of support, treatment and education may begin to respond well to rational-based techniques. Solution-focused therapy, case conference agreements, and notions of responsibility and partnership with parents are likely to work most effectively with individuals classified as 'secure–autonomous' and possibly with those seen as 'avoidant–dismissing' (but *not* avoidant–disorganised) and least well with those classified as 'preoccupied–entangled' and 'disorganised–unresolved'.

Identification and implementation of specific responses, services and treatments

By this stage of planning the intervention process, it will be apparent that a wide range of social work services, treatments and techniques is theoretically available for use in practice interventions. A developmental attachment perspective guides and orchestrates their use. As we have been careful to point out, the actual choice of a particular service, treatment technique or decision depends on the attachment classification (internal working model) hypothesised, the nature of the developmental risks faced by the child, the protective influences to be enhanced, the focus of intervention and the socio-emotional condition of those to be helped. Thus, not any service or technique will do at any time. The appropriateness of a particular intervention has to be judged in terms of its developmental timing and its ability to increase feelings of psychological security and social effectiveness. The individual also has to have the psychological capacity to be able to respond to the intervention in the way intended (that is, the technique and the client have to be able to operate in the same psychosocial domain). The blanket use of a favoured or fashionable technique will therefore more often than not fall on fallow ground.

However, an aim might be achieved by employing a variety of techniques, used as alternatives or in combination. For example, an insecure 9-year-old girl's withdrawn behaviour might be decreased by improving her self-esteem. This might be achieved by training a parent to be less critical and more emotionally available, or by working with a schoolteacher to recognise and respond to the girl's needs at school, or by introducing her to a peer group activity that gives her a sense of belonging and accomplishment, or by some combination of any two or more of these.

A flexible, imaginative and developmentally attuned use of services and techniques based on a careful assessment determines the final choice of intervention at a particular point in time. There will therefore be a rough psychological correspondence between the psychosocial domain in which the technique or service is set, the protective mechanisms that it seeks to increase or introduce and the resiliences that will thereby be strengthened.

13

Conclusion

Developmental attachment theory and child and family social work

We have argued that child and family social work has to be informed by a knowledge of what promotes and impairs children's sound psychosocial development. Although it is increasingly recognised that genes play a major role in the formation and expression of an individual's temperament, personality and behaviour, it is to their dynamic interaction with the environment that we have to look to gain a full understanding of the relationship between nature and nurture. The disciplines that are making the most important advances in this field are developmental psychology and developmental psychopathology. If we are to understand how some children find themselves on maladaptive developmental pathways and how we might help them return to more adaptive trajectories, we need to ground our practice in these determinedly research-based and scientific disciplines.

Child and family social work, and the theory and practice of close relationships

Developmental attachment theory has emerged as a major perspective within the field of child and adult psychology. It has particular relevance and attraction for social workers. They work with the families and parents of society's most vulnerable and disturbed children, in the natural settings of the home, the community, and the school. They are charged with ensuring children's safety and developmental well-being – either by law or because it is the policy and philosophy of the agency for whom they work. The social environment and the factors that affect its quality, such as poverty and poor housing, have been the business of social workers for a hundred years.

Attachment theory is a theory of personality development within close relationships. It is a theory that shows that poor-quality close relationships are where children's developmental prospects first go astray. It helps us to understand why those who have suffered adverse relationships in their past go on to find relationships difficult in the future, relationships with parents, peers, partners, children, neighbours and figures in authority. Attachment theory is also adding to our understanding of how the developmental well-being of children and adults can be recovered within good-quality close relationships. Attachment theory therefore demands that child and family social workers become knowledgable and expert in the business of close relationships – between parents and children, children and peers, parents and social workers, children and social workers – and how these relationships affect behaviour and development.

The disconfirmation of insecure working models

Although it is by no means inevitable that children raised in adversity will, in their turn, become parents who raise children in adversity, there is, nevertheless, an increased risk that those who have suffered poor caregiving will become poor caregivers. The 'intergenerational transmission' of insecure attachment styles, problem behaviours and social incompetence is strong. 'Across the life course and across successive generations,' observe Caspi and Elder (1988: 220), 'problems beget problems.' It is the job of social workers to introduce 'discontinuities' into these intergenerational transmissions of problem family relationships; to break the cycle. By improving the 'felt security' of both children and parents within close relationships, insecure internal working models and negative representations of the self and others can be 'disconfirmed.'

The importance of prevention and early interventions

Some of society's most developmentally impaired, socially disadvantaged and maladapted children have suffered abuse, neglect and maltreatment in their first 2 years of life. This is a powerful reminder of the importance of receiving good-quality caregiving throughout childhood, most critically in infancy and the pre-school years. Interventions to improve the quality of caregiving in the early years of children's lives are therefore the most effective and, in the long run, by far the most economic. Financially as well as morally, prevention is always better than cure.

The value of interdisciplinary, interagency and multimodal interventions

The factors that impinge on any one child's development, both directly and indirectly, are many and various. Neurobiology, temperament, gender, the quality of caregiving, the quality of parent–child interaction, the parent's own relationship history, the availability of material and emotional support for the caregiver, peer groups, school life, community ethos, cultural expectations, the impact of major life transitions, social provisions and many more factors interact in complex ways to propel each child along his or her own unique developmental pathway. No one discipline operating within one single agency favouring one method or technique can hope to deal successfully with the complexities of children's developmental needs, particularly those who have been ill treated. This is a familiar reminder that the most effective work with vulnerable children and their families, in both the short and the long term, is likely to arise out of the combined and coordinated efforts of the welfare, health, mental health and educational services. A developmental perspective provides a theoretical base that is capable of uniting the practices of all those who work with children 'at risk' and their families.

Theory, thought and compassion

The ability to make intellectual sense of people in difficult, distressing and disturbed situations increases social workers' emotional availability. Theoretical understanding helps practitioners to stay with demanding cases and lessens the likelihood of a retreat into procedural ways of working. It is sometimes suggested that social work is most effective with clients who need it least, while the very troubled and troublesome alienate helping agencies by their lack of cooperation, excessive demands and failure to improve. Such work diminishes the professional self-confidence of practitioners and results in clients being considered 'hopeless' cases. If social workers are able to reflect on the dynamics of their relationship with clients and learn to understand its meaning, greater tolerance, compassion and effectiveness result. We attach a great deal of importance to good, reflective, relationship-sensitive supervision when working with children and their families (Pistole and Watkins 1995; Hughes and Pengelly 1998). Reason and emotion have always had to run hand in hand in the turbulent world of social work practice (Howe and Hinings 1995). Attachment theory seeks to encompass reason and emotion, thought and feeling, cognition and affect in the story of human growth and development. Developmental attachment theory is also fundamentally a theory of relationships, and relationships are quintessentially the medium through which social work takes place.

Bibliography

Aber, J.L. and Baker, A. (1990) Security of attachment in toddlerhood: modifying assessment procedures for joint clinical and research purposes. In Greenberg, M.T., Cicchetti, D. and Cummings, E.M. (eds) *Attachment in the Preschool Years*. Chicago: Chicago University Press, pp. 427–62.

Ainsworth, M.D.S. (1973) The development of infant–mother attachment. In Caldwell, B.M. and Ricciuti, H.N. (eds) *Review of Child Development Research*. Chicago: University of Chicago Press, Vol. 3, pp. 1–94.

Ainsworth, M.D.S. and Eichberg, C. (1991) Effects on infant–mother attachment of mother's unresolved loss of an attachment figure or other traumatic experience. In Parkes, C., Stevenson-Hinde, J. and Marris, P. (eds) *Attachment Across the Life Cycle*. London: Tavistock, pp. 160–83.

Ainsworth, M.D.S. and Wittig, B.A. (1969) Attachment and the exploratory behavior of one-year-olds in a strange situation. In Foss, B.M. (ed.) *Determinants of Infant Behavior*, Vol. 4. London: Methuen, pp. 113–16.

Ainsworth, M.D.S., Bell, S. and Stayton, D. (1971) Individual differences in strange-situation behavior of one-year-olds. In Schaffer, H. (ed.) *The Origins of Human Social Relations*. New York: Academic Press, pp. 17–52.

Ainsworth, M.D.S., Blehar, M., Aters, E. and Wall, S. (1978) *Patterns of Attachment: A Psychological Study of the Strange Situation*. Hillsdale, NJ: Lawrence Erlbaum.

Alessandri, S.M. (1991) Play and social behaviour in maltreated preschoolers. *Developmental Psychopathology*, **3**: 191–206.

Alexander, P. (1992) Application of attachment theory to the study of sexual abuse. *Journal of Consulting and Clinical Psychology,* **60**: 185–95.

Allen, J.P., Hauser, S.T. and Borman-Spurrell, E. (1996) Attachment theory as a framework for understanding sequelae of severe adolescent psychopathology: an 11-year follow-up study. *Journal of Consulting and Clinical Psychology*, **64**: 254–63.

Barnett, B. and Parker, G. (1998) The parentified child: early competence or childhood deprivation? *Child Psychology and Psychiatry Review*, **3**(4): 146–55.

Bartholomew, K. (1990) Avoidance of intimacy: an attachment perspective. *Journal of Social and Personal Relationships,* **7**: 147–78.

Bartholomew, K. and Horowitz, L.M. (1991) Attachment styles among young adults: a test of a four-category model. *Journal of Personality and Social Psychology*, **61**: 226–44.

Beckwith, L. and Sigman, M. (1995) Preventive interventions in infancy. *Child and Adolescent Psychiatric Clinics of North America*, **4**(3): 683–700.

296

Beeghly, M. and Cicchetti, D. (1994) Child maltreatment, attachment and the self system: emergence of an internal state lexicon in toddlers at high social risk. *Developmental Psychopathology*, **6**: 5–30.

Belsky, J. and Cassidy, J. (1994) Attachment: theory and practice. In Rutter M. and Hay D. (eds) *Development Through Life: A Handbook for Clinicians*. Oxford: Blackwell Science, pp. 373–402.

Belsky, J. and Nezworski, T. (eds) (1988) *Clinical Implications of Attachment*. Hillsdale, NJ: Lawrence Erlbaum.

Belsky, J. and Nezworski, T. (1988) Clinical implications of attachment. In Belsky, J. and Nezworski, T. (eds) *Clinical Implications of Attachment*. Hillsdale, NJ: Lawrence Erlbaum, pp. 3–17.

Bemporad, J.R. and Romano, S.J. (1992) Childhood maltreatment and adult depression: a review of research. In Cicchetti, D. and Toth, S.L. (eds) *Rochester Symposium on Developmental Psychology*, Vol. 4: *Developmental Perspectives on Depression*. Rochester, NY: University of Rochester Press, pp. 351–76.

Binney, V., McKnight, I. and Broughton, S. (1994) Relationship play therapy for attachment disturbances in four to seven-year-old children. In Richer, J. (ed.) *The Clinical Application of Ethology and Attachment Theory*. Occasional Paper No. 9. London: Association for Child Psychology and Psychiatry, pp. 53–9.

Boswell, G. (1996) The prevalence of childhood trauma in the lives of violent young offenders. In Howe D. (ed.) *Attachment and Loss in Child and Family Social Work*. Aldershot: Avebury, pp. 82–100.

Bowlby, J. (1944) Forty-four juvenile thieves: their character and home lives. *International Journal of Psycho-analysis*, **25**: 19–52.

Bowlby, J. (1951) Maternal Care and Mental Health. *World Health Organization Monograph* (Serial No. 2). Geneva: WHO.

Bowlby, J. (1973) *Attachment and Loss*, Vol. II: *Separation, Anxiety and Anger*. London: Hogarth.

Bowlby, J. (1979) *The Making and Breaking of Affectional Bonds*. London: Tavistock.

Bowlby, J. (1980) *Attachment and Loss*, Vol. III: *Loss, Sadness and Depression*. London: Hogarth Press.

Bowlby, J. (1988) *A Secure Base: Clinical Applications of Attachment Theory*. London: Routledge.

Bradley, R.H., Caldwell, B.M. and Rock, S.L. (1988) Home environment and schools performance: a ten-year follow-up and examination of three models of environmental action. *Child Development*, **59**: 852–67.

Bridge, G. and Miles, G. (1996) *On the Outside Looking In*. London: CCETSW.

Brown, G. and Harris, T. (1978) *Social Origins of Depression: A Study of Psychiatric Disorder in Women*. London: Tavistock.

Brown, G. and Harris, T. (1986) Stressor, vulnerability and depression. *Psychological Medicine*, **16**: 739–44.

Brown, G., Harris, T. and Bifulco, A. (1986) Long term effects of early loss of parent. In Rutter, M., Izard, P. and Read, P. (eds) *Depression in Young People*. New York: Guilford Press, pp. 251–96.

Bruner, J. (1983) *Child's Talk*. New York: Norton.

Burkett, L. (1991) Parenting behaviors of women who were sexually abused as children in their families of origin. *Family Process*, **30**: 421–34.

Byng-Hall, J. (1991) The application of attachment theory to understanding and treatment in family therapy. In Parkes, C., Stevenson-Hinde, J. and Marris, P. (eds) *Attachment Across the Life Cycle*. London: Tavistock, pp. 199–215.

Byng-Hall, J. (1995) Creating a secure family base: some implications of attachment theory for family therapy. *Family Process*, **34**: 45–58.

Byng-Hall, J. and Stevenson-Hinde, J. (1991) Attachment relationships within a family system. *Infant Mental Health Journal*, **12**(3): 187–200.

Cambridgeshire County Council (1997) *Bridge Report and Action Plan*. Cambridge: Bridge Child Care Consultancy.

Carlson, V., Cicchetti, D., Barnett, D. and Braunwald, K. (1989) Disorganized/disorientated attachment relationships in maltreated infants. *Developmental Psychology*, **25**(4): 525–31.

Caspi, A. and Elder, G. (1988) Emergent family patterns: the intergenerational construction of problem behavior. In Hinde, R. and Stevenson-Hinde, J. (eds) *Relationships within Families*. Oxford: Oxford University Press, pp. 218–40.

Champion, L., Goodall, G. and Rutter, M. (1995) Behavior problems in childhood and stressors in early adult life. *Psychological Medicine*, **24**(2): 231–46.

Cicchetti, D. and Lynch, M. (1993) Toward an ecological/transactional model of community violence and child maltreatment: consequences for children's development. *Psychiatry*, **56**: 96–118.

Cicchetti, D. and Toth, S.L. (1995a) A developmental psychopathology perspective on child abuse and neglect. *Journal of American Academy of Child Adolescent Psychiatry*, **34**(5): 541–65.

Cicchetti, D. and Toth, S.L. (1995b) Child maltreatment and attachment organization: implications for intervention. In Goldberg, S., Muir, R. and Kerr, J. (eds) *Attachment Theory: Social, Developmental and Clinical Perspectives*. Hillsdale, NJ: Analytic Press, pp. 279–308.

Cicchetti, D., Toth, S.L. and Hennessy, K. (1989) Research on the consequences of child maltreatment and its application to educational settings. *Topics in Early Childhood Special Education*, **9**: 33–5.

Cicchetti, D., Toth, S.L. and Lynch, M. (1995) Bowlby's dream comes full circle: the application of attachment theory to risk and psychopathology. In Ollendick T. and Prinz R. (eds) *Advances in Clinical Child Psychology*, Vol. 17. New York: Plenum Press, pp. 1–75.

Cline, F. (1992) *Hope for High Risk and Rage Filled Children*. Evergreen, CO: Foster W. Cline.

Cochran, M. and Brassard, J. (1979) Child development and personal support networks. *Child Development*, **50**: 601–16.

Cole-Detke, H.E. and Kobak, R. (1996) Attachment processes in eating disorder and depression. *Journal of Consulting and Clinical Psychology*, **64**: 282–90.

Connell, J.P. (1990) Context, self and action: a motivational analysis of self-system processes across the life-span. In Cicchetti, D. and Beeghly, M. (eds) *The Self in Transition: Infancy to Childhood*. Chicago: University of Chicago Press, pp. 61–97.

Cowan, P.A., Cohn, D.A., Cowan, C.P. and Pearson, J.L. (1996) Parents' attachment histories and children's externalizing and internalizing behaviors: exploring family systems models of linkage. *Journal of Consulting and Clinical Psychology*, **64**(1): 53–63.

Cox, A.D. (1994) Diagnostic Appraisal. In Rutter, M. and Hay, D. (eds) *Development Through Life: A Handbook for Clinicians*. Oxford: Blackwell Science, pp. 22–33.

Cox, M., Owen, M., Lewis, J. and Henderson, V. (1989) Marriage, adult adjustment and early parenting. *Child Development*, **60**: 1015–24.

CPPRG (Conduct Problems Prevention Research Group) (1992) A developmental and clinical model for the prevention of conduct disorder: the Fast Track Program. *Development and Psychopathology*, **4**: 509–27.

Crittenden, P. (1985) Social networks, quality of parenting, and child development. *Child Development*, **56**: 1299–1313.

Crittenden, P. (1988) Relationships at risk. In Belsky, J. and Nezworski, T. (eds) *Clinical Implications of Attachment*. Hillsdale, NJ: Lawrence Erlbaum.

Crittenden, P. (1992a) Quality of attachment in the preschool years. *Development and Psychopathology*, **4**: 209–41.

Crittenden, P. (1992b) Treatment of anxious attachment in infancy and early childhood. *Development and Psychopathology*, **4**: 575–602.

Crittenden, P. (1995) Attachment and psychopathology. In Goldberg, S., Muir, R. and Kerr, J. (eds) *Attachment Theory: Social, Developmental and Clinical Perspectives*. Hillsdale, NJ: Analytic Press, pp. 367–406.

Crittenden, P. (1996) Research on maltreating families: implications for intervention. In Briere, J., Berliner, L. and Bulkley, J. (eds) *The APSAC Handbook on Child Maltreatment*. Thousand Oaks: Sage, pp. 158–74.

Crittenden, P. (1997) Patterns of attachment and sexual behavior: risk of dysfunction versus opportunity for creation integration. In Atkinson, L. and Zucker, K. (eds) *Attachment and Psychopathology*. New York: Guilford Press, pp. 47–93.

Crockenberg, S. (1981) Infant irritability, mother responsiveness and social influences on the security of infant–mother attachment. *Child Development*, **52**: 209–17.

Dean, A., Malik, M., Richards, W. and Stringer, S. (1986) Effects of parental maltreatment on children's conceptions of interpersonal relationships. *Development Psychology*, **22**: 617–26.

DeMulder, E.K. and Radke-Yarrow, M. (1991) Attachment with affectively ill and well-mothers. *Development and Psychopathology*, **3**: 227–42.

Dodge, K.A., Bates, J.E. and Petit, G.S. (1990) Mechanisms in the cycle of violence. *Science*, **250**: 1678–83.

Downes, C. (1992) *Separation Revisited: Adolescents in Foster Care*. Aldershot: Ashgate.

Dozier, M. (1990) Attachment organization and treatment use for adults with serious psychopathological disorders. *Development and Psychopathology*, **3**: 47–60.

Dozier, M. and Lee, S. (1995) Discrepancies between self- and other-report of psychiatric symptomatology: effects of hyperactivating vs. deactivating strategies of attachment. *Development and Psychopathology*, **7**: 217–26.

Egeland, B. and Erikson, M. (1990) Rising above the past: strategies for helping new mothers break the cycle of abuse and neglect. *Zero to Three*, **11**(3): 29–35.

Egeland, B., Jacobvitz, D. and Sroufe, L. (1988) Breaking the cycle of abuse. *Child Development*, **59**: 1080–8.

Elicker, J., Egeland, B. and Sroufe, L.A. (1992) Predicting peer competence and peer relationships in childhood from early parent–child relationships. In Parke, R. and Ladd, G. (eds) *Family-Peer Relationships*. Hillsdale, NJ: Erlbaum, pp. 77–106.

Erickson, M., Korfmacher, J. and Egeland, B. (1992) Attachments past and present: implications for therapeutic intervention with mother–infant dyads. *Developmental Psychopathology*, **4**: 495–507.

Erikson, H. (1963) *Childhood and Society*. 2nd edn. New York: Norton.

Éthier, L.S., Lacharité, C. and Couture, G. (1995) Childhood adversity, parental stress and depression of negligent mothers. *Child Abuse and Neglect*, **19**(5): 619–32.

Fahlberg, V. (1994) *A Child's Journey Through Placement*. London: BAAF.

Farrington, D. (1995) The development of offending and antisocial behaviour from childhood: key findings from the Cambridge Study in Delinquent Development. *Journal of Child Psychology and Psychiatry*, **36**(6): 929–64.

Feeney, J., Noller, P. and Hanrahan, M. (1995) Assessing adult attachment. In Sperling, M. and Berman, M. and W. (eds) (1994) *Attachment in Adults: Theory, assessment, and treatment*. New York: Guilford Press, pp. 128–52.

Finkelhor, D. (1990) Early and long-term effects of child sexual abuse. *Professional Psychology: Research and Practice*, **21**: 325–30.

Fish, B. (1996) Clinical implications of attachment narratives. *Clinical Social Work*, **24**(3): 239–53.

Fonagy, P., Steele, H., Moran, G., Steele, M. and Higgit, A. (1991a) The capacity for understanding mental states: the reflective self in parent and child and its significance for security of attachment. *Infant Mental Health Journal*, **13**: 200–17.

Fonagy, P., Steele, H. and Steele, M. (1991b) Maternal representations of attachment during pregnancy predict the organization of infant–mother attachment at one year of age. *Child Development*, **62**: 891–905.

Fonagy, P., Steele, M., Steele, H., Higgit, A. and Target, M. (1994) The theory and practice of resilience [The Emmanuel Miller Memorial Lecture 1992]. *Journal of Child Psychology and Psychiatry*, **35**(2): 231–57.

Fonagy, P., Leigh, T., Steele, M. *et al.* (1996) The relation of attachment status, psychiatric classification, and response to psychotherapy. *Journal of Consulting and Clinical Psychology*, **64**(1): 22–31.

Fonagy, P., Target, M., Steele, M. *et al.* (1997) Morality, disruptive behavior, borderline personality disorder, crime, and their relationship to security of attachment. In Atkinson, L. and Zucker, K. (eds) *Attachment and Psychopathology*. New York: Guilford Press, pp. 223–74.

Garbarino, J. and Platz, M. (1986) Child abuse and juvenile delinquency: What are the links? In Garbarino, J., Scheelenbach, C. and Sebes, J. (eds) *Troubled Youth, Troubled Families: Understanding Families At-Risk for Adolescent Maltreatment*. New York: Aldine.

Garmezy, N. (1997) Reflections and commentary on risk, resilience, and development. In Haggerty, R., Sherrod, L., Garmezy, N. and Rutter, M. (eds) *Stress, Risk and Resilience in Children and Adolescents: Processes, Mechanisms and Interventions*. Cambridge: Cambridge University Press, pp. 1–18.

George, C. (1996) A representational perspective of child abuse and prevention: internal working models of attachment and caregiving. *Child Abuse and Neglect*, **20**(5): 411–24.

George, C. and Solomon, J. (1996) Representational models of relationships: links between caregiving and attachment. *Infant Mental Health Journal*, **17**(3): 198–216.

Gibbons, J. (1992) Provisions of support through Family Projects. In Gibbons, J. (ed.) *The Children Act 1989 and Family Support*. London: HMSO, pp. 23–33.

Gibbons, J., Thorpe, S. and Wilkinson, P. (1990) *Family Support and Prevention: Studies in Local Areas*. London: HMSO.

Gilligan, R. (1997) Beyond permanence? The importance of resilience in child placement practice and planning. *Adoption and Fostering*, **21**(1): 12–20.

Goldberg, S. (1997) Attachment and childhood behavior problems in normal, at-risk, and clinical samples. In Atkinson, L. and Zucker, K. (eds) *Attachment and Psychopathology*. New York: Guilford Press, pp. 171–95.

Goleman, D. (1996) *Emotional Intelligence*. London: Bloomsbury.

Gore, S. and Eckenrode, J. (1997) Context and process in research on risk and resilience. In Haggerty, R., Sherrod, L., Garmezy, N. and Rutter, M. (eds) *Stress, Risk and Resilience in Children and Adolescents: Processes, Mechanisms and Interventions*. Cambridge: Cambridge University Press, pp. 19–63.

Greenberg, M.T., Speltz, M.L., DeKlyen, M. and Endriga, M. (1991) Attachment security in preschoolers with and without externalizing behavior problems: a replication. *Development and Psychopathology*, **3**: 413–30.

Gregory, D. (1997) Norfolk Family Support Team: Case Studies – Research Presentations. Unpublished transcripts. UEA School of Social Work, Norwich.

Grice, H.P. (1975) Logic and conversation. In Cole, P. and Moran, J.L. (eds*) Syntax and Semantics III: Speech Acts*. New York: Academic Press, pp. 41–58.

Grossmann, K.E. (1995) Evolution and history of attachment research. In Goldberg, S., Muir, R. and Kerr, J. (eds) *Attachment Theory: Social, Developmental and Clinical Perspectives*. Hillsdale, NJ: Analytic Press, pp. 85–122.

Grossmann, K.E. and Grossmann, K. (1991) Attachment quality as an organizer of emotional and behavioral responses in a longitudinal perspectives. In Parkes, C., Stevenson-Hinde, J. and Marris, P. (eds) *Attachment Across the Life Cycle*. London: Tavistock, pp. 93–114.

Harter, S. (1983) Developmental perspectives on the self-system. In Mussen, P. (ed.) *Handbook of Child Psychology*, 4th edn. Chichester: Wiley, pp. 93–114.

Hay, D. and Angold, A. (1994) Introduction: Precursors and causes in development and pathogenesis. In Hay, D. and Angold, A. (eds) *Precursors and Causes in Development and Psychopathology*. Chichester: John Wiley, pp. 1–22.

Hazan, C. and Shaver, P. (1987) Romantic love conceptualized as an attachment process. *Journal of Personality and Social Psychology*, **52**: 511–24.

Hinde, R. (1995) A suggested structure for a science of relationships. *Personal Relationships*, **1**: 1–15.

Holmes, J. (1993) Attachment theory: a biological basis for psychotherapy? *British Journal of Psychiatry*, **163**: 430–38.

Holmes, J. (1997) Attachment, autonomy, intimacy: some clinical implications of attachment theory. *British Journal of Medical Psychology*, **70**: 231–48.

Howe, D. (1998) *Patterns of Adoption: Nature, Nurture and Psychosocial Development*. Oxford: Blackwell Science.

Howe, D. and Hinings, D. (1995) Reason and emotion in social work practice: managing relationships with difficult clients. *Journal of Social Work Practice*, **9**(1): 5–14.

Howe, D. and Fearnley, S. (1999) Disorders of attachment and attachment therapy. *Adoption and Fostering* 22 (3).

Hughes, L. and Pengelly, P. (1998) *Staff Supervision in a Turbulent Environment*. London: Jessica Kingsley.

Jones, M.A. (1985) *A Second Chance for Families: Five Years Later*. New York: Child Welfare League of America.

Juffer, F., van IJzendoorn, M. and Bakerman-Kranenberg, M. (1997) Intervention in transmission of insecure attachment: a case study. *Psychological Reports*, **80**: 531–43.

Kagan, J. (1989) *Unstable Ideas: Temperament, Cognition and Self*. Cambridge, MA: Harvard University Press.

Kagan, J. (1994) *Galen's Prophesy: Temperament in Human Nature*. London: Free Association Books.

Kasl, C. (1989) *Women, Sex and Addiction*. New York: Mandarin.

Kazdin, A. (1987) Treatment of antisocial behavior in children: current status and future directions. *Psychological Bulletin*, **102**: 187–203.

Kazdin, A., Esveldt-Dawson, K., French, N. and Unis, A. (1987) Problem-solving skills training and relationship therapy in the treatment of antisocial children. *Journal of Consulting and Clinical Psychology*, **16**: 76–85.

Keck, G. and Kupecky, R. (1995) *Adopting the Hurt Child*. Colorado Springs, CO: Piñon Press.

Kendall, P. (1993) Cognitive-behavioral therapies with youth: guiding theory, current status and emerging developments. *Journal of Consulting and Clinical Psychology*, **61**: 235–47.

Kobak, R.R. and Sceery, A. (1988) Attachment in adolescence: working models, affect regulation and representation of self and others. *Child Development*, **59**: 135–46.

Koestler, L., Papouček, H. and Papouček, M. (1989) Patterns of rhythmic stimulation by mothers with three-month olds: a cross modal comparison. *International Journal of Behavioral Development*, **12**: 143–54.

Kotler, T., Buzwell, S., Romeo, Y. and Bowland, J. (1994) Avoidant attachment as a risk factor for health. *British Journal of Medical Psychology*, **67**: 237–45.

Lally, R., Mangione, P. and Honig, A. (1988) The Syracuse University Family Development Research Program. In Powell, D. (ed.) *Parent Education as Early Intervention*. Norwood. NJ: Ablex, pp. 79–104.

LeDoux, J. (1998) *The Emotional Brain*. London: Weidenfeld & Nicolson.

Lewis, M., Feiring, C., McGuffog, C. and Jaskir, J. (1984) Predicting pathology in six-year-olds from early social relations. *Child Development*, **55**: 123–36.

Lieberman, A. (1992) Infant–parent psychotherapy with toddlers. *Development and Psychopathology*, **4**: 559–74.

Lieberman, A.F., Weston, D.R. and Pawl, J.H. (1991) Preventive intervention and outcome with anxiously attached dyads. *Child Development*, **62**: 199–209.

Lieberman, F.G. and Pawl, J.H. (1988) Clinical applications of attachment theory. In Belsky, J. and Nezworski, T. (eds) *Clinical Implications of Attachment*. Hillsdale, NJ: Lawrence Erlbaum, pp. 327–51.

Lojkasek, M., Cohen, N. and Muir, E. (1994) Where is the infant in infant intervention? A review of the literature on changing troubled mother–infant relationships. *Psychotherapy*, **31**(1): 208–20.

Lopez, F.G. (1995) Contemporary attachment theory: an introduction with implications for counseling psychology. *Counseling Psychologist*, **23**(3): 395–415.

Lyons-Ruth, K. (1996) Attachment relationships among children with aggressive behavior problems: the role of disorganised early attachment patterns. *Journal of Consulting and Clinical Psychology*, **64**: 64–73.

Lyons-Ruth, K. and Block, D. (1996) The disturbed caregiving system: relations among childhood trauma, maternal caregiving, and infant affect and attachment. *Infant Mental Health Journal*, **17**: 257–75.

Lyons-Ruth, K., Alpern, L. and Repacholi, B. (1993) Disorganized attachment classification and maternal psychosocial problems as predictors of hostile aggressive behavior in the preschool classroom. *Child Development*, **64**: 572–85.

Lyons-Ruth, K., Connell, D., Grunebaum, H. and Botein, S. (1990) Infants at social risk: maternal depression and family support services as mediators of infant development and security of attachment. *Child Development*, **61**: 85–98.

McCrone, E.R., Egeland, B., Kalkoske, M. and Carlson, E.A. (1994) Relations between early maltreatment and mental representations of relationships assessed with projective storytelling in middle childhood. *Development and Psychopathology*, **6**: 99–120.

McDonough, S.C. (1995) Promoting positive early parent–infant relationships through interaction guidance. In Minde, K. (ed.) *Child and Adolescent Psychiatric Clinics of North America*, **4**(3): 661–72.

McMillen, J. and Rideout, G. (1996) Breaking intergenerational cycles: theoretical tools for social workers. *Social Services Review*, September pp. 378–99.

Main, M. (1991) Metacognitive knowledge, metacognitive monitoring, and singular (coherent) vs. multiple (incoherent) model of attachment. In Parkes, C., Stevenson-Hinde, J. and Marris, P. (eds) *Attachment Across the Life Cyle*. London: Tavistock, pp. 127–59.

Main, M. (1995) Recent studies in attachment: overview, with selected implications for clinical work. In Goldberg, S., Muir, R. and Kerr, J. (eds) *Attachment Theory: Social, Developmental and Clinical Perspectives*. Hillside, NJ: Analytic Press, pp. 407–74.

Main, M. (1996) Introduction to the special section on attachment and psychopathology: 2. Overview of the field of attachment. *Journal of Consulting and Clinical Psychology*, **64**(2): 237–43.

Main, M. and Goldwyn, R. (1984–94) *Adult Attachment Scoring and Classification System.* Unpublished scoring manual. Department of Psychology, University of California, Berkeley.

Main, M. and Solomon, J. (1986) Discovery of an insecure-disorganized/disoriented attachment pattern. In Brazelton, T. and Yogman, M. (eds) *Affective Development in Infancy.* Norwood, NJ: Ablex, pp. 95–124.

Main, M. and Solomon, J. (1990) Procedures for identifying infants as disorganized/disorientated during the Ainsworth strange situation. In Greenberg, M., Cicchetti, D. and Cummings, M. (eds) *Attachment in the Preschool Years.* Chicago: University of Chicago Press, pp. 273–310.

Mattinson, J. and Sinclair, I. (1979) *Mate and Stalemate.* London: Institute of Marital Studies.

Mayseless, O. (1996) Attachment patterns and their outcomes. *Human Development,* **36**: 206–23.

Meisels, S., Dichtelmiller, M. and Liaw, F. (1993) A multidimensional analysis of early childhood intervention programs. In Zeanah, C. (ed.) *Handbook of Infant Mental Health.* New York: Guilford Press, pp. 361–85.

Miller, L., Rustin, M., Rustin, M. and Shuttleworth, J. (eds) (1989) *Closely Observed Infants.* London: Duckworth.

Morris, J. (1996) A Social Work Assessment of Children's Attachment. Unpublished M.Sc. thesis, School of Psychiatric Social Work, University of Manchester.

Mueller, N. and Silverman, N. (1989) Peer relations in maltreated children. In Cicchetti, D. and Carlson, V. (eds) *Child Maltreatment: Theory and Research on the Causes and Consequences of Child Abuse and Neglect.* Cambridge: Cambridge University Press, pp. 529–78.

Murray, L. and Cooper, P. (1994) Clinical application of attachment theory and research: change in infant attachment with brief psychotherapy. In Richer, J. (ed.) *The Clinical Application of Ethology and Attachment Theory.* Occasional Paper No. 9. London: Association for Child Psychology and Psychiatry, pp. 15–24.

Nezworksi, T., Tolan, W. and Belsky, J. (1988) Intervention in insecure infant attachment. In Belsky, J. and Nezworski, T. (eds) *Clinical Implications of Attachment.* Hillsdale, NJ: Lawrence Erlbaum, pp. 352–86.

Norwood, R. (1985) *Women Who Love Too Much.* New York: Arrow Books.

O'Connor, M.J., Sigman, M. and Brill, N. (1987) Disorganization of attachment in relation to maternal alcohol consumption. *Journal of Consulting and Clinical Psychology,* **55**: 831–6.

Olds, D., Henderson, C. and Tatelbaum, D. *et al.* (1986) Preventing child abuse and neglect: a randomized trial of nurse home visitation. *Pediatrics,* **78**: 65–78.

Patterson, G. (1982) *Coercive Family Process.* Eugene OR: Castalia.

Pearson, J., Cohn, D., Cowan, P. and Cowan, C. (1994) Earned- and continuous-security in adult attachment: relation to depressive symptomatology and parenting style. *Development and Psychopathology,* **6**: 359–73.

Pianta, R.C., Egeland, B.E. and Adam, E.K. (1996) Adult attachment classification and self-reported psychiatric symptomatology as assessed by the Minnesota Multiphasic Personality Inventory – 2. *Journal of Consulting and Clinical Psychology,* **64**: 273–81.

Pistole, C. and Watkins, C.E. Jr. (1995) Attachment theory, counseling process, and supervision. *Counseling Psychologist*, July, pp. 457–78.

Plomin, R. (1994) *Genetics and Experience: The Interplay between Nature and Nurture*. Thousand Oaks, CA: Sage.

Provence, S. and Naylor, A. (1983) *Working with Disadvantaged Parents and Children*. New Haven, CT: Yale University Press.

Quinton, D. and Rutter, M. (1988) *Parenting Breakdown: The Making and Breaking of Intergenerational Links*. Aldershot: Avebury.

Quinton, D., Pickles, A., Maughan, B. and Rutter, M. (1993) Partners, peers and pathways: assortive pairing and continuities in conduct disorder. *Development and Psychopathology*, **5**(4): 763–83.

Radke-Yarrow, M. (1991) Attachment patterns in children of depressed mothers. In Marris, P., Stevenson-Hinde, J. and Parkes, C. (eds) *Attachment Across the Life Cycle*. London: Routledge, pp. 115–26.

Richards, I. and Sullivan, A. (1996) Psychotherapy for delinquents? *Journal of Adolescence*, **19**: 63–73.

Robertson, J. and Bowlby, J. (1952) Responses of young children to separation from their mothers. *Courrier Centre, Internationale Enfance, Paris*, **2**: 131–40.

Robins, L. (1966) *Deviant Children Grow Up*. Baltimore: Williams & Wilkins.

Rodning, C., Beckwith, L. and Howard, J. (1991) Quality of attachment and home environments in children prenatally exposed to PCP and cocaine. *Development and Psychopathology*, **3**: 351–66.

Rogosch, F. and Cicchetti, D. (1994) Illustrating the interface of family and peer relations through the study of child maltreatment. *Social Development*, **3**: 291–308.

Rogosch, F., Cicchetti, D. and Aber, L. (1995) The role of child maltreatment in early deviations in cognitive and affective processing abilities and later peer relationship problems. *Development and Psychopathology*, **7**(4): 591–609.

Rosenberg, D. (1984) 'The quality and content of preschool fantasy play' cited in Main, M. (1995), p. 429.

Rosenblith, J.F. (1992) *In the Beginning: Development from Conception to Age Two*, 2nd edn. Newbury Park, CA: Sage.

Rosenstein, D.S. and Horowitz, H.A. (1996) Adolescent attachment and psychopathology. *Journal of Consulting and Clinical Psychology*, **64**(2): 244–53.

Rothbaum, F. and Weisz, J. (1994) Parental caregiving and child externalising behaviour in nonclinical samples: a meta-analysis. *Psychological Bulletin*, **116**: 55–74.

Russ, S. (1995) Play psychotherapy research. In Ollendick, T. and Prinz, R. (eds) *Advances in Clinical Child Psychology*, Vol. 17. New York: Plenum Press, pp. 365–92.

Rutter, M. (1975) *Helping Troubled Children*. Harmondsworth: Penguin.

Rutter, M. (1990) Psychosocial resilience and protective mechanisms. In Cicchetti, D., Nuechterlein, A. and Weintraub, S. (eds) *Risk and Protective Factors in the Development of Psychopathology*, Cambridge: Cambridge University Press, pp. 181–214.

Rutter, M. (1991) A fresh look at maternal deprivation. In Bateson, P. (ed.) *The Development and Integration of Behaviour*. Cambridge: Cambridge University Press.

Rutter, M. (1995) Psychosocial adversity: risk, resilience and recovery. *Southern African Journal of Child and Adolescent Psychiatry*, **7**(2): 75–88.

Rutter, M. (1997) Stress research: accomplishments and tasks ahead. In Haggerty, R. Sherrod, L., Garmezy, N. and Rutter, M. (eds) *Stress, Risk and Resilience in Children and Adolescents: Processes, Mechanisms and Interventions*. Cambridge: Cambridge University Press, pp. 354–86.

Saarni, C. (1990) Emotional competence. In Thompson, R. (ed.) *Socioemotional Development: Nebraska Symposium on Motivation 1998*, Vol 36. Lincoln, NE: University of Nebraska Press.

Schaffer, H. (1996) *Social Development*. Oxford: Blackwell.

Schofield, G. (1996) Parental competence and the welfare of the child: issues for those who work with parents with learning difficulties and their children. A response to Booth and Booth. *Child and Family Social Work*, **1**(2): 87–92.

Schofield, G. (1998) Inner and outer worlds: a psychosocial framework for child and family social work. *Child and Family Social Work*, **3**(1): 57–67.

Schofield, G. and Brown, K. (1999) Being there: a family centre worker's role as a secure base for adolescent girls in crisis. *Child and Family Social Work*, **4**:(1): 21–32.

Shaw, D., Owens, E., Vondra, J., Keenan, K. and Winslow, E. (1996) Early risk and pathways in the development of early disruptive behavior problems. *Development and Psychopathology*, **8**: 679–99.

Simpson, J.A., Rholes, W.S. and Phillips, D. (1996) Conflict in close relationships: an attachment perspective. *Journal of Personality and Social Psychology*, **71**(5): 899–914.

Smith, T. (1992) Family centres, children in need and the Children Act. In Gibbons, J. (ed.) *The Children Act 1989 and Family Support*. London: HMSO, pp. 9–22.

Solomon, J. and George, C. (1996) Defining the caregiving system: toward a theory of caregiving. *Infant Mental Health Journal*, **17**(3): 183–97.

Solomon, J., George, C. and DeJong, A. (1995) Symbolic representation of attachment in children classified as controlling at age 6: evidence of disorganization of representation strategies. *Development and Psychopathology*, **7**: 447–64.

Spangler, G. and Grossmann, K. (1993) Biobehavioral organization in securely and insecurely attached infants. *Child Development*, **64**: 1439–50.

Sroufe, A. (1988) The role of infant–caregiver attachment in development. In Belsky, J. and Nezworski, T. (eds). *Clinical Implications of Attachment*. Hillsdale, NJ: Lawrence Erlbaum, pp. 18–38.

Sroufe, A. (1989a) Relationship, self and individual adaptation. In Sameroff, A. and Emde, R. (eds) *Relationship Disturbances in Early Childhood: A Developmental Approach*. New York: Basic Books, pp. 70–96.

Sroufe, A. (1989b) Relationships and relationship disturbances. In Sameroff, A. and Emde, R. (eds) *Relationship Disturbances in Early Childhood: A Developmental Approach*. New York: Basic Books, pp. 97–124.

Toth, S.L. and Cicchetti, D. (1996) Patterns of relatedness, depressive symptomatology, and perceived competence in maltreated children. *Journal of Consulting and Clinical Psychology*, **64**(1): 32–41.

Trevarthen, C. (1979) Communication and cooperation in early infancy: a description of primary intersubjectivity. In Bullowa, M. (ed.) *Before*

Speech: The Beginnings of Interpersonal Communication. Cambridge: Cambridge University Press.

Trevarthen, C. (1987) Brain Development. In Gregory, R.L. (ed.) *The Oxford Companion to the Mind.* Oxford: Oxford University Press.

Urban, J., Carlson, E., Egeland, B. and Sroufe, L.A. (1991) Patterns of individual adaptation across childhood. *Development and Psychopathology,* **3**: 445–60.

van IJzendoorn, M.H. (1995) Adult attachment representations, parental responsiveness, and infant attachment: a meta-analysis on the predictive validity of the Adult Attachment Interview. *Psychological Bulletin,* **117**: 387–403.

van IJzendoorn, M.H. and Bakermans-Kranenburg, M.J. (1996) Attachment representations in mothers, fathers, adolescents, and clinical groups: a meta-analytic search for normative data. *Journal of Consulting and Clinical Psychology,* **64**: 8–21.

van IJzendoorn, M.H., Goldberg, S., Kroonenberg, P. and Frankel, O. (1992) The relative effects of material and child problems on the quality of attachment: a meta-analysis of attachment in clinical samples. *Child Development,* **63**: 840–58.

Vizard, E., Monck, E. and Misch, P. (1995) Child and adolescent sex abuse perpetrators: a review of the research literature. *Journal of Child Psychology and Psychiatry,* **36**(5): 731–56.

Wachs, T. (1992) *The Nature of Nurture.* Newbury Park: Sage.

Walden, T. and Garber, J. (1994) Emotional development. In Rutter, M. and Hay, D. (eds) *Development Through Life: A Handbook for Clinicians.* Oxford: Blackwell Science, pp. 403–55.

Watanabe, H. (1994) The application of attachment and amae to clinical problems in Japan. In Richer, J. (ed.) *The Clinical Application of Ethology and Attachment Theory.* Occasional Paper No. 9. London: Association for Child Psychology and Psychiatry, pp. 36–43.

Westen, D. (1996) *Psychology: Mind, Brain, and Culture.* New York: Wiley.

Whittaker, J. (1993) Changing paradigms in child and family services. In Ferguson, H., Gilligan, R. and Torode, R. (eds) *Surviving Childhood Adversity: Issues for Policy and Practice.* Dublin: Social Studies Press, Trinity College, pp. 3–13.

Winnicott, C. (1964) *Child Care and Social Work.* London: Bookstall Publications.

Winnicott, D. (1964) *The Child, the Family and the Outside World.* Harmondsworth: Penguin.

Woods, J. (1997) Breaking the cycle of abuse and abusing: individual psychotherapy for juvenile sexual offenders. *Clinical Child Psychology and Psychiatry,* **2**(3): 379–92.

Zeanah, C.H. (1996) Beyond insecurity: a reconceptualization of attachment disorders of infancy. *Journal of Consulting and Clinical Psychology,* **64**(1): 42–52.

Zeanah, C.H. and Emde, R.N. (1994) Attachment disorders in infancy and childhood. In Rutter, M. and Hay, D. (eds) *Development Through Life: A Handbook for Clinicians.* Oxford: Blackwell Science, pp. 490–504.

Zeanah, C.H., Boris, N.W. and Larrieu, J. (1997) Infant development and developmental risk: a review of the past 10 years. *Journal of American Academy of Child Adolescent Psychiatry,* **36**(2): 165–78.

Author Index

Subject Index

therapy   254, 259, 270–1, 282
positive chain events   257
positive cognitive processing   261
possessiveness   110
poverty   3, 106, 119, 232
pre-attachment   19
pretend play   52–3, 66, 143–4, 194
prevention   262–3, 293
primary intervention   262–3
problem-solving   52, 58, 238, 253
projection   96, 100, 144, 225
projective story-telling   35–6, 53, 66,
    93–4, 143–4, 192
prosocial behaviour   16–17, 19, 46, 274
protective influences, definition of
    237–40
proximity seeking   13–15, 22, 26–7
psychiatric illness   78, 158
psychopathology   10, 26, 61, 126, 232
psychosocial development   1, 4–5,
    9–10, 13
psychotherapy   256, 262, 268, 271–5,
    284–5

R
reactive attachment disorder   136
reflective function   21, 57, 112, 159,
    171, 225, 234–5, 237, 243, 278,
    282–3
reflexivity   10, 30
relationship play therapy   254
repression   73
resilience   29–30, 49, 55, 58, 60, 171,
    187, 231, 233–6, 238–9, 244–5
resistance   91
reunion behaviour   12, 32–3, 35–6, 66,
    91
risk factors, definition of   231–3
risks, reduction of   240–2, 249–50
role reversal   129–30, 133–5

S
scaffolding   47
school   54–5, 70–1, 98, 100, 104,
    116–17, 125, 140, 150, 155, 239,
    257–8, 260
secondary intervention   262, 265
secure attachments   19, 25, 27, 29, 33,
    36, 38–9, 45–60
secure base   42, 45, 59, 246, 273
self, formation of   9
self-disclosure   26, 58, 74
self-endangerment   102, 138

self-reflection   26
self-reliance   59, 61, 70–1, 75, 182,
    217
self-sufficient behaviour   65
semantic memory   94, 127, 133, 282
separation   12–14
separation anxiety   87, 89, 91, 93, 95
signalling behaviour   15
social competence   5, 9, 17, 46, 47, 55,
    145
social isolation   79
social understanding, importance of
    9–10
social withdrawal   107, 119, 145, 149
social work process   169–70
socially reserved   71
splitting   36, 43, 94, 108–9, 111, 225
STEEP Program   262, 284
stoicism   75
Strange Situation procedure   31–3, 35,
    48, 63, 66, 91, 123
suicide, attempts at   99, 113–14, 147
suicidal thoughts   152
supervision   295
symptom expression   111, 200
synchronised caregiving   17, 19, 47, 59,
    88

T
theory, role of   13, 169, 228
temperament   3, 9, 231–2, 234, 237–40
    and attachment behaviour   34–5
tertiary intervention   262, 265
therapeutic alliance   246, 279
trance-like behaviour   125, 139
turning points   243, 259–60

U
uncertain caregiving   42, 45, 115–16,
    219–24
unemployment   239
unresolved patterns   39–40, 45

V
victims   97, 100, 120
video-training, with parents and
    children   248, 252–3

W
withdrawal   12

Y
Yale Child Welfare Project   263